Days Made of Glass

Also by Laura Drake

Sweet on a Cowboy series:

The Sweet Spot
Nothing Sweeter
Sweet on You

Widow's Grove series:

Her Road Home
The Reasons to Stay
Twice in a Blue Moon
Against the Odds

For more about me and my books, visit:

http://LauraDrakeBooks.com

Copyright © by Laura Drake

ISBN 978-0-9970721-0-5

ISBN 978-0-9970721-1-2

Printed in the United States of America

Book design by Laura Drake

Heart of a Hawk

Acknowledgments:

Thanks to the courageous bullfighters who keep riders safe.
And those who helped a city girl get it right: Shorty Gorham,
Rob Smets, Greg Dohering, Marsha Miller, Cody Burelison,
Bill and Jan Pearson, and Mike Story, Orin Buchanan. A
special thanks to Lyle Sankey and Buddy Bush. If you're
looking for a Rodeo School, you won't find one more giving
and wonderful than Lyle Sankey's.

I've taken liberties with the dates and times of the rodeos in the
book, but the locations all exist, and they put on bang-up
rodeos. If you want to learn more, visit:
https://www.facebook.com/WSRRA
http://www.pbr.com/
http://www.prorodeo.com/

A thank you to Uprock of Midland, for the Tattoo deets.

Special thanks to my friend, plot whisperer and inspiration
partner, Orly Konig Lopez, for making me dig deeper. Thanks
also to my critters Jessica Topper and Kimberly Belle.

For Nancy.

Wherever you are, save me a seat.

Your absence has gone through me
like a thread through a needle.
Everything I do is stitched with its color.

W.S. Merwin, 'Separation'

The First Day

The world is round and the place which may seem like the end may also be the beginning.

Ivy Baker Priest

Chapter 1

Harlie Cooper watched the pair of giggling college coeds seated four rows ahead on the Salinas city bus. *BFF's.* From Harlie's high-school-hall observations, 'forever' lasted somewhere between a few hours to six months. They leaned into each other, bumping shoulders and whispering. Why did girls need people hanging off them all the time? Why let people in, when they'd only mess you up, then let you down?

I don't have trust issues. I just know better.

She turned back to the window and watched the straw-colored hills rushing past.

It wasn't like family. Family was everything. Even if hers was down to only two.

Lacing her fingers, she stretched her arms over her head, her muscles resisting with a slight tug of tired. Calf roping at the rodeo team practice had gone well today — she'd shaved a second off her time. The smell of horse drifted off her jeans. *Borrowed horse.* Batting away the soft wish, she sat up straight. No sense in wanting.

"Hey, isn't that Mack Tyler's place?"

At her guardian's name, Harlie shot a look across the aisle, where several grown-ups stood out of their seats, pointing out the window.

Smoke rolled into the sky, spreading over the dairy like an angry fist.

Angel!

An electric current jerked her to her feet. "Stop the bus!" She snatched her backpack and rushed down the aisle, grabbing seat backs for balance. "Stop!"

She reached the front, ducking her head to keep her eye on the dystopian horizon. Panic swirled in her belly, rising, rising. Grabbing the silver pole, she took the steps to the well in one leap. "Let me out!" She grabbed the handle and rattled the door.

"I'm working on it." The driver pulled over with a squeal of brakes.

The door lurched open. Her boots hit the pavement and she took off, heart battering her ribs, the frantic wing-brush of her sister's name in her skull. *Angel.* Her feet flew, barely touching the ground. But like in a nightmare, the dread-laced smoke column never seemed to get closer. *Angel.*

A half-mile down the road, she reached the yard, littered with fire trucks and police cars, strobes flashing. Leaping the ditch, she scrabbled through the weeds on the other side, her eyes locked on the flame-licked smoke pouring from the broken windows of the porch. *Angel!*

A yellow-coated fireman backed out the front door holding the handles of a stretcher. A limp, blanket-shrouded body came next, another firefighter hefting the trailing end. Harlie's vision narrowed to a tunnel. She dropped the backpack as her legs buckled. She fell to her knees, fingers clenching the dusty soil. Her panicked brain took a second to process what she was seeing.

Too big.

Mack, then.

When her starved lungs hitched a breath, dizziness receded and the world righted.

Where is Angel? She leapt up and ran to where a fireman stood, shouting into a two-way radio. She snatched at his arm and he started.

"My sister." She screamed up at him. "My sister's in there!"

Arms grabbed her from behind and she twisted, fighting.

"She's not!" His fingers dug into the flesh of her arms. "She's okay. Calm down."

Harlie stopped struggling and he let go. She whirled, chest heaving. "Where?"

The uniformed cop pointed to the side yard.

She dashed around the corner of the house. Angel, blanket-wrapped and clutching a dirty child, stepped out of the barn, led by a fireman. Sound, previously dulled by fear, surged to full volume. Water blasted the side of the house with a liquid roar. Men shouted. A lone siren wailed a warning in the distance, getting closer.

Angel's gaze fastened on Harlie. Prying the sobbing child's arms from her neck, Angel handed her to the fireman, then ran to launch herself into her sister's arms.

Harlie was shorter than most of her classmates but at thirteen, Angel's head still fit easily under her chin. The scent of smoke drifted off her sister's hair — musty ash with the bite of alkaline, leaving a taste like spent adrenaline in Harlie's mouth. She ran her hands over her sister's bony back, still reeling from the gaping hole of a future without Angel. Finally, she leaned back, breaking the embrace.

"What the hell happened here?" The fear came out growling – angrier than she meant.

Under the soot, Angel's face shone slick and pasty. "I – I don't know." She glanced at the house, then away. "Jenny's mom wasn't due to pick her up for hours. We were in the bedroom playing Old Maid. I smelled smoke. The kitchen was filled with it. I couldn't even get near the living room. It was full of fire." A deep, hacking cough shook her narrow chest.

Arm around her sister's shoulders, she led Angel to the two rusty-white wrought iron chairs resting in the shade of the barn. They sat. "Mack didn't make it."

Angel studied her hands, curled in her lap. "I know." She glanced up, her deep brown eyes reminding Harlie of those dime-

4

store paintings of soulful-eyed puppies digging in garbage cans. Angel whispered, "What're we gonna do *now*, Harlie?"

Harlie hugged her sister, fierce protectiveness snapping her muscles taut. "It won't be nothing we don't want this time, Angel. I promise." Harlie had begged the judge last year for custody of her sister. He'd been kind, but told Harlie she was too young – that she shouldn't give up her own childhood so early. What a joke.

Knowing the system would offer slim odds of them staying together, they discussed it, then chose the devil they knew.

"No one but Mack would take us before. Now they're gonna split us up. Make us go to foster homes." Hopelessness threaded through Angel's raspy whisper.

Mack was dead. He and Mom hadn't been married, and he had no blood kin. Likely the dairy would go to the state. They'd be allowed to take just their belongings. With a start, Harlie pictured her mother's photo on the nightstand next to their bed. And the box of her books beneath it. All they had left of her.

An ambulance wheeled into the drive and cut its siren. A county unmarked car pulled up behind it and parked.

Harlie's glance slid to her fidgeting sister. Easy to see they had different fathers. Angel had always been a dark little fairy, with pixie features and delicate bones. Harlie'd inherited her mom's fair hair, but her narrow, strong-boned face must've come from her father. Harlie wouldn't know, having never met the loser. Angel's dad hadn't been around long either.

Maybe they could wander away in all the commotion . . .

"Well. Harlequin and Angelique Cooper."

Angel jerked beside her.

Harlie winced. Mom's romance books had been the inspiration for their names. Harlie'd been grateful that Angel wasn't born a boy. Knowing Mom, she'd have named him Rhett. Or, God forbid, Fabio. She looked up to the wary gaze of Sheriff Bowman. His eyes reminded Harlie of a hawk she'd gotten close to once.

"I'd hoped to never see you two again in sad circumstances." He looked sad. "What happened out here today, girls?"

"I —" Angel's thin voice cracked and she cleared her throat. "I don't know."

Harlie heard the 'want to' between the 'don't' and 'know.' She hoped the sheriff hadn't.

Angel continued. "Jenny's mom wasn't due to pick her up for hours. We were in the bedroom, playing Old Maid when I smelled smoke. The kitchen was filled with it. The living room was full of fire."

Sheriff Bowman's hound-dog face settled in mournful lines and he shook his head. "Mack Tyler was a good man. The town is going to miss him. And what he did for all those poor kids."

Mack was involved big time in local kid's charities.

Had been.

The Cooper girls had a different perspective. Everything about Mack had been hard: his eyes, his voice, his hands. Not that he'd been abusive, exactly. He was even nice to them when other people were around. But he made it clear he kept them only for the free labor they afforded. Harlie was stronger, so the outside work had fallen to her. Angel had house duty, cleaning up and waiting on him.

And he drank. Not so anyone who didn't live with him would know, but . . .

Be careful.

"Mack takes a . . . nap, some afternoons, Sheriff." She looked at her dirty hands, clenched in her lap. "Took, I mean." She forced herself to meet his eyes. "I've taken a lit cigarette from between his fingers more than once."

A cop walked up and whispered in the Sheriff's ear. He nodded, then held up a hand. The cop stepped away, but not far.

The Sheriff heaved a sigh. "Girls, you know we'll need to talk later, about what comes next."

Angel grabbed Harlie's hand, tight, as if someone were already pulling them apart.

6

Goddamn it, they weren't going to be farmed out as slave labor again. This time would be even worse. They wouldn't have each other.

Not an option. Harlie's muscles were strung tight, ready to run. For all the good that would do. Where would they go? How would they get there? Harlie pushed the thoughts away.

Focus on what you can do, not what you can't.

Those questions wouldn't matter if they didn't escape first.

Be ready when you get your chance.

"You know, funny thing about that fire." The sheriff stood, head cocked with that hunting hawk look. "The fire crew said there wasn't a piece of glass intact in that house. Even the mirrors were broken. Any idea how that happened?"

***

The sun was nearing the horizon when Harlie and Angel stepped out of the police cruiser. Sawhorses stood sentinel, blocking the bottom of the driveway. Plywood sheets covered the windows, the raw wood garish against the sooty façade. Yellow, 'Do Not Cross' tape wove through the slats of the porch railing like a new ribbon through a battered basket.

She and Angel had just caught a big break in the form of a domestic dispute involving firearms, two miles away. It hadn't taken a lot of convincing to get the lady cop to drop them off to get their clothes.

"You stay away from the living room. I'll be back in just a little while, and I want to see you waiting right here with your stuff. You hearing me?"

"Yes'm, we will. Thank you." Harlie gave a sad little wave as the cruiser pulled onto the road. She waited until the taillights disappeared over a hill, then grabbed Angel's hand. Skirting the sawhorses, they sprinted up the driveway.

"You get our clothes and gather all the food that won't spoil." Harlie took the steps to the kitchen door in one leap and pulled the key from her pocket. "Bring everything out here and dump it." She unlocked the door.

"But Harlie –"

"Just do it, Angel. I'll get our stash, then pull the truck around." She vaulted off the steps.

The clock ticking in her head matched the cadence of her feet as she pounded through the barn. Grabbing a shovel against the wall, she burst through the back door, startling the cows that gathered at the paddock fence.

Shit. The cows.

Harlie hesitated, hand on the knob. Mack sure wouldn't be doing the evening chores. Recognizing her, the Guernseys lowed.

Double shit.

Harlie weighed: hungry cows versus Social Services. Gritting her teeth, she trotted on, ignoring the look in their soft eyes and the pinch in her heart.

About fifty feet behind the manure pile, she stopped at the crushed soda can marker, half buried in the dirt. She started shoveling.

Someone will remember to feed them. Eventually.

Mack had forbidden her to join the rodeo team at first, since getting home late would cut into her chores. So she offered to take on the morning chores instead. He agreed fast, which should have been her first clue. Turns out, the bulk of the work on a dairy happened in the morning.

Getting up at four a.m. seriously sucked, but once she stepped into the barn it wasn't so bad. The overhead light fell soft on the friendly shadowed shapes. No matter how hard the wind whistled outside, the barn was a warm haven full of animals and the smell of alfalfa and manure. She'd move down the row, attaching milking machines to udder after udder. Something about having her head tucked into the warm side of a willing cow eased the hollow ache that had dogged her the past year.

The tip of her shovel clunked. Harlie bent to uncover their hope chest — a mildew-stained cigar box. Opening it, she pulled out the sandwich baggie full of cash, mostly fives and tens. Every bit they'd squirreled away for the past year. Angel's babysitting money and Harlie's earnings from odd jobs: mowing, fixing fence, feeding cattle. They'd been saving, just in case.

'Just in case' showed up today.

Hurry.

She rounded the manure pile. Cattle followed her along the fence, milling in a pod at the gate. She glanced to the sun, dipping at the horizon. Time was evaporating like rubbing alcohol in open air. She jogged for the barn but skidded to a stop halfway to the door.

"Shit." She hissed under her breath. Changing course, she ran to the wall's shade where hay bales lay under blue plastic tarps. No time to grab gloves. Whipping off the tarp, she lifted the closest one. She grunted as the twine bit into her hands, almost *feeling* the cruiser rolling toward them.

She humped the bale to the edge of the fence, then ran for another. A trickle of sweat rolled down the hollow at the base of her spine.

Hurry! The voice screamed in her head.

Pulling her pocket knife, she bent, cut the twine and kicked at the bales, splitting them open. Hungry faces pushed through the pipe fence, snatching mouthfuls.

She turned and ran for Mack's truck, praying her weakness hadn't just cost them their freedom.

Piles of trash-bagged clothes sat in the driveway alongside cartons of canned goods. *Thank you, God.*

Slamming the truck in park, she hopped out and started heaving everything into the bed.

The screen door slapped. Angel stood on the porch, eyes wide, and a familiar battered box in her arms.

Mom's romance books? Really?

"Angel, we seriously don't have room to take books we're never gonna read." She tossed the last bag into the truck bed, ticking off their inventory in her head. "Did you bring a can opener?"

Angel stood rooted to the porch as if she'd been slapped.

Regret pricked the back of Harlie's throat. *Mom.*

No matter what people thought, mom was *not* a slut. Just soft-hearted and overly optimistic, sure that the *next* man would be the shining prince from one of those romance novels, come to rescue them from the trailer park. Harlie had always been the responsible one, taking over the shopping and the checkbook as soon as she was old enough to subtract. And subtraction was a skill she needed much more than addition.

A tear trail cut through the soot on Angel's face.

It cut into Harlie, too. She took the box from her sister, laid it on the concrete and pulled her into a fierce hug. "It's okay, Angel. We just need to get through this to get to the good stuff that's waiting for us." The familiar words rolled off her tongue. She kissed her sister's hair. "You know I'll take care of you, right?"

Angel's arms tightened and though her chest hitched once, her head moved under Harlie's chin in a nod.

Harlie would have liked to stay in that hug. She needed the comfort as much as Angel. But time was passing. Seconds they couldn't get back.

It wasn't like Harlie didn't have feelings. She just seldom had the luxury of time for them.

She released her sister and took a step back. "It's okay. Put Mom's books in the back – we'll make room."

Angel's head bowed over the box on the cement. "No, you're right."

"Goddamn it, I said we have room." She lifted the box and laid it in the bed, her stomach jumping like she's swallowed a cricket.

"Now hop in. I'll be right back."

Harlie mounted the stairs, pulled open the screen door and stepped into the silent, shadowy, smoke-smelly kitchen. She moved fast, photograph-memories flashing in her brain as she passed. Their bedroom – waking Angel for school and tickling her into a good mood. Their bathroom — combing out Angel's wet hair after a bath.

She stepped into the bedroom that had become only Mack's a year ago. It used to be bursting with her mom, tidy and smelling of her perfume. Harlie scanned the unmade bed, nose wrinkling at the smell of dirty clothes and sour, booze-sweated sheets. Glass from the shattered window covered everything in glittering slivers. She shuddered, a goose walking over her grave.

Hurry.

She ducked into the bathroom.

Lifting off the back off the toilet tank she reached into the cold water, around the bottle of Wild Turkey, to the jar tucked behind it. Mack likely thought it a secret, but Harlie'd known about his stash for a year. She lifted the jar and set it on the counter. Unscrewing the lid, she pulled out the sheaf of cash, then replaced the lid to the toilet tank and threw the jar into the bathtub. It shattered, the shards joining those from the broken window above it. It was enough to hope the sheriff would ignore the missing truck. No need to leave more evidence of thievery.

The lies would weigh heavy on her shoulders, but not as heavy as her responsibility. It was her job to keep them safe.

If stealing from a dead man would ensure that, she could live with it.

She ran back through the house, stopping only to scoop up Angel's schoolbooks from the kitchen table, half expecting to see the cruiser idling out front. Barreling through the screen door, she almost slammed into her sister.

The manic clock ticked in her head. "*What* Angel?"

Her sister stood, big-eyed, glancing from the truck to the wad of money. "You told that lady we wouldn't touch anything that wasn't ours."

Harlie crammed the bills into her pocket. She shot a glance to the empty road. "I'd say we've earned at least this much. What do you say?"

Jaw tight, Angel nodded, her eyes skittering over the outside of the house.

Harlie snatched open the truck door. "Then let's bounce."

The Second Day

"Joy and sorrow are inseparable . . . together they come and when one sits alone with you . . . remember that the other is asleep upon your bed."

Kahlil Gibran

Chapter 2

Three years later — *Rancho Ramona, Temescal Canyon, California*

Harlie swept off her hat and used her sleeve to blot the sweat-sting in her eyes. The air was shiny with dust stirred by cattle's hooves. It coated everything: her horse, her clothes, the inside of her mouth. Watching for strays, she donned her hat and tugged the brim to block the blazing sun. She smiled, grit sliding over her teeth. God, she loved this job.

She and Angel had fled Salinas, looking for big-city anonymity. But when they hit LA, every neighborhood seemed old, tired and used up. People gathered on the corners, trash gathered in the gutters. Gone were the friendly faces of the valley. Unease had skittered over Harlie's skin with repulsive little spider feet. People there seemed foreign in a way she'd never seen before – their faces were hard, cold, dangerous. Or maybe she was just paranoid. But she and Angel were alone in the world and if Harlie made the wrong decision, they'd both pay.

Angel had held her tongue, but the barely controlled panic in her eyes convinced Harlie. She cruised neighborhoods until she found what she sought: a For Sale sign in the window of a car that looked like it would run. A burnt-paint '93 Caddy with gangster whitewalls and orange shag carpet in the back window. Angel promptly named it, "Yolanda."

They'd bought it, and left the truck in a supermarket parking lot with a note to Sheriff Bowman on the seat. Harlie only hoped her anonymous call to the police would give them a head start on the car thieves.

Then they backtracked, searching for a fringe town. One big enough to hide them, but with a bit of open country.

Santa Clarita fit the bill. So did this job.

"Whup, cow. Move it, Mama." Harlie eased the cow and its calf into the bunch, then fell back to trail the small herd, trying to stay out of their dust cloud. The ranch outbuildings and corrals lay ahead.

Maybe they had been due some luck. She'd found this job just as the money ran out. Oh sure, the manager looked her over hard, but by working for free that first week, Harlie'd proven to him that she knew cows. Rancho Ramona wasn't just a movie location; it was a working ranch. She had the calluses to prove it.

Whistling, she twirled the end of her rope, urging the cattle into the corral. A small knot of businessmen stood beside the porch of the ranch office, deep in conversation. When the last calf cleared the gate, she swung it closed and latched it, then reined her horse to the hitching post and dismounted. With her back to the well-dressed men she loosened her horse's girth, picturing the cold, sweat-beaded soda can waiting for her in the office.

"Shit! Do you have any idea of how much money this is costing me, Sid? I'm going to hold up production because a goddamn extra can't get on a fucking plane?"

A whiny voice answered. "Her mother didn't check with me before she died, okay? And she's not quite an extra. It's not like I can just pick up a Western stunt double shopping on Rodeo Drive, Brad. What the hell do you expect me to do?"

"I *expect* you to find someone. Now. That's what a fucking Associate Producer does."

Her mount cared for, Harlie walked to the office porch. All buildings on the place did double duty. This one had served as a sheriff's office in more than one Western. Not like she'd

14

seen it – she had no money for movies. She went up the stairs and crossed the porch, head down, practically invisible.

"Hey! You. Girl!"

Not quite invisible. Harlie hesitated, hand on the knob. Maybe she could act like she hadn't heard . . .

"Come over here." No mistaking the order in that bark.

She turned. The short man of the group waved her over. Licking grit from her teeth, she recrossed the covered porch and took the steps.

The men watched her approach.

"She's the right height. Built like a boy, but we've got padding, and on a horse you wouldn't notice." The short man addressed the obvious leader. "The blonde isn't right but we can fix that."

Now she knew what a heifer felt like in the auction ring. Hot blood throbbed in her face. She lifted her chin. The cords in her neck tightened. All she wanted was her soda, and to get back to work. She'd love to flip them off. But she had Angel. And bills. She halted in front of them and hid her fists in the front pockets of her jeans. "Yessir?"

The man she pegged as the director stood, arms crossed, the air around him thick with authority. "Maybe if she were cleaned up . . ." He looked her over as if she were a prop. "At least we know she can ride." He waved a hand in Harlie's direction. "Handle it, Sid." He walked away. The other men followed, like pilot fish around a shark.

Sid's lips lifted in a used-car-salesman's smile. "How old are you?"

"Twenty-one as of last week. Why?"

"You want to make some good money for a couple weeks, Girl? What's your name, anyway?"

"Harlie." Maybe she'd earn enough to catch up on the rent. Maybe there would even be enough to take Angel shopping. Maybe that would pull her out of the funk she'd fallen into. "How much?"

He named a wage that would buy new shocks for Yolanda *and* put money in the bank. She'd watched the shoots. She knew

15

it'd be a lot of waiting around, a lot of doing the same thing, over and over. Harlie hadn't known her stomach muscles were tight until they relaxed. *Money for nothing.* And hey, she'd be in a film. They might even go see it. She imagined sitting in a crowded movie theatre with Angel, watching the screen. She'd ride up . . . *Wait.* Her stomach cramped. Her sphincter tightened, remembering the truck she'd stolen. "My face wouldn't have to be on camera, would it?"

***

Harlie clicked open the last deadbolt and burst into their studio apartment, a sparkler of happiness fizzing in her chest. "Hey, Angel!" She panted, only partially from the three-floor climb. The air inside the apartment hit her like an invisible wall. Their walk-up had no air conditioning. *Why didn't she open the windows?*

"Angel?" Stepping around the edge of the tiny kitchen, the rest of the apartment came in view: bean bag chairs, battered coffee table. The mattress in the corner, a blanket-covered lump in the middle. The sparkler winked out.

Oh, not again. She crossed the room, threw open the window, then turned and dropped to her knees on the mattress. "Come on, Sista. We're gonna go celebrate!" She shook the lump.

It groaned.

"Get up, Angel." Harlie jerked down the covers. Her sister made an irritated sound in the back of her throat and threw an arm over her eyes.

Excitement leaked from Harlie like air from a balloon. Angel wore the same faded blue t-shirt and underwear she'd worn to bed the night before. "You didn't go to school. Again."

When Angel lowered her arm, apprehension whooshed into the places vacated by excitement. Angel's dark, greasy hair was matted, her face swollen – with sleep or tears, Harlie couldn't tell. But it was the look in her eyes that iced Harlie's nerves. They looked like photos she'd seen of concentration camp victims. Haunted, hollow. Dead.

Harlie knew from experience it was no use asking Angel what was wrong. She'd just go away in her head. Angel had been depressed since their mom died, but since they left Salinas, she'd gotten worse. *Dysthymia—chronic depression.* Harlie'd learned the word when she'd gone to the library to research. She wished she hadn't, because giving something a name gave it power. The word had burned into the covering of her brain.

And the hormones of fourteen weren't helping any either. She could feel her sister slipping away. Fear made Harlie shake her sister harder than she'd meant. "Come on Angel. Get in the shower. We're going out!" The happy-voice sounded fake, even to her.

Angel stirred, as if coming alive. "Out?"

"Yeah. I told you that if we worked hard, things would get better. We're on our way to that great future we planned." Harlie stood and took the few steps to the closet, shifting the sparse hangers, looking for something decent for Angel to wear. She settled on a pair of shorts and a slightly less faded t-shirt than the one Angel had on. "We're celebrating tonight. I got a raise!"

Two hours later they sat in a booth at the Hometown Buffet, stuffed to groaning with their first restaurant meal in a year. Harlie carefully counted out bills to pay the check. "You'll get your diploma, and get a decent job. I'll make head wrangler, get more film work. And we can live in an apartment in Studio City, with A/C." She looked up and winked at Angel. "And a pool. And you'll see movie stars walking around every day."

The sparkle was back in Angel's eye. "Do you really think so?" She breathed it soft as a wish.

There was her sister. "Stick with me, kid." She ruffled Angel's hair and scooted out of the booth. "Let's bounce."

They walked out into the dragon's-breath desert air. If it was this hot in March, what would their apartment be like in July?

It'll be what it is.

Harlie threw an arm around her sister's neck. "Next week, after I get paid, I'm taking you clothes shopping." She bent to check Angel's expression. "You'd like that, wouldn't you? Have something to show off at school?" Angel's smile helped dilute the worry-laced food in Harlie's stomach.

"That'd be cool." Angel scanned the shop-lined street.

"Let's check out the stores. At least they'll have air-conditioning." They strolled the sidewalk in the tourist section of town. Angel wasn't getting better. Harlie did her best, tutoring Angel at night to help her catch up on work she missed from frequent absences, but . . .

Screw it. Just put it down for one night. It's not like she had any answers, anyway.

Harlie opened the door to the next shop, not caring what they sold; there was no money to buy anything. The cool air brushed her sweaty exposed skin. Angel ducked under her arm.

It was a china shop. Aisles of display shelves held fragile curios. Painted plates circled the walls in an orderly line.

"Cool."

She hadn't seen open wonder on Angel's face since Mom had taken them to the Fourth of July fireworks. Harlie eyed the fragile knick-knacks. "Just be careful."

Angel wandered off, leaving Harlie to her thoughts. Yolanda's shocks could wait. Maybe she'd look into a psychologist instead. *Yeah, right.* This stunt gig would last a couple of weeks at best, and whatever was wrong with Angel wasn't going away in a couple of sessions. Therapy would take a steady stream of extra cash. Harlie had tried working part time at the Stop-n-Go, but with Harlie being gone so much, Angel did worse.

"Oh. Wow."

The whispery wonder in Angel's voice brought Harlie's head up. She rounded the end cap to see her sister leaning over a clearance table.

"Look." She picked up a rose colored stained-glass box and laid it on the palm of her hand. "A glass house. Isn't it pretty?"

Harlie stepped alongside her sister. Angel held a square jewelry box, made for a ladies' dressing table.

"This reminds me of us." Angel's finger traced the curled black and white enamel design on the lid. "What is it?"

"They call it Yin and Yang. It's the Chinese symbol for infinity."

Angel nodded, cradling the box. "See? Told you it was us."

In the simple immaculate innocence of Angel's smile, Harlie caught a flash. Not a memory – more the brush of a feeling – back when had Mom made the world special, like it was made just for them.

How could she have forgotten that?

Taking the box from her sister, she turned it over. Twelve dollars. They could buy a lot of food for twelve dollars. Trying to think of a gentle way to say no, Harlie noticed the disappointment on Angel's pinched lips.

Then it was gone, smoothed once more to practiced indifference.

Angel took the box and gently set it back on the table. "Let's bounce." Her fingers stroked the glass in a reluctant release.

"Hell, that's a steal." Something in her throat made the words come out wavery. Harlie snatched up the box. "Next month is your birthday anyway, Punk."

Chapter 3

The makeup artists flitted around Harlie like hummingbirds around a feeder, bemoaning split ends, sunburned skin and powdering her shiny nose, even though most of her on-camera work was at a dead gallop with a hat shading her face. Just more evidence that these people were well disguised space aliens—they obviously didn't live in Harlie's world.

Watching the shoot was amusing, as was the actor's off-screen demeanor. But after a few days, Harlie felt antsy—her hands missing the heft of fence pliers, her feet missing the broken-down comfort of her own boots.

The movie was a modern Western about the life of a Pro Bull Rider. Harlie was a stand-in for the lead actress. Patrice (not Pat, not Patty) Paige refused to stand downwind of a horse, much less get on one. Today they'd shot a rodeo sequence. The metal bleachers set up around the corral had been filled with cheering extras. A contingent of men from the PBR had trucked in bucking bulls and had stayed to see that the film represented the sport accurately.

The waning sun blazed its way down her back as Harlie leaned with her forearms on the corral fence. She should be home by now, but hadn't been able to make herself leave the drama. Apparently the actors felt the same, since most watched from the bleachers.

20

Pomeranian in her lap, Patrice lounged beside her beefcake boyfriend. The director had banished the yappy rat dog from the set but one of Patrice's people had retrieved it the second the cameras finished filming the final bull ride.

Past time I got home. Angel would be waiting to hear stories of the filming while Harlie fixed dinner. The stars may seem like aliens to Harlie but they were gods to her sister, who parked herself at the checkout stand reading tabloids while Harlie shopped. Angel had gone on and on about Patrice's steamy romance with her former bodyguard, Bo. Harlie studied the pair, memorizing the details for Angel. When Patrice wasn't in a shot, she was the picture of studied indifference, Pomeranian in hand, checking her manicure.

Bo sat beside her. Harlie had to admit, he had a body. Hard to miss, since his favorite attire was too-small wife beater t-shirts, tight jeans, and spanking new ostrich skin cowboy boots. But something about the way his eyes slid, oily, over any pretty girl made Harlie think his morals weren't as strong as his muscles. His cylindrical head rose from the powerful muscles of his neck, and keeping with fashion, he had more hair on his face than his shaved head. He looked like a pencil eraser with a goatee.

The dog had barked from the second they'd put it in Patrice's lap. It bounced on her knee, struggling to get down.

God, doesn't she hear that yapping?

"That's it people." The director yelled from across the arena. "I need you here at seven tomorrow morning."

Clang!

The metal gate swung, and they released the last unbucked bull into the arena. An old, red-coated Hereford-Brahma cross, small, with wicked horns.

The rat dog used the distraction to make his break, joyfully bounding down the bleachers and through the pole fence, long fur flying behind him.

Patrice jumped up screeching. Bo smiled behind her back, as did most of the onlookers. No one liked the irritating little snake-food dog. Most weren't fond of its owner, either.

Yipping in triumph, the dog shot like a flaxen arrow to the center of the arena and faced Patrice with a panting grin.

The bull stood before the gates, snorted, threw his head up and with white rimmed eyes, regarded the irritant. Harlie watched, frozen. The bull strutted, looking around, deciding. It might have walked to the open exit gate if the Pomeranian hadn't challenged it with a cascade of furious yapping.

The bull wheeled to the center of the arena, dropped its head, and with a heavy snort, charged. The dog held his ground, barking at the charging one-ton animal like a drunk with little-man syndrome.

Patrice shrieked from the bleachers.

Why isn't anyone doing anything? Harlie jerked her hands from the pole fence. The dog was a pain in the ass but it was about to be pummeled to a bloody rag under the bull's hooves.

She didn't think. Ducking between the poles, she judged the bull's trajectory and ran on a diagonal that would allow her to scoop up the dog without getting stomped.

Maybe.

She barely heard the shouts of the onlookers. Instead, she focused on the speed of the bull, gaining, gaining.

No way she'd make it to the fence.

The sweet rush of adrenaline hit her like a heroin-mainlining junkie. It sang through her veins, lifting her, making her impervious—superhuman. She sped up, heart thundering in her ears—or maybe that was bull's hooves.

Everything seemed to slow. Details stood out in perfect focus: the shine of spit on the dog's bared teeth, the whorl of hair at the center of the bull's forehead, a small scar next to its white-filled eye.

In full stride, Harlie reached the center of the arena, snatched the now cowering fur ball by the nape and kept moving. The ground shook with pounding hooves. She tensed her muscles for impact, but felt only a sliding rub of horn on her butt and the rush of air at her back as the bull passed. Clutching the suicidal mutt in a death grip, Harlie sprinted for the fence.

She'd taken only a couple of steps when the panicked yells of the onlookers penetrated the swelling adrenaline chorus in her head. Harlie didn't have to look. She knew bulls. The animal had wheeled, and from the vibrations in the soles of her fancy cowgirl boots, was bearing down to gore her.

No time. She heaved the dog toward the red-faced men on the opposite side of the fence. Her brain registered a stop-action photo of the little dog flying through the air, hair blown back, mouth open.

She hadn't known dogs had an expression for terrified but this one sure did. It hit the ground running and streaked for the line of boots at the fence.

Harlie spun on her heel. The bull was farther away than she'd guessed, but closing fast. She shot a glance to the fence. It seemed as if she were seeing it through the wrong end of a telescope. A bull will beat a human in a race, every time. She'd never make it.

No choice.

Tension zinged through her. The timing had to be just right. Failure would come in the form of lunging horns and bone-snapping hooves. Head down, the bull came on.

Decision made, the fear in Harlie's chest lay down before a rising exaltation of *knowing.* Crouched in a marathon runner's stance, she shook the jitters out of her hands and gauged the bull's closing speed.

One more step –

Harlie exploded, launching herself straight at the bull.

She took two long-jumper strides.

The bull charged in, lowering its head to hook her.

On the third stride, perfectly timed, her foot came down in the center of the bull's broad forehead. He threw his head up and she was launched, flying over the beast's back

It seemed she rose forever, her stomach dropping, shooting the sparkly fireworks of a roller coaster's first hill. A quiet, high-pitched sound escaped her lips. It might have been a giggle.

When the arc finally began its downward tail, Harlie looked for a place to land.

She hit the ground running, shooting a look over her shoulder for the bull. A cowboy on horseback entered the arena and roped the bull. The horse pulled it to the exit gate.

As Harlie ducked through the fence she was surrounded by the onlookers, clapping her on the back, expressing admonishment, amazement, fear. One had retrieved her hat and clapped it on her head. Her heart and lungs slowed from a gallop to a trot, and her muscles released their iron grip on her bones. But still the on-the-edge wildness sang through her. The crowd parted for a Patrice that Harlie barely recognized. Mascara tracked from her reddened eyes over blotchy skin. Her hair, normally a smooth helmet, stood up in snatches. The cause of all the trouble lay squeezed tight in her embrace, panting a smug grin.

"I just don't know what to say. You saved my Pookie – and I couldn't have *lived* without him!" Undone, Patrice threw herself at Harlie, breaking into theatrical weeping. "You're my hero!"

Embarrassed to be the center of attention, Harlie winced at the wail in her ear and almost sorry for the dog sandwiched between them, she just stood there, wearing Patrice like a necklace. Mortified, she gave Patrice an awkward pat on the back. Harlie had no doubt the woman's emotion was genuine, but damn. Even in real life Patrice overacted.

Bo stepped up, extricated Patrice from Harlie's neck, and murmuring support, led her away. Show over, the crowd broke up heading for the parking lot in small groups.

The adrenaline hangover hit. Harlie leaned on the fence, not wanting to test if her knees would support her, as a wave of dizzying emptiness scoured her chest. She was thirsty. She wanted to go home. She wanted her mom. Nightmare scenarios of what could have happened ran through her mind. Bloody, painful, expensive scenarios. What the hell had she been thinking? Sure, she'd loved vaulting when she'd been on the gymnastics team when they'd lived in Kentucky, and she'd watched a guy jump a bull once when the high school rodeo coach wasn't around. But what if she'd been hurt? They had no insurance, and Angel—

"Pretty fancy work out there today." A young dude in boots, razor-creased Wranglers, and a tweed sport coat walked up and touched the brim of his cowboy hat. "When'd you learn to do that?"

She snorted. "Today, I guess."

His gaze sharpened, and Harlie braced herself. She knew that look.

"I'm Steve Rawlings, a marketing rep for the PBR, and I have a crazy idea." He looked her over, head to heel. "But it could be crazy enough to work." Resting a boot on the bottommost pole, he leaned a forearm on the fence. "And *you* may just be crazy enough to try."

Oh man, what now? "With smooth talk like that, you must be a huge success in marketing." She pushed away from the fence. She needed to be standing for this.

He chuckled and tipped his hat back. "You know, there's never been a female professional bullfighter. It could be a huge draw. Good for the PBR, good for you. *If* you could make the cut."

Do this, every day? Oh yeah, she could handle that. She squinted up at him, "What's it pay?"

***

Fifteen minutes later, Harlie raised a hand to wave as Steve made his way out of the almost deserted parking lot. She allowed herself a secret smile. How cool would that be? The PBR would pay her way to Bullfighter school, then pay her a salary while she worked herself up the rodeo circuit, gaining experience. If she did well they'd take her in the Touring Pro Division, with hopes that she'd make the big time.

She slid his business card into the back pocket of her jeans. Of course, she'd turned him down. No way she could travel, with Angel still in school. Mom had dropped out of high school, so she hammered the value of an education into their heads from the time they could understand. And after they fled Salinas, Angel hounded Harlie until she sat for the GED.

Still, her step was light in the aisle between stalls.

She walked into her 'dressing room,' the tack room of the barn. Wardrobe wouldn't allow her to wear her 'set clothes' home. Closing the door, she leaned her head against it. Just for a moment, she imagined herself in the center of an arena working a bull, pulling him away from a downed bull rider.

"Rider Protection." Now there was a cool job title.

A shadow of the emotion she'd felt today passed through her and she shivered in a delicious, secret thrill. Standing in the arena today, she'd breathed in the rare ether of alive. In those frozen seconds before the bull charged, her senses seemed to crystallize — she could touch, taste, savor it – feeling poised on the knife-blade edge of the future.

Where this love of danger had come from, she couldn't have said. Maybe because life had been precarious from her earliest memory, Harlie had developed a high tolerance. Or maybe she'd come into this life with it. Early on, when she realized that that others feared the risk she embraced, Harlie learned to hide it. It became her secret shame, this craving for danger that throbbed in the deepest part of her. Besides, she and Angel's lives were precarious enough.

But it sure was a happy dream. She turned with a sigh, unbuttoning her western shirt. Light streamed in the high window, illuminating the tack-crowded room. She shrugged out of her shirt and hung it on a peg on the wall.

Behind her, the door clicked open. *What the* – She whirled, crossing her arms over her bra.

Patrice's boyfriend, Bo, filled the doorframe.

"What the hell are you doing? Get out!" Keeping her eyes on him, she crouched to hide as much skin as possible. She groped for her t-shirt on the peg behind her.

He smiled. "It's okay. Patrice is tucked into a load of roofies, snoring away."

"Get the fuck out of here!" Harlie's hammering heart sent a flush of heat down her limbs and up her neck. When her questing fingers finally touched cotton, she ripped her shirt off the peg. Not taking her eyes from Bo, she threw it over her head, not caring if she got it backwards. She jerked her arms though and pulled it down. The flimsy barrier didn't make her feel any less naked.

"You know; I was a bodyguard for a drug runner before Patrice." Bo stepped into the room and kicked the door. It slammed closed behind him. "Until today, watching you, I'd forgotten how much I missed the rush."

"I don't give a crap." She put all the hardass she had into her voice. Damn, he was big. A picture of the empty parking lot flashed in her mind. She strained to hear over the pounding of her heart. The barn was silent, empty.

"Oh, sure you do." Bo moved slow, taking a step toward her. His deep, mellow voice poured over her. "You know what it's like. You can feel the danger in the air, all around you. Before you even think, you've stepped up to meet it." The light from the window bounced off the shiny skin of his head. His dark eyes bored into her, looking, seeing. "You're invincible. Because in those few seconds—you're a god." His last words slid out in a whisper.

Only their breathing disturbed the quiet. Hers rapid, his deep, calm.

She felt as if he'd reached out and touched her intimate hidden pleasure — stroking it with a filthy finger. Mesmerized by his eyes, she shivered in revulsion. "I'm nothing like you."

His slow, slimy smile bared her lie. "Oh yeah, you are. I saw it when you came out of the arena." His smug, greasy smile exposed perfectly bleached teeth. "You know what it's like to be on the edge. You *like* it." His next step brought him too close. His huge hand circled her bicep. He leaned in, his breath brushing her face. "It turns me on." His fingers darted in. He twisted her nipple. Hard.

An electric bolt of agony jolted her chest, shock freezing her in place. A freight-train realization of what was coming slammed into her. The muscular wall of him blotted out the room.

27

Harlie knew her only hope was surprise. Her fist snapped out, connecting with his nose. The cartilage gave under her knuckle with a sickening crack. Bo jerked upright, flinging hot spatters of blood on her face. The hand clamped over her bicep like a manic blood pressure cuff, squeezing off the blood supply. Hot urgency poured through her. She pushed off the floor, driving a knee into his groin.

Just for a moment, his hand spasmed tighter on her arm, then was gone. Air whooshed out of him, tailing out to a moan. His body made a sound like a bag of wet cement when it hit the floor.

Harlie didn't stay to gloat. Wary of his long reach, she skirted the edge of the room, hugging the wall, then ran like hell.

Chapter 4

When Harlie walked in, Angel sat at their rickety Goodwill table, studying. She looked up. "What's wrong?"

At the sight of open schoolbooks and scattered papers, Harlie released a breath she held every night as she walked in the door. *Angel's having a good day.* She slapped on a smile, batted her eyelashes, and lowered her voice to sultry. "Are you kidding? How could the day of a *Star* be less than perfect?" She put a hand on her hip and flipped her hair over her shoulder as she'd seen Patrice do a quad-zillion times.

The Oscar for her performance came in Angel's smile. A smile made all the more precious by its rarity.

Besides, today hadn't been *that* bad. Nobody died.

"So? Tell me." Angel closed her book and walked to the stove to stir something in a pan, which given their pantry and Angel's culinary skills, had to be boxed macaroni and cheese. "What was Patrice wearing?" She turned to Harlie, the spoon dripping on the worn linoleum. "Was Bo there?"

The reverence in her sister's voice made Harlie want to wash Angel's mouth out with soap. "They were shooting background scenes today. She wasn't even on the set." No need to worry Angel. Harlie crossed the room to take their two plates from the drain board, then bent to wipe the drips from the floor with a rag.

After dinner, Angel retrieved the cheap radio alarm clock from beside the bed, set it on the sink and plugged it in. She tuned it to an oldie station, and they washed the dishes to their Mom's songs; Love Shack, Sweet Dreams, Love Cats.

Harlie dried the last dish and put it in the empty cupboard. The Motels came on, singing 'Suddenly, Last Summer.' Mom had listened to this tape, over and over. She'd take turns dancing the girls across the floor.

They looked at each other and without a word, clasped each other's wet hands and danced with a ghost in the hot, cramped kitchen. At the end, Harlie dipped Angel until her hair brushed the floor. She came up laughing, a sheen in her eyes.

They lay in bed that night with just a sheet over them, the fan barely stirring the hot air. Harlie studied her sister's soft-featured profile in the glow of the parking lot security light. There was potential in the slope of her nose, her strong chin. If Angel wanted college, Harlie would find a way to make it happen.

Harlie smoothed the hair back from her sister's forehead. "If you could be anything when you're grown up, what would you be?"

Angel lay unmoving, staring at the ceiling. "Someone else."

The weight of sadness in the words crashed onto Harlie. "Don't say that, Punk. I like you just the way you are."

No change in the dark profile, except maybe a blink. "I'm like mom. 'Mentally unfit.'"

Shame burned in Harlie's chest, and spread over her skin like acid. This was her fault. "Don't you say that! She wasn't. You're not."

One mistake. Would Angel ever let it go?

Harlie had been eleven. Too innocent to know not to tell. When the nice lady in the apartment next door asked, Harlie told her about mom working nights at the bar. She hadn't realized why the woman was asking . . . until the Social Service lady showed up with a policeman that night. Harlie told her they were fine, that she always took care of her little sister.

They must have called mom, because a half hour later she came in the apartment crying, and yelling at the government people. She didn't calm down until they threatened to take Harlie and Angel with them.

Mom worked out a babysitting swap with another single mom in the apartments, and that should have been that.

Except it wasn't. Kids have big ears and must've heard their parents talking. Harlie could handle herself, but she didn't even know Angel was getting crap at school until she asked Harlie what 'mentally unfit' meant.

Harlie beating that kid up was her second mistake; Angel took it as proof that the kid had been telling the truth, and Harlie did it to shut him up. "Angel, those people were just being mean. They didn't know what the hell they were talking about."

"Yeah. Whatever."

Harlie felt the retreat in her sister's dead monotone. Darkness crashed. Angel had fallen into the black hole again.

"Angel." She shook her shoulder. "Please, don't leave me."

No response.

"You're frightening me." Her wavery voice echoed loud in the empty room. It was her job to keep Angel safe. And she did. But something had snuck past her to steal the most precious part of Angel: her mind.

On the heels of fear came desperation. Give Harlie something to fight and she'd go down swinging. But this . . . this was like trying to punch her way through miles of filthy cotton.

"It was Mack, wasn't it?" When Angel didn't respond, Harlie shook her. "Mack messed with you, didn't he? Goddammit it! I should have—"

"I *told* you before. He *never* touched me." Angel rolled away, leaving only the armor of her frail back to deflect questions.

But it was enough. Harlie heard the finality. Knew she could tear out Angel's fingernails and she'd say nothing more. She also heard the rock-solid truth in the words. Mack really hadn't touched her. But there was something there. Harlie knew her sister. She felt sometimes they were one person living in two bodies, separated only by a flimsy barrier of skin.

31

Angel was sliding away, and Harlie didn't know what else to do.

And that scared the spit out of her.

The next morning in the ranch parking lot, Harlie stepped out of Yolanda, slammed the door and watched two men walk toward her. They should be coming to apologize for Bo's assault but given her luck, and their firing-squad bearing, she doubted it. Her intestines growled and she had the sudden urge to find a bathroom.

The set boss, Sid, and Tonio, her ranch boss, stopped in front of her. They exchanged glances, as if each expected the other to start.

Sid lost the stare-down. He turned to her. "Listen, Kid. You're out." His steel-wool tone was as gruff as ever.

*Oh no. T*his was one of the scenarios she'd imagined, lying in sweat-tangled sheets last night long after Angel's breathing evened out in sleep. Dammit, she'd counted on that money.

Well, if she was getting canned, she was done with, 'yessir'.

"No need to sugar-coat it, Sid. I *can* call you Sid, right? If you're screwing me, I think we're on a first name basis."

He stuck out his chin. "Hey, my being sorry about it doesn't make a difference, Kid. You're just as fired."

Harlie leaned her butt against Yolanda's hood and crossed her arms. "So? What's his story? I'm assuming that my side doesn't matter, since you didn't ask to hear it before firing me."

His eyes sidled away. "Bo said you accosted him in the barn last night. When he told you he was devoted to Patrice, you attacked him." He gave her a sickly smile. "Kind of a hell-hath-no-fury kinda thing."

Sonofabitch. Sure, she'd known this was a possibility. But the indignity still hit like a slap. She shook her head. "And you believed him? Really, Sid?"

He really looked at her for the first time. "You're new to this, Chickie, so let me tell you how it is. I can replace you. I can't replace Patrice. That means *you* have a problem. Not Patrice. Not me. Not Bo. You're the lowest animal on the food chain. The slowest antelope. Know what I mean?"

Damn, she was going to miss that money. She didn't need Sid to tell her they didn't matter. She and Angel were just part of the vast underground economy of L.A., scrambling to get by alongside illegals and parole dodgers. Getting screwed was a given she'd accepted long ago.

But acceptance didn't mean it didn't hurt. She glanced to the corral. Extras lounged, waiting. No stars, or their bodyguards, in sight. She turned to Sid. "I just hope your butt isn't ever the one hanging out at the back of the herd, Sid. From what I've seen, I'd invest in a pair of steel underwear if I were you."

She turned to Tonio, who watched uneasily, hands in his back pockets. "I guess I'm all yours again, Boss. Where do you want me today?" She pushed away from the car.

"Um," His mouth opened, then closed. Then opened. Nothing came out.

A fist of panic hit and air whistled out through her teeth. *Shit!* This was the scorched-earth scenario she couldn't bring herself to contemplate last night. What would they do if she lost this job? "No. Please. You know I'm committed to this ranch. I work hard. You know I do."

Don't beg. Thoughts whirled around, caught in the huge wind roaring in her ears. *Whatever you do, don't beg.* "Sir. You don't understand. I *need* this job. Please." Her voice kept rising, even as the volume decreased. She made herself stop. Almost.

"Please."

"I don't have a choice, Harlie. The ranch needs the revenue from the production companies. If we're blackballed, we're out of business."

He looked sorry. For all the good that did.

She'd heard enough. Pulling the car door open, she dropped into the seat. Ignoring the two men, she took one last look at the ranch. Money aside, she was going to miss the freedom of working outdoors, with the cattle. *It doesn't help, wanting.*

She winced, imagining herself standing at the bottom of a conveyor belt, plastic bag between her legs, waiting for the groceries to slide toward her.

That's if I'm lucky.

She cranked the engine. Time for the slowest antelope to haul ass.

She had to change clothes. Harlie pushed the key into the apartment deadbolt. Cowhand couture wouldn't work, even for a 'do-you-want-fries-with-that?' interview. When the last lock clicked, she pushed the door open. A slight breeze brushed against her face.

At least Angel left the window open when she left for school.

She sniffed. Something smelled off. A funny, almost metallic smell she couldn't place. Had she forgotten to take out the trash? In the quiet came an odd two-note hum. Her fingers spasmed, and her heart leapt to a rat-a-tat rhythm. Dread infused her blood, and her frenzied heartbeat spread it through her body. She wrestled to extract the key from the lock and when her fingers wouldn't work, she abandoned it. Leaving the keys dangling, she rushed through the entry.

It doesn't sound happy. It sounds –

She turned the corner and stepped into hell.

Both bean bag chairs had been slashed — tiny Styrofoam peas shifted in a line across the floor, dancing in the breeze from the broken windows. Tiny shards of glass strewn on every surface winked like silver glitter in the sunlight. Shock froze her feet. Someone had broken in! Realization hit. *Angel!*

"Angel!" She ran the few steps to the bedroom area, but the mattress on the floor held nothing but crumpled sheets and slivers of glass. Two steps to the right, the bathroom looked like a Marquis de Sade torture chamber. The towel she'd dried herself with not two hours ago stirred in the breeze of the broken-out window, the tub beneath bristled with glass. The sink was filled with silver slivers from the mirror above it.

Over the manic rush of blood in her ears, Harlie heard the two-note moan–from behind her. She sprinted the few steps to the kitchen, then skidded to a stop, her brain trying to comprehend what her vision telegraphed.

In the corner, Angel sat slumped against the wall in a pool of crimson. Spatters coated her t-shirt and shorts, her legs and arms were painted in it. Head down, she seemed to be writing on her forearm. But in place of a pen, she held a wicked glass shard.

"Help!" Harlie's scream echoed in the closed space, shattering her paralytic shock. "Somebody help me!" Ignoring the dish shards, she snatched the dishtowel from the sink and fell to her knees beside her sister. "Honey! It's okay, it's me."

Focused on her grisly task, Angel didn't notice.

Harlie pulled the glass from her sister's hand, feeling the edges slice through her fingers. She tossed it up and it tinkled into the sink.

"Help me. Somebody help me!" Her screech hurt her own ears, but Angel didn't react. She sat head down, looking like a broken, paint-spattered doll.

Towel in hand, Harlie's brain chugged in slow motion. She couldn't decide where to start. Arms? Legs? Which wound was deepest? There were too many! Scarlet gaping mouths oozed.

There! An artery at Angel's wrist pumped with her pulse. Harlie tore a strip from the dishtowel, wrapped it around Angel's wrist twice, and tied it tight as she could.

"Eieeeeee! Madre de dios!"

Harlie turned her head.

A small brown woman, hands to her cheeks, looked on in horror.

"Call 911!" When the woman didn't move, Harlie groped through her memory for her few bones of Spanish. "Llame la Policia!" She turned back to triage the next most urgent cut, only vaguely aware of the woman running out, yelling.

So much blood. She worked like a robo-nurse, tearing strips from the towel until it was gone. Then she tore off the bottom of her own shirt. More time ticked away on the kitchen clock.

Hurry!

Finally, down to the oozing cuts, Harlie wiped the inside of Angel's forearm—the one she'd been cutting when Harlie found her. Between blottings, she glimpsed a pattern. She wiped again, and her horrified mind made the connection. Angel had carved the yin-yang symbol of the glass house into her skin.

Eyes half closed, Angel raised her head and leaned it against the wall as if it were too heavy. "I had to let it out." Her eyes slipped closed.

Her barren whisper blew through Harlie like a December wind. "It's okay, Angel. It'll be okay, I promise."

The sweet sound of a siren getting closer drifted in through the broken-out windows.

Chapter 5

Harlie cracked open an eyelid. Florescent light stabbed her eyeball, waking her headache with a snarl. Wincing, she shifted to her other sore hip in the meagerly padded chair of the visitor's lounge. Giving up even the pretense of sleep, she stood and crossed the scarred linoleum to the window. She didn't know the time, but dawn couldn't be far away . . . if there was a God.

It's okay. You've been through worse than this.

But had she, really?

For the first time in a long time, Harlie longed for her mom. Not to lean on—mom had never been much good in a crisis. But just to have someone to wait with . . . someone to talk to who shared their history. They would reminisce about Angel, in happier times. Someone who knew all their worn-to-softness stories.

Harlie'd never felt like an orphan before, but she did now.

Looking back at the past few years, they seemed a long dirt slope that began when mom died. Harlie hadn't been aware of going downhill, but looking back now, the top seemed very far from where she now stood. There were claw marks in the dirt where she'd scrabbled for purchase, trying to keep them fed and a roof over their heads. Here and there were narrow ledges, where they'd rested. But those were few. Looking back, she could see the signs she'd made herself ignore; signs that Angel wasn't getting better.

God, she'd screwed up so bad.

But this had to be the bottom, didn't it? She didn't know. Only the past seemed clear. The road ahead was blacked out. No job, no money, no Angel.

Oh yeah, this had to be bottom.

Harlie had followed the ambulance to the hospital, but was stopped from following Angel's gurney at the admissions desk. There she began the red-tape gauntlet of check-in, billing, and MediCal application. Hours later, spit out at the end, she felt like a grateful but processed package of meat.

Rules didn't allow her to stay with Angel in her room overnight—not on this floor. Her sister wouldn't know anyway. They'd drugged her in the ER last night, following two pints of blood and seventy-eight stitches. When they finally let Harlie see her, Angel was sleeping, a study in white: sheets, bandages, skin. With her dark hair, long eyelashes, and waxen face, she looked like a vampire in one of those movies she loved.

Maybe Angel wasn't missing her, but Harlie made up for that. This was the first night of her life she hadn't slept beside her sister, and there was a hollow place in her chest.

Funny how she'd always thought about Angel needing *her*. In this interminable night she learned that she needed Angel more. Her palms itched to feel her sister's skin beneath her hands, soothing the hurt. She wanted to be by Angel's bed, making sure the sheet on her chest rose and fell.

Who was she if she wasn't being Angel's big sister?

Harlie watched the reflection of the sunrise on the face of the ragged mountains. It was a new day.

Two hours later Harlie noted the fine shake in her fingers as she reached for the gas nozzle to cram it in Yolanda's greedy mouth.

Long term care. The doctor had explained all the medical terminology, but this was the only scrap that stuck in Harlie's overworked brain. They said that Angel needed more help than Harlie could give, and that sent panic skittering through her like lightning. Trust the most precious thing on earth to someone else's casual care?

The run-down, overused hospital facilities hadn't surprised her. Everyone knew California was broke. But she was more alarmed by the employees that came through the locked doors at shift change. The dulled hopelessness in their eyes mirrored their patients' – as if they, too, were prisoners here. They shuffled through the hallways, as unplugged as their charges.

I can't leave Angel there.

How would her vibrant pixie survive that depressing place, much less get better? Harlie leaned her forearm on the car's roof and rubbed her gritty eyes. Gravity pulled at her body, harder than usual. Or maybe she just never noticed the pull before.

Angel had gone away in her head. The doctors couldn't tell Harlie when, or if she'd ever come back.

Anger surged, muscling aside exhaustion. What the hell did they know? When the nozzle clicked, Harlie slammed it on the pump cradle and replaced Yolanda's gas cap. For all she knew, those doctors didn't know their ass from a hot rock. She walked to the squat building to retrieve her change. After all, what good doctor would choose to work in that environment? If Angel woke in that place, she'd probably go away again, just to escape.

I sure would.

But Harlie had made calls this morning. The price of a private clinic left her breathless. She snatched the station door and stepped in, ignoring the full bodied smell of coffee that woke her stomach with a vicious growl. It was going to take some serious money to get Angel where the halls didn't smell like shit and the doctors weren't drowning in hopeless cases.

A minimum wage job wouldn't cut it. And after yesterday, she didn't even have *that*.

The swarthy man behind the counter counted change into her hand. She folded the two ones and shoved them in the back pocket of her jeans. She could live in Yolanda, but that still wouldn't leave enough . . . something scraped the back side her finger. She pulled a business card from her pocket. The PBR logo brought it back. That man's offer to learn bullfighting.

Her brain scurried through the maze of possibilities, waiting to hit a dead end. She did the math. Given the numbers the marketing guy had thrown out; she could afford the cheapest private clinic for Angel. If she gave up eating. She could give up the apartment since she'd be on the road. All the time.

Leave Angel?

Harlie couldn't rest last night, even knowing that Angel slept safely just down the hall. How would she ever get to sleep, hundreds of miles away? How could she focus on bullfighting, when she couldn't come home to Angel?

Funny how Harlie'd always thought of herself as independent. People called her a loner. But it had always been Harlie and Angel, and two people weren't alone. One was.

Well she was about to find out what a loner was, because there was no other choice. She couldn't leave Angel locked in that human warehouse.

Maybe bullfighting would be great. She remembered the thrill of jumping the bull — could it have only been the day before yesterday? A rainbow bubble of hope swelled in her, rising, breaking on her face in a smile.

She turned it on the cashier. "Do you have a phone I can borrow?"

School Days

Adversity is the diamond dust Heaven polishes its jewels with.

Thomas Carlyle

Chapter 6

Harlie spent most of the five-hour plane flight foot-bouncing, looking out the window. She'd never been in a plane before, and realized she liked the odd perspective of seeing the earth through the cloud tops. Though it didn't seem quite real — as if the plane was just an airlock with painted scenery scrolling by the window.

Maybe this was just a five-hour intermission while God arranged the set for the next act. Instead of 'Houston', her ticket should read, 'The Rest of Your Life'.

And she could hardly wait to get started.

A stab of guilt set her hands jittering on the arm rests. If she was flying off to her future, didn't that mean she was leaving Angel in her past?

Angel was settled in her new home, a slightly threadbare but 'Skilled Care' facility. Harlie had met the doctor, and though she wasn't in a position to judge the young man's credentials, at least he appeared to care.

She had left the box of their mother's books beside Angel's bed, in case they made her feel more at home. She'd laid the rose glass box on the dresser, but then reconsidered and tucked it into her spare underwear in her backpack. She'd bring it back when Angel was better. Harlie needed the touchstone more.

Her goodbye made no ripples in the deep pool of her sister's catatonic state.

She leaned her forehead against the airplane's plastic window, closing her eyes against the memory of walking out of that room. Angel had stared unseeing, while Harlie tore out her heart and left it on the bed. And now, with every passing mile, something tugged in her chest, as if her arteries were stretching to accommodate the distance, a tether, keeping her and Angel connected. It wasn't a bad feeling; after all, it allowed her body to survive without her heart.

Alone. The word echoed back from the hollow place. Her people—the only people that mattered, had dropped away leaving only Harlie. She'd never been alone before. She'd been her little family's protector since she could remember. Odd, how keeping them safe together had made her feel safe. Like she had a place; somewhere she belonged.

Opening her eyes, she focused forward. She didn't have time for self-pity. The only way she could help Angel now was to keep the money pouring in for her care and hope for a breakthrough.

Steve Rawlings had laid it out clear. The PBR was taking a big chance, laying out a bunch of money on her, sight unseen, solely on his recommendation. His reputation was at stake. He'd grilled her: Was she single? Able to travel? No ties to take her mind from the arena?

She'd only had to lie to the one.

Bullfighter School. Who knew there was such a thing? For that matter, who knew there was a place called Chilly, Texas? Steve had warned her the next week wouldn't be easy. There'd never been a woman professional bullfighter. He'd convinced the school's owner to enroll her, but the man warned that he wouldn't lower his standards for a female.

He wouldn't vouch for the attitudes of the students, either.

But once the school was over, it was the rodeo road for her. After she proved herself, on to the PBR. The money would come in. Angel would be past this bad patch, and Harlie would take Angel on the road with her. She'd have to look into online courses so Angel could finish high school. The adventures they'd have. The fun . . .

The plane's nose dropped, beginning the descent into Houston. Her stomach went weightless. She *would* make the cut.

Because she *wanted* this future.

Because Angel needed it.

***

Passengers milled around the luggage carousel like cows around a feed trough. Harlie squeezed between a businessman and a kid with a skateboard to snatch her nylon duffel from the conveyor. She backed out of the herd with her duffel, her backpack slung over her shoulder, feeling a bit lost. Trying not to think too far ahead, she reined in her worries and glanced around the room. Steve had said someone would pick her up.

A young rangy brown-haired guy in jeans, boots and cowboy hat held up a sheet of cardboard with her name on it. A canvas bag rested at his feet.

When she walked over, he doffed his straw Stetson. "Are you lost, Miss? Cuz I'm not from around here."

"Not hardly." She dropped her duffel. "That's my name on your sign."

He lowered the sign, read the name, then looked back at her, smiling at what he must assume was a joke. "A girl bullfighter? Get out."

She'd expected it. Steve had warned her about it. Still, his snort of incredulity stung like a whip's lash. She slipped her hands into her back pockets and pulled out some attitude. "You'll get out before I do, Kid."

"Kid?" He settled his hat back on his head and, eyes slitted, looked down on her. "I guess we'll see, won't we?" He held out a hand, to shake. "I'm Deuce McAllister."

She just stood there, caught between manners and munitions. If she didn't take it, did that make her a bitch? If she shook, what message would it send? If—

Beep-beep-beep-beeeeep!

A battered red ranch truck idled at the curb, a swarthy Hispanic waving from the rolled down window.

45

"That's our ride." He reached for both their bags.

She jerked hers away as if he were a purse snatcher. "I got it." Her embarrassment made it come out belligerent, and she felt blood rush to her face.

"Suit yourself, *Miss.*" He managed to make fingering his hat brim look sarcastic before he turned and marched away. Shaking his head, he dropped the sign in the trash on his way out the door.

A half hour later, Harlie swiped at the sweat that gathered on her face in spite of the hot wind blowing in the open window. *They sure misnamed this burg.* The sign at the Chilly City limits boasted one-hundred twenty-six citizens. The dusty town crouched in the urban sprawl of Houston like a squatter's shack on a country club golf course.

When the truck pulled up a long dirt drive and stopped, Harlie opened the door, crawled out of the jump seat and stepped out. The small ranch reminded her of the Western movie set back on Rancho Ramona. Only older. And more run-down. Chickens scratched in the dusty dooryard rimmed by a modest clapboard ranch house, what looked like a long bunkhouse and a faded-to-pink leaning barn.

An old man strode by the truck with bandy-legged speed that belied his stooped shoulders and the furrows in his grizzled face. "Y'all meet up with the rest in the bleachers." His voice had raspy edges, like a file dragging across wood.

Deuce stepped out of the passenger seat on the opposite side of the truck.

Manuel slammed the driver's door behind him. "You're the last ones. Y'all better hustle. I'll put your things in the bunkhouse."

"Today, people!" The old man bellowed from a pipe pole corral about fifty yards from where she stood.

How could you dread something even as you had to keep yourself from running to it? She lifted her battered cowboy hat from the seat, settled it firmly on her head. Pulse pounding in her ears, she took the first step to meet her future.

A set of weather-worn, two-step wooden bleachers sat at the side of the corral. She perched on the edge of one and checked out the other four students who eyed her as if she'd just wandered into their Good 'Ol' Boys Club. Deuce, the tall baby-face from the airport sat on the top step. Below him sat twins, identical ginger flat-topped, jar-headed farm boys with the square stocky build she recognized from steer-wrestlers on her high school rodeo team. The guy next to them didn't dress any different, but something about the angle of his hat, the ironed-to-white razor creases in his Wranglers and the toothpick in the corner of his mouth said, 'genuine cowboy'. He appeared around twenty and handsome, with blond hair curling to his collar. As if feeling her stare, he turned, clicked out of the corner of his mouth and winked at her.

She snorted. *Make that an arrogant genuine cowboy.*

"All right. You're all here, and 'bout time." The old guy stood, one hand on the pipe corral. "Today's a bust for working bulls, but I'll let you know what to expect, and we'll get the howdy's out of the way." He rested a broken down boot on the fence behind him. "I'm Hoot Leonard, and this here's my spread. I was a rodeo clown for fifteen years 'fore they started callin' what we did bullfightin'. I can teach you technique and I can teach you how to be safe. As much as you can be, anyway." He spit tobacco into the dust. "But there's two things I can't teach you, because nobody can. That's agility and bull savvy. You either got those comin' in, or you're goin' home." He paused for effect. "And I get to decide what's what."

His stare fell on her. Harlie swallowed anxiety that was trying to crawl out of her stomach, and refused to look away.

"You'll obey my instructions at all times. Men have been killed by bulls, but never on my watch. I expect that streak to continue. But I can't save you from being stupid, so when a bull is around, even if you're not in the arena, keep your head up and stay alert. Shit can and does happen. No showing off." He turned his head, his laser focus on her. "No jumping bulls."

Oh great. Rawling must have told him. Though Harlie's cheeks flamed, she gritted her teeth. She'd only been acting on instinct. Damned if she was going to feel bad about it. Especially since that's what had gotten her this chance.

He turned back to the others. "Are we clear?"

"Yessir." They said, in unison, as if they'd practiced.

"Now, look around."

They stared at him.

He sighed. "Not at me, you idjits, at the man next to you. You're going to get to know each other better'n you know your brothers." He glanced at her. "Or whoever. You're gonna know what the other does before he does it. Why? Because your lives, and more important, the lives of the riders are going to depend on it.

"I don't care what you've come in here thinkin', or what you've seen. You're not here to fight bulls. Or to look like a stud, or to be on TV. These are the *only* jobs of a bullfighter." He held up his fingers to tick off his points. "First, keep the rider safe. Second, keep other bullfighters safe. And third, keep yourself safe." A stream of tobacco juice hit the dirt, raising a little cloud of dust. "Then you keep the stock safe. You got that?"

They nodded.

"Okay, tell your name, where you hail from, and why you're here." Hoot tipped his chin at the real cowboy.

"I'm Cash Campbell, from Austin. I've been competing in rodeos since I was a kid." When he leaned back, the sun flashed off his huge gold trophy belt buckle. "Bullfighting is about the only thing I haven't tried, so I thought I'd give it a shot. It looks like fun."

Hoot grunted, then looked to the twins.

Who looked at each other. No words were spoken, but something must have passed between them, because the one on the left spoke up. "I'm Levi, and this is Jonah. Morgan. We're from Black Springs, Arkansas. Our Pa is a rodeo stock contractor, and bullfighters are scarce in our neck of the woods."

Hoot waited, but apparently that's all the twins had to say. "Okay, you." He spit tobacco juice, then pointed at Deuce.

"I'm Deuce McAlister, from Kinta, Oklahoma. I've wanted to be a bullfighter since I was old enough to know what one was. I plan on being a PBR bullfighter. It's all I ever wanted to be." Chin out, he shot a look around like someone was going to argue with him.

"Now you." He squinted at Harlie.

She considered. The truth? Or what he'd want to hear? She ran her hands down the thighs of her jeans. "I'm Harlie Cooper. From Santa Clarita, California. I like working cattle."

"Lots of safer ways to work cattle."

"I'm not looking for safe." She slammed her lips closed before 'I'm looking for money' could slip out.

"Well, you better be, cuz you can't help in the arena ifn' you're dead."

The guys snickered.

Hoot dropped his heel from the fence and stood as straight as his bandy legs allowed. "Y'all get settled in the bunkhouse. There'll be a run before supper." He pointed to her. "You. Follow me." He strode off.

Harlie shook off the curious glances of the other students and hustled to catch up. "Where are we going, Sir?"

"House. The Missus has a room made up for you."

She followed, but stopped at the foot of the porch.

Hoot took two steps, stopped and turned, his wrinkles falling into an irritated frown. "What?"

"Sir, can't stay at the house." Even though her heart beat pounded her eardrums like a garage band, she kept her chin up. "Sir, I -"

"A kid tells me 'no' within an hour of meeting me? You call me Hoot."

This was a minefield, and it would be Angel who paid if she put a foot wrong. "Hoot, Sir, how do I get to know them 'like brothers', if I'm bunking at the house? I can handle myself. I've worked around men all my life."

He glared from under wiry, straggly gray brows. "But I'll wager you never bunked with 'em, though, did you?"

"Nosir. But if I'm ever going to be accepted as one of them, I think it has to start now." She shoved her fists into her back pockets and forced her jitters to still.

49

He ran a hand over his two-day-whiskered chin. It sounded like sandpaper. "The Missus ain't going to like it." His green eyes bored into her. "But, you asked for it. Follow me." He set off for the screen door of the bunkhouse, where the other students had disappeared a few minutes before.

Harlie grabbed her duffel and backpack from the porch and hustled after him. Her drumbeat heart cranked to 'Wipeout' speed and the crickets in her stomach started rocking out. She tightened her stomach muscles.

For Angel.

Which was almost altogether true – except for the tiny blackened spot on her soul that had recognized the whoosh of the electric doors at LAX this morning as a cage door opening.

Hoot put his hand on the door handle. She touched his arm. "Sir? I think I have to do this alone."

He looked at her a long moment, his leathery face unreadable. Then he turned on his heel and walked for the house.

Grabbing a breath, the door handle and all her courage, she stepped in.

She stood a moment, eyes adjusting to the lack of blazing sunshine. The room wasn't exactly silent—echoes of words spoken before she walked in hung in the hot dusty air.

Four simple iron beds made up with green army surplus blankets marched down the right wall of the rectangular room, her fellow students reclined on all but the last, against the far wall.

This might have been easier if she'd had brothers. But the men's thoughts were as foreign to her as ancient Greek. She strode the silent gauntlet head up, bearing the stabs of stares without flinching. Outside.

"Oh no, she's not."

She whirled to face the voice she recognized as Deuce's. "What's the matter, not mature enough to handle sleeping in the same room with a woman?"

Deuce lay back, propped on his elbows. "It's not seemly."

The twins nodded like identical bobble-heads. Cash, the genuine cowboy, hands laced behind his head, just watched with an amused smile.

"Seemly?" A dusty chuckle of surprise popped out before she could stop it. "Do people really still worry about that?"

"Where I come from, they do."

"Where are you from? Nineteen-fifty?" Her boots thumped the silvered plank floor to her bunk, and she dropped her duffel and backpack on the bed. A scarred end table sat next to it. For some stupid reason, she felt an unreasonable rush of liquid to her eyes.

Screw them. They're sure as hell not the first to disapprove of your choices. You're just tired, and the past few days have been a long strange trip.

Seeing only two doors on the opposite wall, she walked to the farthest and pushed it open to find a tiled shower room. No dividers, no curtains. A gang shower. Just three aluminum shower heads along one wall, a drain in the middle of the floor, a sink opposite the door.

Well, maybe she'd have to shower at the house. Not ideal, but . . .

She stepped out, trying to ignore the stares of the men and pushed open the other door. A sink on the wall straight ahead, a urinal on the wall to the left. She looked right, then let out a breath. Thank God. Two toilet stalls with doors. She could live with that. She walked over, stepped into a stall, took care of business, then looked for somewhere to put her used tampon. She couldn't flush it; this far out of town, they had to be on a septic system. She agonized a moment, but seeing no other alternative, she buried it in a wad of toilet paper and, wincing, tucked it in the waistband of her jeans, under her t-shirt.

Gross never killed anybody.

Luckily, this was her last day. She unlatched the door, walked to the sink and washed her hands, eyeing the trash can next to the urinal. Much as she dreaded walking out with the evidence, leaving it in the trash here was just too . . . personal. She dried her hands, checking in the mirror to be sure there wasn't a bulge at the waist of her t-shirt. With a last check to be sure her expression showed no weakness, she turned and pushed the door open.

The guys hadn't moved, but from the whispering echoes, they'd been talking. Probably getting to know each other. Probably talking about her.

Feeling the familiar needle stab of otherness, she considered sitting and trying to interject herself into the conversation. Imagining the silence that would ensue, she kept walking. A trash barrel stood on the side of the bunkhouse closest to the barn, and after a glance around, she buried the wad of TP under an empty feed sack, then brushed her hands on the back of her jeans.

Sweat tickled her scalp. She took off her straw hat to scratch her head. The sunrays hammered harder here than in California. She felt marinated in the liquid heat and her own sweat. She glanced back at the door. Dammit, she should march back in there and demand that they talk to her. She took a step.

But what if they wouldn't? It wasn't like she could make them talk. Maybe she'd just give them some time to get used to the idea of a lady bullfighter. Of bunking with a lady bullfighter.

The dooryard was deserted. Even the chickens were smart enough to take up residence under the porch, out of the sun. The barn door stood open, so she headed for some blessed shade.

The barn wasn't cool, but seemed so in comparison. Slits of sunlight slipped between the warped boards of the walls as if the sun begrudged the shade within. The wide aisle was lined with wooden stalls, and the tops of the Dutch-doors stood open, sills worn with the rubbing and cribbing of many generations of horses. Feeling at home for the first time today, she walked from stall to stall, whispering hellos and rubbing friendly forelocks.

"Baaaaah!"

The outrage in the bleat brought her head around. A short white Billy goat with dirty knees and oversized curling horns stood in the middle of the aisle, scraping the dirt floor with a hoof. Then he reared, lowered his head and charged.

"Hey!" She sidestepped, but the goat swerved at the last second, colliding with her hip. The impact shook her bones and drove her back. She tripped over a hay bale and fell on her ass.

"Damn, goat. What'd I ever do to you?" She snatched her hat, which had fallen in the dirt.

"Baaaaah!" The dirty demon scraped a hoof and prepared to charge again.

She scrambled to her feet and hopped onto the hay bale, hopefully out of range.

A stall door down the way swung open, and Hoot ambled out, leading a saddled chestnut horse. "I see you met Banjo."

The goat pawed, watching her with alien eyes, waiting for his next chance.

"I didn't do a thing to him. What's his problem?'

The horse clomping placidly behind, Hoot wheezed an arid cough that she took as a chuckle. "Ah, Banjo's okay. A bit contrary, maybe."

"Contrary?" She rubbed her bruised hip. "I think you need to call an exorcist."

Hoot patted the goat's head on his way by. "Stand down, Banjo."

Banjo didn't hear well. Or didn't listen well. He shook his head and continued the stare-down.

Hoot kept walking. "Are you coming, or are you gonna play with my goat all day?"

She hopped down and trotted after the horse, throwing glances over her shoulder to be sure the devil wasn't sneaking up from behind.

"You plan on running in those boots?"

"Um. Nosir." The sun pounced as they walked out of the shade of the barn. Her head throbbed with the beat of her heart.

"Then get a move on. Daylight's burnin'. Roust those lazy dogs while you're at it."

"Yessir." She jogged to the bunkhouse, pulled the screen door and stepped in.

Still sprawled on the cots, the guys stopped mid-laugh.

Head down, she strode for her cot. "Hoot wants us to fall out for a run." She opened her duffel, pulled out a pair of shorts, tennis shoes and a ball cap, then headed for the bathroom to change.

***

In spite of the hot damp air making it feel like she was more swimming than running, Harlie beat all the boys back from the two mile run. She walked into the bunkhouse, wondering how she'd get a shower. Hoot was still trotting his horse alongside the guys.

A flash of color caught her eye. "What the . . ."

A bright yellow shower curtain hung from a rod suspended by wire from the bare beams of the ceiling, separating her cot at the end from the others.

At a metallic click, she turned to see the driver who'd picked her up at the airport walking out of the shower room holding a screwdriver and a plastic bag. "What's going on, Manuel?"

"I just installed a lock for you on the shower room door."

"And this?" She waved at the hideous curtain.

"Senora Leonard's orders. She said to tell you sorry about the color. It was all she had on short notice."

"I sure appreciate the lock. But the curtain —"

"The Missus's orders." His expression told her that was the end of that.

That someone had thought about her situation, her feelings . . . for the second time today, emotion took her unawares, taking out her sandbagged defenses like Katrina took the levees. She turned away so he wouldn't see. Would this day never end? "Will you thank her for me?"

"Sure." She heard his footsteps retreat.

"Thanks, Manuel."

"De nada." The screen door slapped behind him.

She pushed the ridiculous shower curtain aside, grabbed her duffel and dug through it for clothes, shampoo and a towel. She wanted to get in the shower room and lock it before the guys got back.

54

The lock snapped with a satisfying *snick*. She hung her fresh clothes and towel on a peg by the door and dropped her dirty ones on the floor. Even knowing she was alone and the door was locked, she felt overly naked, walking across the room to turn on the shower.

Well, she expected the guys to get used to this. She'd better too.

Turning the handle to 'cold', she sucked a breath when the deliciously frigid water hit her sweaty skin. A hollow yearning burst in her chest, so vast and unexpected, she crossed her fists over her breasts and hunched her shoulders, trying to ease it.

Angel.

The image of her sister staring sightlessly at the industrial beige wall of the facility made the hollowness expand. The pressure built in her chest. She searched for a happier memory.

A younger, more innocent Angel, ran at the edge of the beach, the splashing surf breaking in flashes of crystal. Their mother chased her, pants rolled to her knees, blonde hair bouncing, feet delicate as pale porcelain. Both were laughing, graceful, caught in a freeze-frame photo that had never been taken.

But that was okay, because Harlie remembered it. The hollow ache in her chest eased enough for her to straighten and turn finish her shower.

You'll be okay. It's just that you're far away, and everything is strange. You'll get used to it.

She'd have to, because this was her life now.

The deep rumbling of voices through the wall announced that the guys were back. Dressing in her other pair of jeans and a fresh t-shirt, she ran a comb through her hair. She wrapped her dirty clothes in the towel, took a breath, tightened her stomach and unlocked the door. "Your turn." She addressed the room in general.

They didn't look at her directly, which, for some stupid reason, made her remember she'd been naked moments before.

She clutched her bundle tighter to her chest and walked to her cot.

"Nice run."

Deuce's voice came from behind her and she turned to see if he was being sarcastic. His small smile appeared sincere. It threw her off-balance, as his offer to shake had, in the airport. Was this an olive branch? Or a switch, to hit her with? She ducked her head. "Thanks." She pulled the curtain, grateful for the flimsy privacy, even though the guys had all trooped to the shower. She dumped her dirty clothes in a garbage bag she'd brought, then dropped onto the bed, fishing under it for her backpack.

The light from the window hit the sides of Angel's glass house, making it glow as if it were made of rubies instead of carnival glass. She traced the black and white yin-yang symbol on the lid, feeling the hole in her where Angel should be. Opening the box, she touched the sable lock of Angel's hair she'd snipped . . . could it only be this morning? She knew Angel wouldn't have minded.

A bell clanged out in the yard. "Dinner, five minutes. You're not here then, you don't eat!" Hoot's gravel voice carried easily through the screen.

She closed the lid, pulled open the top drawer of the scarred nightstand, and tucked the glass house safe inside.

They ate on the back patio of the house, at an oversized picnic table shaded by a corrugated tin roof. While the guys settled on the benches, Harlie vacillated by the back door. Her mother would switch her for not offering to help the hostess, but in this case she wasn't here as a guest, but a student. One of the guys.

But still, she was a woman. Would Ms. Leonard think badly of her if she didn't behave like one?

She shifted from foot to foot, watching the guys settle, laughing and elbowing each other for room. Dammit, this wasn't fair. These thoughts would never cross a man's mind. She chuffed a sigh of disgust.

Since when did you start looking for fair?

The screen door swung open and a thin gray-haired woman in a flowered apron emerged with a platter of fried chicken.

"Thank you, Ma'am. For the lock." Reflexively, Harlie reached to ease the woman's burden. "And for . . . stuff." She couldn't speak of the thoughtfulness. It was so rare; she didn't know how. Besides, five men sat within earshot.

The woman reared back, eyeing Harlie as if she'd tried to snatch her child. "You are a paying student. You sit."

Stung, Harlie stuffed her hands in her pockets. Well, that answered that. She'd taken a step to the table when the soft voice came from behind her.

"But thank you, child."

She kept walking, and sat in the only narrow space left, beside Deuce.

He sighed, but scooted over, making room.

Ms. Leonard set the platter in front of Hoot, who sat in a plastic-webbed lawn chair at the head of the table. Mashed potatoes and gravy, snap beans and corn on the cob followed, the plates clustered as close to Hoot as space provided.

Cash reached for a golden chicken thigh.

"Hey," Hoot barked.

Cash froze, chicken halfway to his plate.

Hoot looked through his bushy gray brows at the offender. "On this ranch we say grace before we eat."

Cash replaced the evidence, mumbling "Sorry," he bowed his head.

Hoot reached a hand to Cash on his left and Levi, on his right. They grasped it, and reached to the person beside them.

Given no choice, Harlie loosened her fist in her napkin and took Deuce's offered hand, then stretched the other across the table to Jonah. She'd do what she had to for the sake of decency, but she wasn't closing her eyes. Harlie believed Bible stories about as much as Mom's romance novels. She'd learned early that time was much better spent trying to fix something than wait for help that didn't come.

"Lord, make us truly grateful for this bountiful meal prepared by your humble woman, my wife. I thank you for her, this ranch and all the animals upon it. Please keep these poor fools here safe. Amen."

Harlie took her hands back as soon as the last word was out. Hoot's raspy voice saying the soft words made them more sincere. The Leonard's had probably been married for longer than she'd been alive. How strange was that? She tried to imagine caring enough about someone to want to spend the rest of her life with them. No picture came to mind. Sure, there was her and Angel, but they were sisters. That was genetic. Trusting and depending on someone she wasn't related to? How could that even happen?

Hoot lifted a platter of chicken and passed it to Levi. "We eat family style here. You'll have three squares. Good solid food." He didn't fill his plate until all the students had taken what they wanted.

They all sat, waiting.

"Well? Aincha hungry? Dig in."

They did, and soon the conversation flowed like the iced tea.

Cash elbowed the silent Jonah. "Hey, better luck next time, Dude. You almost beat me."

Blushing, Jonah focused on his plate.

"Yeah, but I wouldn't brag." Hoot rasped. "You got beat by a girl."

Harlie smiled and sat straighter.

"Too bad, the most you'll have to run in the arena is twenty feet. Speed don't count for much if'n you can't sidestep a goat." Hoot cackled and Deuce raised an eyebrow at Harlie.

Face burning, she speared some beans onto her fork. *You came in first. That's what matters.*

Damned goat.

"Tomorrow we get started. Y'all better get a good night's sleep. You're gonna be on your toes all day."

The door opened, and Mrs. Leonard descended, carrying a lattice-crust cherry pie.

58

Dark had fallen, but the temperature hadn't. Harlie left the lights behind and walked the dirt drive to the road for a bit of solitude and quiet. Didn't those guys ever shut up?

She took in a deep breath of the night. Plants released their scents of sage, dust, and the flowers Miz Leonard had hanging in pots on the porch, as if sighing in relief from the brutal sun.

The security light in the yard gave her enough to see by, but not enough to throw back the dark. The muscles in her core relaxed and she slowed her pace, letting anticipation build. And the worry.

The cheap knockoff phone she'd bought with the advance Rawling had sent was the first she'd ever owned. But it wasn't an extravagance—it was a lifeline. She'd worked it out with the nurses before she left; she'd call every night and they'd hold the receiver to Angel's ear, so Harlie could say goodnight.

She pulled the phone from her back pocket and hit speed dial to its only stored number.

"Hello, Harlie, its Crystal. Let me ring through to your sister's room and I'll run in and pick it up."

"Wait! How is she today?" But she was speaking to hold music. She paced across the drive and back.

"Okay Harlie, I'm here."

"Crystal, how is she?"

"We're about the same today, but we're eating well, aren't we, Angel?"

Do they teach that 'we' thing in nursing school?

Rustling came across the line and Crystal's faraway voice said, "Go ahead, Harlie."

"Hey Littlest." She used Mom's old nickname for Angel, hoping.

Nothing.

"Well, I started bullfighting school today. I'm living with a bunch of noisy, sweaty guys."

Silence.

"But I did whup their butts on a two mile run tonight. It's really hot and humid here. You'd hate it." She rambled on, not caring that she sounded as stilted as a high school valedictorian. "I was thinking about that time it was so hot that mom took us to the beach. Remember how sand got in our shorts and the salt rubbed our skin raw? Man that was a good day." Her voice cracked.

She felt lost. Alone. But then, so was Angel. Maybe they could be alone, together? She cleared her throat. "Anyway, I just called to tell you goodnight, sleep tight, and don't let the boogeyman bite." It was their nighttime ritual since Angel was little, a spell Harlie had created to keep bad dreams away.

"I'm okay Angel. You be okay too, okay? I love you."

She waited a few seconds, letting the sound of Angel's breathing soothe her.

Then she made herself hit 'end'. As she trudged back up the drive, the dirt beneath her boots didn't feel solid. Probably because most of her existed in room twenty-two of Compadres Medical Center.

She walked in the bunkhouse. The stream of conversation flowed around her without a ripple. Why would they notice a ghost?

She rounded the ugly curtain and sat on the bed, too heart-weary to change to shorts and lie down.

Someone turned off the light.

". . . so Pa paid our tuition and plane fare to get us here. God knows where he scraped up the money. I only hope we don't let him down."

Funny how in the absence of light, you notice voices. Levi's was made for the dark – deep and rumbly, like water over rocks.

Maybe, in the dark, I can talk to them.

"How'd you get here, Deuce?" Levi asked.

Springs creaked.

"I'm from nowhere, Oklahoma." His voice wasn't as deep as Levi's but his drawl was rich as the soil of his home state. "My dad has a hardscrabble ranch outside town. Don't get me wrong; I love home. But I never planned to trail skinny cows for the rest of my life."

"Did he expect you to?" Cash's brassy baritone matched his personality.

"He would have liked it if I did. He's outnumbered with me gone. See, I've got four younger sisters, each one with a stronger bent for disaster. I'm just so tired of females. The products in the bathroom. The drama. The helplessness." He sighed. "I was looking for a break from saving women." He stopped, maybe remembering who was listening.

So much for her night-talking.

Cash's chuckle filled the silence. "Sucks to be you."

"Nah. I'm proud of where I grew up. It's just that Kinta is a great place to be *from*. The PBR is where I'm going *to*."

She'd heard enough guy-bonding for one night. Harlie pushed herself to her feet and walked to the bathroom to change.

Chapter 7

"**G**rab your socks and drop your coc— um . . . daylight's burnin'!" Hoot's raspy shout came through the screen door of the bunkhouse. "Breakfast is ready in five!"

Harlie jerked upright. There wasn't much to see in the pre-dawn light. Squeaking springs and groans came from the other side of the shower curtain.

Running a hand through her hair, she blinked in an attempt to congeal the sludge between her ears. She'd lain awake it seemed forever last night, sweating in her nylon shorts and t-shirt, listening to the snores of the men and the rebounding echoes of her separateness: from Angel, from home, from a friendly face. At night, the wall of detachment she built to survive the day became a pen, holding her captive with only her downward spiraling thoughts for company. Talking to Angel wasn't near enough. She missed her sister's voice, her smell, the half of herself Harlie'd left behind.

It doesn't help wanting.

Marshaling determination, she threw the covers back. She grabbed her jeans and t-shirt, then pulled back the curtain and headed for the bathroom, toiletry bag in hand.

Deuce stood shirtless at the sink, brushing his teeth. When he saw her in the mirror, he froze, mid-brush. His eyes darted, as if looking for a way out.

"Oh please. I know you brush your teeth." She walked to the only unoccupied bathroom stall. Might as well start getting used to this now.

"Hey, Deuce, are we working bulls today, do you know?"

Cash's voice from the stall beside her made her jump.

"Hont ooh." Deuce said through his toothbrush.

She lowered her jeans and sat. Glimpsing Cash's boots under the stall door, her bladder muscles clamped down. Oh God, was she going to be able to do this?

Dammit, you're not going to be able to avoid peeing for ten days. Get over yourself and just do it. It'll get easier. She stuck her fingers in her ears, closed her eyes and imagined herself anywhere but in a bathroom with two men.

The toilet next to her flushed.

After, she stepped to the sink to wash her hands and brush her hair and teeth. Deuce was alone at the sink. He wiped his hands on his towel, gave her the stink-eye, turned on his heel and walked out.

That guy's attitude was getting old. It wasn't her fault he had a brood of simpering sisters at home. She glared at the tough-girl mask in the mirror.

You just go out there and kick their butts today. That'll earn you respect.

The bunkhouse was empty when she walked out of the bathroom. They'd left her! She tossed her bag on her cot and sprinted out the door.

She rounded the corner of the patio at a dead run.

Hoot looked up from his full plate. "This morning is your one pass. After this, if you're not sitting when I pass the food, you don't eat."

"Yessir." Head down, heart hammering, she stepped to the table. Everyone sat in the same places as last night, so the only space was again beside Deuce. She slid in.

They again held hands while Hoot said grace. At the foot of the picnic table an old, clunky TV perched on a metal TV tray like a big man on a Shetland pony. When he rasped 'Amen', she dropped the large hands like they were radioactive.

Hoot passed her plates of scrambled eggs, thick bacon, hashed browns, and fluffy golden biscuits. The guys dug into Ball jars of homemade strawberry jam.

"Later today there'll a batch of wannabe bull riders coming."

Cash paused, biscuit halfway to his mouth. "Oh, good, we get to show you our stuff."

Hoot shot him a look. "None of you are getting in an arena with a bull until I know you know something. Today's ground school."

"Are you going to work the bulls, Mr. Leon – Hoot?" Levi asked.

Hoot made that cough-wheeze that passed for a laugh. "No, boy. After the last time I broke my neck, the missus threatened me with worse than what a bull could dish out if I ever got in the arena again." *Wheeze.* "No, I'm bringing in a couple'a local boys to fight the bulls. They're not great, but teachin' you what not to do is a good lesson too."

The last time he broke his neck? Harlie force-swallowed a bite of egg. In spite of the clammy heat, she shivered as an ice water trickle of reality ran down her spine. She hadn't thought much about the medical paperwork Steve Rawling had sent, just signed and returned it.

No longer hungry, she touched her paper napkin to her lips and set it alongside her plate. If she got hurt, her medical bills may be covered, but if she didn't work, she didn't get paid. And Angel would be sent back to that human warehouse.

She glanced around the table as a cloud of impending failure moved in. Hoot made it clear yesterday that they'd have to work together in the arena. How could she do that, when they didn't even acknowledge her presence half the time? Steve had warned her this wouldn't be easy—he didn't know the half of it.

"Y'all done? We got work to do." Hoot carried his plate to the screened back door. It opened, and wet hands emerged from the shadows to take it. "Take your plates to the Missus, then come sit."

64

Harlie was last in line. Ms. Leonard didn't reach for the plate, just looked her over. "You makin' out okay in that stable of studs?"

"Yes'm" Harlie shot a look over her shoulder to be sure the guys weren't within earshot. Being singled out would be one more reason—

"Well, you let me know if it gets bad, or just if you just need some 'woman time', y'hear?"

Squirming inside, Harlie shifted her feet. She couldn't be rude to the only one on the place who'd been nice, but she had to get back before the guys noticed. "I'm fine, Ma'am." She ducked her head. *Let me go!*

The older woman finally took Harlie's plate. "Well, you let me know if you have anything you can't handle."

"Yes'm. Thank you." Free at last, she hustled to her seat.

Hoot walked to the foot of the table. Lifting the remote from the top of the TV, he turned it on, pushed in a VCR tape, then paused it.

When they'd all returned and sat, he asked, "How many of you have fought a bull?"

Cash's hand was the first in the air, but the others followed. Harlie's fingers twitched. Given Hoot's comment about her bull-jumping, she didn't think he'd count that. So she crossed her forearms on the table to keep her hand from rising and avoided the glances of the other students.

"Most often in the lower ranks, you're going to only have two 'fighters' in the arena. The PBR has lotsa' money, so they have three. We'll go over what that means in the way of strategy later." He started the tape. The camera panned the chutes at a PBR event, then zoomed in on the one full of bull, a rider perched atop it.

"Look where the bullfighters are standing." Hoot paused the tape before the gate opened. See how there's one on either side of the gate? Part of your job is to help turn the bull into the spin. The top flight PBR bulls don't need it, but the ones you're going to run into might."

He paused the tape. "Let me back up, in case some of you don't know this." He scanned his students as if it wasn't Harlie he was talking to, but he needn't have bothered; they all knew. "Half the ride's score is cowboy, half the bull. The stock contractors are asked for their druthers for bullfighters all the time, so if you want to work, you're going to want the contractors in your corner.

"You do that by making their bulls look good. A bull that turns into a spin scores higher than one that hauls ass for the other end of the arena. Now watch." He moved the tape to where the gate opened. When the bull had taken one jump out of the chute, he paused it. "See how the gates on the left open from the left, and the ones on the right open from the right?" They nodded. "A bull has a lead, just like a horse does. Think of it as being right or left handed. This bull is left-handed. They load him on the left, because he bucks better that way." He pointed to the screen. "First thing you watch for is the bull's head. He goes where he looks. That's how you know which way he's gonna spin." He advanced a few frames.

"If he gets in the spin on his own, you just stand ready. Not so close to distract the bull, but close enough to step in when you need to."

And how do you know which is which? Harlie pulled a tiny notebook and pen from her back pocket, and started taking notes.

"See how this one is looking straight ahead? That's when you step in. Whichever of you is closer to his head, you run in a circle in front of him, and he'll follow you into a spin." He raised a finger. "As long as you're not too close. If you're close, he'll get a bead on you, and chase you down. Then you'll not only have the contractor pissed at you. If you're not quick, the bull's gonna run you over."

Harlie wrote as fast as she could.

"Get the bull started. Then you step back an' watch. But now, you watch the rider." He let the tape roll. "Watch his hips." He pointed at the screen. "See how he's getting outta shape?" The rider was leaning to the inside, and with every jump, leaned more. "We call that falling into the well. Odds of him makin' it out are small."

Sure enough, the rider fell to the inside of the spin. Hoot fast forwarded to the next ride. A huge dun bull lunged from the chute and the cowboy was left behind, thrown back on his hip pockets. When the bull kicked his back feet like he was trying to kick out the lights, Hoot froze the tape. "See how his arm got straight? That's another sign that he's coming off. Or he can lose holt' with his spurs. The bull can come up and hit him in the face, or pull him down on his horns. There's a buncha' ways this can go bad." He looked up at them. "Point is, you have a better chance a bein' in a good position, if you know early. So once the bull is bucking good, you watch the rider, and stay outta the way."

He fast forwarded through the ride.

"Aren't we going to get to see the bullfighters work?" Cash huffed.

Hoot's grizzled eyebrows came down. "Son, you too good for all this? Cuz if you are, you sure don't need to be here."

"No sir. I just –"

"Then you'd best just ferget what you think you know, and open your ears, boy." He turned back to the TV. "When you see the rider's in trouble, you don't rush in. You wait. You get too close; you'll be part of the problem." He raised a liver-spotted hand, index finger extended. "You're gonna distract the bull and he'll come outta the spin. That might help or hurt the rider, but you already done screwed up the ride." He extended his second finger. It was missing the end from the last joint on. "You get kicked, horned, or stepped on." He let loose another finger. "The rider will come off and land on you." He dropped his hand and shrugged. "You can't help a wreck if you're flat in the middle of one. Nuthin' good is gonna happen if you step in too fast."

He advanced to the next ride, stopping when the rider was well on his way to being ejected. "See where the fighters are?" He pointed at the screen. The two men were caught, frozen midstride, heading for the bull. "Here's where you go to work. You've gotta get in there, and get the bull's head up. Get him to follow you out of the spin and away from the cowboy. Watch." He let the tape advance. The man stepped in and tapped the bull's head on the spin. The rider flew off, landing on his butt in the dirt six feet away. The bull stopped spinning, lowered his head and went after the bullfighter. "That's what you want, right there. See how he pushed that bull's head down? Bull's gonna push back. That brings his head up. And you're standin' right in front of him, a perfect target."

Harlie swallowed a wad of worry as wildness sang through her veins. How could she long for the danger, even as she feared for her life? She didn't know. It just was.

A cowboy with a whistle swinging from his neck rounded the edge of the house. "Hey, Hoot, the boys are here. You ready?"

"Yeah, ready." He turned off the TV. "Y'all, this is Deke, the coach of the high school rodeo team. Let's go buck some bulls."

The men headed for the corral. After jotting a final note, Harlie rose and jogged after the crowd.

She'd watched the bull rider's practice on the rodeo team back home, but she hadn't paid much attention to the bullfighters. Now she sat sweating in the sauna heat, listening to Hoot and taking more notes.

"See how Bubba got that bull's head up? Once he did, the bull lit out after him, and the rider had a clean getaway. Meanwhile Luke hung back 'til he was sure the rider got up and was heading for the fence, then he took off after the bull, to be sure Bubba got away." Hoot turned to them. "Remember your priorities: the rider, the other bullfighter, yourself, the bull."

Levi retrieved bottles of water from the cooler beside the bleachers and passed them around. Harlie rolled the sweating plastic bottle over her forehead, then slid it over the back of her neck, shivering when drips rolled down her spine. Cash may grumble about wanting to get in the arena, but she wanted all the 'ground school' she could get.

Thanks to the dairy, and her job working with cattle on the ranch in California, she had 'cow savvy', but there was a big difference between range cattle and these bulls.

Namely, attitude. And proximity.

Safety helmet or no, these kids were nuts.

"Watch 'im, this a mean'un!" Hoot yelled to the bullfighters who stood waiting as the rider in the chute prepped his rope. The baseball-bat-sized horn jutting from the slats had what must have been a wicked tip trimmed off. When the bull kicked the metal slats, the other chutes wobbled in a wave and the cowboys grabbed for a handhold. The bullfighters backed up a step.

"Still in a hurry to get out there?" Deuce asked Cash.

"Oh hell yeah. Once we gathered wild ones from the mountain back home, and –"

The gate swung, and a huge brindled bull took one long leap into the arena. The move left the rider behind, his arm pulled straight. The bull reared then plunged, overbalancing the rider. He lost hold with his spurs and his heels came up behind him. His head came down.

The bull's came up.

It seemed to happen in slow motion. There was a *crack* of plastic hitting bone, then the rider was off in a flight of boneless unconsciousness.

"Stop." Hoot commanded, his arm shooting in front of Harlie's chest.

She stopped, hand on the top pipe of the corral, not aware of having stood, much less running to the fence.

Alongside her, Deuce looked as surprised as she.

When the rider hit the dirt, Harlie felt the thud through the soles of her boots.

Bubba slapped the bull on the nose and his head came around, sighting a new target.

Luke stepped between the rider and the bull, prepared to take a shot if he had to.

Bubba was fast, but the enraged bull was faster. He lowered his head and charged, catching Bubba on the hip and tossing him six feet ahead, directly in his path. Bubba landed on his feet, the bull inches away. He spun, his baggy shorts and jersey flaring, and took off at a ninety-degree angle. The bull took up the chase.

A kid on a horse moved in and roped the bull's horns and dragged him, snorting and head tossing, out of the arena.

Luke squatted beside the unconscious cowboy, but didn't touch him. The second the bull cleared the gate, the coach and another man ran in and knelt beside the downed rider.

"Did you see that? The 'fighters worked that just perfect." Hoot demonstrated with his hands. "Luke protected the rider, Bubba drew off the bull. Beautiful. Just like they were dancing."

Harlie shot a look at the other students. Their eyes showed the shock she felt.

"What? You think I'm hard?" Hoot's brows slammed together and he spit into the dust. "If you get all soft and sappy in a wreck, you can't do your job. Sometimes that means taking a hit, like Bubba did. Like Luke could've. You cain't fix everything. You do your best, and leave the rest to God."

In the arena, the men were helping the dazed rider sit up.

Thank God. Taking a deep breath, Harlie willed her heart to slow from its machine-gun-fire cadence. Her stomach sloshed her breakfast in a greasy wave.

She'd known this was a dangerous job. She was okay with that. But sitting helpless as the wreck unfolded was horrible. Just watching was much worse than facing down a pissed off bull. At least she wouldn't have to feel that paralytic powerlessness when she was in the arena.

She always felt best *doing*.

When her mom dropped responsibilities like breadcrumbs in her wake, Harlie picked them up. After mom died, she'd looked after Angel. When Mack died in the fire, she'd kept them from the do-gooder clutches of Social Services. As long as she could *do* something, she had a chance of making things better. Even if she made a mistake, she could do something else and right things again.

The only truly terrifying thing was not being able to do anything.

Well, that and the possibility of getting hurt, and not being able to earn money to help Angel.

She pushed away the memory of Angel, staring sightlessly at the industrial green wall of the county hospital. Compared to that, bullfighting was easy. Because it was doing.

Turning from the fence, she returned to her seat.

Four riders later, they took a break. Harlie took off her hat and swiped sweat from her forehead. Living in a non-air-conditioned apartment, she was used to heat, but this humidity melted a hole in her and her strength had trickled out, leaving her a spent puddle.

"You think this is hot, you should try two hours of football practice in August." Cash stepped from the bleacher and walked to the cooler.

Harlie rolled her eyes. *Of course he was on the football team. Dude is a legend in his own mind.*

He reached into the cooler and pulled out a bottle of water. "They refill these you know." There was no distinctive click when he unscrewed the cap. "Cheapskate."

"That's rude." Slipped out before Harlie could stop it.

Cash snorted. "A chick who's living in a bunkhouse with a bunch of guys, sharing their bathroom, is gonna explain polite to me?"

"Listen ass—"

"Toss me one, willya?" Deuce held out a hand.

Cash tossed one into it, then handed them out to the rest. He snagged another, screwed off the top, doffed his hat, and dumped the contents over his head.

"Hey, don't waste it. He may not have more." Harlie drank half the bottle in one swallow.

Cash shook his blond locks like a wet dog, scattering drops over Harlie. She half expected them to sizzle on her skin. The dots of cool didn't last for more than a sigh.

"He'd better. I paid good money to be here, and he sure isn't spending it on the accommodations."

Harlie added 'entitled' on her list of adjectives for this idiot. He was what her old boss, Tonio, used to call, 'All hat and no cattle'.

71

Well, they'd find out soon enough. Hoot told them that tomorrow, they'd get in the arena. Her stomach gave a rumble, the kinetic potential in far-off summer thunder.

And it felt good.

Chapter 8

Having given up her fits-and-starts attempt at sleep around four, Harlie was showered and waiting when Hoot yelled through the screen door of the bunkhouse at dawn. What dreams she'd had were dark and bloody, of mauled riders and glass-shard etchings in her sister's skin. She lay on her cot, suspended between a room in Compadres Mental Health Center, and whatever would happen today.

She rounded the shower curtain as the guys shuffled for the bathroom, looking like little boys in their pajama bottoms, sleepy eyes and unguarded expressions. They must've still been asleep, because each mumbled 'Good mornin', on their way by. Well, all but Cash.

But she'd take what progress she got. She returned their greeting.

Smiling, she let the screen door slap behind her and took a deep breath of the faint hint of cool. The heavy morning air wouldn't be called 'fresh' but it seemed so, compared to what the rest of the day would be. The first rays of dawn weren't kind, spotlighting a strip of peeling paint here, a loose porch board there, casting the dooryard in an abandoned, falling-to-ruin, light.

She didn't want to be late for breakfast, but she also didn't want to be found sitting at her place like a good little girl when the guys rounded the corner of the house.

Imagining working in the arena today, the familiar-odd mix of trepidation and thrill fizzed in her blood, making it hard to stand still. Maybe a few minutes of warm up. Her boots raised dust as she jogged into the wide alley between the barn and an empty corral.

"Baaaaah!" The dirty white goat stood barring the way, shaking his beard at her.

Yesterday she'd been caught unawares. Not today. "You want some? Bring it on, Dude." Scowling, she shook out her hands, bouncing from one foot to the other like a boxer.

"Baaaaah!" The billy goat charged.

She waited until the last second, until his horns were inches from her thigh, then sidestepped, like she'd seen in the films yesterday. The goat plunged by.

Smug spreading with her grin, she began a turn. "Banjo is a stupid name for a—"

The beast's horns slammed into the back of her knees, knocking her legs from under her. "Shit!" On her hands and knees, she scrambled to the wall of the barn.

"Dang it." Hoot's raspy voice came from the front of the barn. "Will you quit messing with my goat and get your behind to the breakfast table?"

"Bah." The goat sauntered by, head up, a triumphant gleam in his eye.

Harlie stood, grumbling under her breath as she brushed the dirt off her jeans and walked to breakfast, her face hotter than the fires of hell that produced that goat.

Of course the other students were already seated when she came around the corner to the patio.

Once grace was said and the pancakes had been passed, Cash rubbed his hands together. "Finally. Today we get to work some bulls."

Hoot squinted down the table at him. "We'll see."

Cash's smile slid off. "But you said—"

"I said no one dies on my watch. I'll decide when y'all get in with a bull." Hoot poured himself more orange juice.

Cash opened his mouth like he wanted to say something, but stuffed in a forkful of pancake, instead.

Jonah, an entreating look on his face, elbowed his brother who elbowed him back, hard enough to rock the picnic table. "You got a mouth. You ask him."

"Y'all gonna tussle, take it in the yard," Hoot barked.

Jonah's red face matched his hair. He cleared his throat. "Hoot, sir?" His voice was small, as if he hadn't used it in so long he wasn't sure of the volume control.

You could have heard a spider fart as everyone at the table waited to hear what was important enough to force a question from the silent twin.

Hoot's eyebrows hovered at his hairline. "Well? Spit it out, Son."

"Do you think, if'n a person's big. And slow. And um, not so graceful . . . can they still fight bulls?" He sighed as if he'd just completed an arduous task.

Hoot fingered his whiskers and eyed them each in turn. "Yer all gonna have weak spots. Some, you can get over by workin' hard. What you need most is bull savvy. If you're smarter'n the bull, you got a shot."

"What was *your* weakness?" The challenge in Cash's tone was as clear as the arrogance of his curling lip.

Harlie sucked in a breath. *Guy's in the right profession – he has a death wish.*

"Well, I'll tell you." Hoot's raspy voice was soft. And, like a whisper in a dark room, all the scarier for it. "Had me a weakness, same as anybody. Never would abide' a man who could strut sittin' down." He wiped his mouth with his napkin and stood. "If you're done slappin' lips about bullfightin', let's go do it."

The arena stood empty, save a wheelbarrow with a plastic steer's head bolted on the front. Hoot leaned on the pipe fence. "Well, what're y'all waitin' for? Get in there."

They stepped through the fence, then stood looking at each other.

"You, girl. You be the bull." He waved at the

wheelbarrow. "Don't jest stand there with your face hanging out!"

Harlie walked over, and feeling like a fool, lifted the handles.

"You. Smartass. Let's see if you can work *this* bull afore you get in with a real one."

Cash strolled the center of the arena, thumbs in his belt loops.

"Now, get after him."

Harlie gave a half-hearted thrust at Cash.

"Come on! You saw bulls work yesterday. *Be* the bull. Put his butt in the dirt!"

Ears burning, hands clenching the splintery wood, Harlie looked for an opening, knowing Cash wasn't he only one being tested.

He crouched like a front lineman, waiting for the snap.

Remembering the goat-from-hell's moves, Harlie charged.

Cash hopped out of the way.

She pivoted on the front wheel and hit his knees from behind. With the same result she'd had.

Cash bounced to his feet and brushed dirt from the knees of his jeans. "Dammit, a bull can't spin that fast!"

Harlie ran two steps and hit him in the thigh. The vibration ran through the wooden handles, jolting the bones of her hands. *That had to hurt.*

"Wait a damned minute. I wasn't ready!" He rubbed his thigh.

"You tell that to a bull. See where it gets you." Hoot cackled. "If you're in an arena, you best be ready for anythin'."

Harlie charged again. Up on his toes, Cash dodged the thrust. She wheeled around and came at him again. He sidestepped, but she caught him in the butt with the horn and kept coming, knocking him down and running the wheel over his back.

"That's not fair!" He popped up again and brushed himself off.

Hoot bent and stepped through the fence, slow and easy, like it hurt. "Tell you what. I'll go round up all my 'fair' bulls, fer ya." He walked to where Harlie and Cash stood panting. "Course, they'll have teats under 'em."

Cash's fists clenched, his face turning a blotchy shade of plum.

"Here. I'll show you how it's done." Hoot stepped four feet in front of the wheelbarrow, relaxed, feet spread. "Bring it on."

What if she knocked the old guy over? She took two steps forward and stopped, waiting for him to move.

"Dang it, move! Yer a bull, not a butt-sprung turtle!" He backed up and waved her forward. "Come on!"

Glancing at the others, who looked very happy to be bystanders, she tightened her grip and charged.

Hoot leaned left, so she steered that way. But at the last second, he whirled to his right, pirouetting so when she passed him, he faced her. Wow. Who knew the old guy could move so smooth and pretty?

She wheeled around again. This time, not buying the fake, she turned the other way. He was in front of the horns, then he wasn't, spinning away. Not sure what to do, she stopped.

Hoot's shoulders lost their rigid line and his back rounded, transforming him back to an old man. He limped in his odd gait, back to her. "That's a fake, and a step-through. You're gonna use that move more than any other in the arena." He stood in front of them, feet spread shoulder width. "You fake the opposite way you're gonna spin. But you really gotta sell it, or the bull won't buy it. Lean that way, throw your arms that way, but keep the other foot planted." He demonstrated. "Watch the bull's head. Remember, where his head goes is where he's a-headin'." He shifted his weight to the other foot and spun, doing an about-face. "By the time you do a step- through, the bull is past you, and comin' around. Then you'll throw another fake." He did the move again. "You can do this all day. The bull's never gonna catch on."

Deuce rubbed his chin. "That's one slick move."

Even Cash looked impressed.

"Now, the bull might not charge you every time. He might try an' get in close so's he can hook ya'." He waved Levi over. "Turn around me."

Levi stayed a step away and walked in a circle around Hoot.

"No, ya' dummy." He grabbed Levi's large bicep and tugged him closer, until they stood shoulder to shoulder. "The bull's gonna try to muscle you, get you down where he can stomp you. You'll want to use your hands, to grab a horn. Don't do it. You're never going to be able to shift him, and if he throws up his head it's gonna put you off-balance. Instead, you make a pitcher frame." He put up an arm, his skinny bicep beside his ear protecting his head, his forearm just touching Levi's shoulder.

With his arm at a ninety-degree angle, Harlie could see that it was like one half of a frame. She lifted her arm, mimicking.

"Now, move around me, and tryn' push me over."

Levi stood chewing his lip.

"Jes do it, ya' big lunk."

Levi shrugged and did as he was told.

Hoot again morphed into a dancer, stepping light in a small square pattern, on the inside of the spin. "See how you can stay safe, even this close? The bull cain't hurt you, tucked into his shoulder. The horns won't reach, and as long as you stay on your feet, he cain't trample you."

"I see." Harlie practiced, arm up. Her mom had taught her that dance. "It's like a waltz. Step-turn, step-turn."

"Yeah. Like that." Hoot nodded. "Now, y'all practice those moves. Take turns on the wheelbarrow. And really work it. If you don't learn this, you'll be in deep shit in the arena."

He limped away, ducked between the pipe fence and lowered himself onto the bleachers to watch.

***

They practiced until the bell on the porch tolled lunch. By then, even the twins were pirouetting like ballerinas. Large, sweaty ballerinas. Harlie followed the group across the dooryard to the house.

"I knew you could do this, Jonah." Deuce clapped him on the shoulder, raising a tide of red from the silent twin's shirt.

"I just hope we can do okay when the horns aren't plastic." Jonah said.

Walking in hollow aloneness, Harlie studied the male bonding taking place ahead of her. She may live among these men, but she understood them about as much as an iguana did a polar bear.

And she had no desire to be a bear. But it must be nice, being able to fit in like that.

Cash slowed, falling in step beside her.

The corners of her mouth lifted. Maybe —

"Just stop it," he said out of the corner of his mouth.

She cocked her head. "Huh?"

He stared ahead. "I know what you're trying to do." Cold rolled off the ice-tipped words.

"What is your problem? I'm trying to be a bullfighter. Just like you are."

"You're trying to make me look stupid." His eyes glittered with malice. "And you don't want to go there."

Irritation stung like the sweat in her eyes. "You're trying to *scare* me?" There were men who had, but they were bigger and badder than this pretty-boy. "Get over yourself. In spite of what your momma says, you're not the center of the universe. I'm here to get through this and learn to do the job. That's it." She sped up and left him behind.

After grace, they dug into bowls of pinto beans and homemade yeast bread.

"You can listen while you eat." Hoot picked up the TV remote. "There's two different kinds of bullfightin'. Rider protection and freestyle." He clicked on the TV. "Freestyle is you n' the bull in the arena, puttin' on a show for the folks."

The sixty second film clips were from the World Bullfighting Championship, clips of bullfighters dancing with bulls.

"They judge on your level of control, and how close you get to the bull." A fighter on the screen got caught and with a toss of the bull's head, was vaulted into the stands. Hoot chuckled, "That one was too close."

"I thought we were only there to protect the rider," Deuce said.

"At rodeos, yer also hired to entertain the crowd." Hoot clicked pause. "You can do that a couple a ways. You can tell jokes, dance, do pratfalls, chatter with the arena announcer, or freestyle. It's up to you, an' what you like."

Staring at the stop-action frame of a bullfighter in yellow baggy pants fluffed out in a spin, his hand on the bull's forehead, Harlie's heart took a happy skip. She'd leave the comedy for others. *This* was her idea of entertainment.

Hoot clicked off the TV. "Did y'all bring bullfightin' gear?"

The guys all nodded.

Harlie felt, 'oh shit', rising from her neck, bursting onto her face in a flash of heat. "Gear?"

Hoot rolled his eyes heavenward. "There's always one."

Cash snickered.

The tips of her ears were on fire. "Nobody told me—"

"It was in the paperwork. Black and white." Deuce cocked his head.

She'd never seen that paperwork; Rawlings had filled it out. It hadn't been a secret, exactly. But she knew the guys would be even more hostile if they found her tuition had been paid by the PBR — the employer they most wanted to work for. *Dang, Steve didn't say a thing about gear.*

"I got extra in the barn." Hoot dropped the remote and stood. "Y'all go get geared up and meet us at the arena."

The barn may be shabby, but the tack room was neat. Fancy hand-tooled show saddles sat on wooden saddle trees alongside worn working ones. From the wording on the skirts, they were rodeo prizes: bull riding, bareback bronc riding, calf roping. On her way by, she brushed dust off one that read 'All-around Cowboy'.

Wow. He sure fell a long way. Must not have planned for retirement.

She followed Hoot, his leathery neck sprinkled with silver hairs.

He opened a door at the end of the tack room. "Should be able to find somethin' that fits in here."

She stepped into an office of sorts. A massive WWII-vintage metal desk took up one wall, a butt-sprung cracked leather chair in front of it. Hoot opened a large closet on the opposite wall and rooted around.

The framed photo-covered walls drew her. She stepped closer to study a bull riding action shot, black and white, featuring a painted-face clown in baggy clothes in a full run, his hand on the head of a bull charging from behind. In a color one, the same clown, wearing pink and green, crouched in a protective stance between a bull and a downed cowboy, staring the bull down.

She scanned the walls filled with more photos like these. A larger one, centered over the desk caught her attention. It wasn't an action photo. A much less worn version of Hoot stood bowlegged in typical cowboy clothes, grinning beside a handsome cowboy, their arms around each other's shoulders.

"Holy crap. Is that Lane Frost?" She'd seen a documentary with the rodeo team, about the legendary bull rider's life.

Hoot's head appeared from around the door. "Quit your gogglin' and come over here. I don't wanna be at this til sundown."

She stepped over.

He handed her a padded vest. "Flak jacket. Fighter's are different than rider's. Gotta be able to move more. You got shorts?"

"Cutoffs."

He snorted. "Gotta have ones like basketball players wear. Big, so they flare when you move. Then you stick handkerchiefs outta the pockets. The bull might hit them instead'a you." He dug through a pile of clothes in the back corner. "Most people think that red draws a bull. It doesn't. They're color-blind. They go for the movement." He pulled out

81

a pair of baggy shorts. "Here, try these."

He handed her silky lime green shorts with a wide pink stripe down the leg that she'd seen in the photo on the wall.

"These are yours. I can't wear them."

"I'm biggern you, but we'll jest hitch em up with some baling twine and —"

"No, I mean, these are special. What if I trash them?" The silk felt good under her fingers, even if it caught on her calluses.

"Then you don't never get in a clinch that's gonna rip or get blood on 'em." He pointed at her. "Put 'em on." He stepped to the desk, pulled out a drawer, and handed her a hank of twine. "I'll see you in the arena." He closed the door behind him.

She stood a moment, looking at the walls, at the shorts. Maybe this wasn't a big deal to Hoot, but it was to her. She shimmied out of her jeans and into the shorts. They were three sizes too big, but the twine took care of that. She looked down at her burnt orange t-shirt, then to Hoot's pink and green shorts that ended where her rundown cowboy boots started.

She ran her fingers over the silk. She may not match, but she wouldn't trade these shorts for anything.

Chapter 9

The other students laughed. Of course they did. They looked like bulky basketball players. She looked like a homeless clown. Still, it was easy to hold her small smile. They didn't have charmed shorts.

Yeah, that was stupid. Juvenile, even. She knew she wasn't special. Hoot would have loaned them to whoever needed them. But as the silk slid over her legs, she felt changed. As if the shorts fused to that yearning need for excitement she'd hidden away, forming a ball of something solid. Something strong. Something right.

She probably ought to be committed. In spite of the guy's stares, she chuckled. A woman bull fighter? Oh yeah.

At the memory of Angel's haunted, unfocused eyes, the chuckle dried to grit that coated the inside of her mouth. She wasn't here to be proud, or to play. This was deadly serious stuff, for more reasons than the danger.

"Git your butt in here. Bull's are awaitin'." Hoot barked.

She ducked under the pole fence and into the arena. The clang of a hoof hitting metal rang out. In the pen behind the chutes, bulls milled, raising a dust cloud. The ball of tension in her chest thrummed, spreading through her body, resonating in her bones. She bounced on her toes, and shook it off the ends of her fingertips. Still it built.

This was what she'd wanted, all those years. This thrill.

This on-the-edge of life awareness. This *aliveness.* "I'm ready."

Hoot squinted at her and nodded. "When you make yourself stand when a sixteen-hundred-pound bull is comin' at you at twenty miles an hour, you find out who you are." He yelled over his shoulder. "Manuel, you ready?"

"Si, el patrón."

He turned back to the students. "We'll go over rider safety tomorrow. But first, I need to know you can stay ahead of a bull. I'm not puttin' riders in your hands afore I know you can get outta your own way." He scanned the corral and yelled, "Bubba, where are you?"

One of the bullfighters from the demonstration yesterday ducked into the arena. "Right here, Hoot."

"Bubba's jest there to pull a bull offn' you if you're gettin' stomped. Otherwise, you're on your own."

He had her full attention. Deuce's throat clicked when he swallowed. Even the twins' faces had lost their perpetual pink. They looked downright scared. Cash sported his usual cocky grin but it was pulled as thin and tight as a cheap Halloween mask.

Hoot looked them over from under his brows. "Jest remember about throwing fakes and the picture frame I taught you. Now, get back behind the fence." Hoot's bony arm stopped her from following. "You. Stay here. You're first."

Hers bowels gurgled a warning. She slammed her muscles tight and turned to face the gate that separated her from the bulls.

Manuel was on a chestnut horse in the corral, culling out a bull.

Angel.

The fear lay down before the image of her little pixie face, smiling, vibrant with life.

The gate opened and a dun colored bull trotted into the arena, head up. Short deflated horns framed his white face.

"Watch 'im. Those banana horns may not poke holes but he kin still kill you." Hoot yelled from the cheap seats. "When you hear the whistle, break off and head for the fence."

The bull spotted her and stopped, curious.

The thrumming sped up until her feet felt two inches off the ground. Harlie threw up her arms to make a bigger target. "Whup, bull. Bring it."

Head low, he charged slow. She leaned left, then at the last second, spun right. Faster than she'd thought, he spun after her, and his next step brought him even with her shoulder.

The bull thought he had a longhorn's rack. He leaned in and lowered his head to gore her. She threw up her arm to hold him off and turned. The bull bowed around her and kept coming.

They moved in perfect synch, like they were dancing. Sparkles of joy streaked through her chest, and a high-pitched giggle escaped her clenched jaw. Her arm brushed the bull's rock-hard shoulder and she laid a hand on his forehead, to feel for his next move.

"Off his head!" Hoot's raspy bark came at the same time as the bull's head-toss.

A sharp pain hit her elbow, and off balance, she fell away. Four faltering steps and she caught herself and shot a look behind her.

The bull's head was six inches from her ass.

Adrenaline burned through her veins in a searing wave. Panicked, she took a few running steps before she remembered.

She couldn't outrun a bull.

The shouts of the students were a staccato counterpoint to the beat of the bull's hooves, and the thundering in her head. Throwing a look over one shoulder, she cut the other way.

The bull missed, swung around and stopped, gathering himself for his next move.

A coach's whistle pierced the air. "Hit the fence!"

She took advantage of the bull's indecision and hauled ass. She leapt and caught the top pole, her momentum carrying her feet over. When they hit, she bent her knees, then straightened, lifting her arms in a gymnast's 'nailed-the-landing' salute.

Hoot was right. She'd found out who she was. And dammit, she was a bullfighter!

The guys actually smiled back at her. Deuce even

clapped.

Grinning like a fool, she basked in the acceptance. She didn't need it. But it sure felt good, just the same.

Hoot's wrinkles collapsed in, making him look like a wizened apple. "What the hell did I tell you 'bout not leanin' on his head?"

When he didn't say more, she assumed he wanted an answer. "Not to do it?" She panted.

"Damned right I did." He turned to the guys in the bleachers. "'Member I told you every plus has a minus?"

The bobble-heads bounced.

He cut his eyes to her. "You may think you're smart cuz you got fast reflexes. That works, right up til the bull catches you." He spit in the dust. "And a bull is gonna catch you sometime." His bony fingers closed around her bicep. "How you think you're gonna do compared to this brute here?" He grabbed Jonah's bicep, but his fingers didn't come close to encircling it.

"Um. Not so good." She swallowed.

"He's wood. He can take a hit and get up with only a dent. You're glass. You're gonna shatter." He closed one eye and squinted at her. "Remember that when you're out there playing like this is a game."

A flush of heat radiating from every pore, she made herself hold his stare. "Yessir."

She rubbed her throbbing elbow. She may be embarrassed, but she wouldn't trade what she'd just learned in that arena. About technique. About timing. About herself.

This was what thrill seekers sought—for those few rarefied seconds she'd held her life in her own hands and understood—that the only way to be fully conscious of being alive was is to be on the edge of the opposite. But that feeling was, by nature, as fleeting as it was glorious.

And like a junkie, she couldn't wait to get back in that arena and get another fix.

Hoot turned to Cash. "You, Smartass. You're up next."

Cash's signature strut was missing as he shuffled to the center of the arena in brand new cleated tennis shoes, his hockey shorts hanging six inches from his crotch. Instead of the straw cowboy hat the rest of them wore, he sported a backward-facing baseball cap. He looked cool – until you saw the fear, as plain as the sheen of sweat on his face.

Jazzed, but stinging from both the tongue-lashing and her bruised elbow, Harlie sat.

Deuce offered a covert fist to bump. Grinning, she did.

The arena gate swung, letting in a Hereford-cross bull, much smaller than Harlie's had been. Dust bounced off his red coat with every trotting step.

"He's just a punk!" Some of the swagger was back in Cash's voice. "Come on, little dude!" He took off his hat and waved it at the bull.

The horns were only about a foot long, with no curve — toothpicks that would grow to baseball bats. The animal lowered its head and pawed the ground, throwing dust over his back.

"Whatsa' matter, you scared?" Cash waved his arms.

The bull charged, much faster than Harlie's.

Cash threw a fake, but when he turned, the bull caught his billowing hockey shirt on the way by. It jerked him off his feet and he landed on his butt in the dirt.

The loud thud reached the bleachers. *That had to hurt.*

Bubba moved in, but Cash was up, waving at the bull. "That the best you got? Come on, dumbshit!"

Hoot's whistle blew. "Get your butt on the fence!"

There was no arguing with Hoot's orders, but Cash's tight jaw showed he wanted to. He limped for the fence without a look behind him.

Bubba covered him, watching the bull.

"Get your ass over here." Hoot barked.

Cash stepped through the fence and stood by the bleachers, slapping dust from his shorts.

"Now you know why 'fighters wear baggy shorts, but not baggy shirts. If a bull snags your shorts, it's your center, where all your weight is. You're not likely to go down. But your shirt? You saw what happens. Go change and come back."

Cash limped off, grumbling.

"You." He pointed to Deuce. "You're next."

She wondered if Hoot didn't know their names, or if this was a drill sergeant's tactic. No way to tell.

Deuce hopped through the fence and looking like he was facing a firing squad, waited on the bull. Manuel opened the gate to a black Brahma cross with short horns and a large hump on his shoulders. Muscles bunching, the bull strutted, head up. Spotting Deuce, he charged.

Deuce morphed from a cowboy to a dancer. Up on his toes, he threw a fake and spun away. With the second fake, the bull came so close a horn brushed Deuce's flaring shorts. On the third, Deuce tucked into his shoulder and they pirouetted. Until the bull stepped on Deuce's foot, and he went down.

Harlie jumped up, took the two steps down, and ran to the fence. The bull danced on top of Deuce.

Bubba ran in, slapped the bull between his horns. The bull jerked his head up, snorted, and took off after Bubba.

"Get up. Get up, dammit!" Hoot yelled.

The gate swung open and Bubba ran for it, the bull close enough to snotify the back of his shorts. Once the bull cleared the arena, a ranch hand swung the gate shut. Bubba hit the fence, and safety.

Deuce was slow to get up but finally gained his feet and limped for the fence, clutching the back of his right thigh.

"What the *hell* were you doing out there?" Hoot started in before Deuce had taken two steps. "Even if you're knocked out, you get your ass up and head for the fence. The other 'fighter has enough to do without you lying around. They can get hurt saving your sorry butt."

"Sorry to be in the way." Deuce stepped through the fence, hobbled to the bleachers and sat beside Harlie, slow and gentle.

"You okay?" She whispered.

His lips peeled back in a grimace, he nodded.

"Y'all learn from that. You get in trouble, the worst place in that arena is anywhere you're lyin' down. Nothin' good is gonna happen next. So get up. If you got a broke leg, you get up.

88

You can hurt later." He spit. "At least you'll live to hurt later. Got it?"

"Yessir." They recited.

He worked them until the sun neared the horizon. They all got two more bulls in. The twins were slow but seemed to somehow know what the bull was going to do before he did, so they stayed out of trouble.

Hoot's normally gravelly voice had worn to sand by the end, sliding and at times giving way entirely. He never ran out of derision though. No one was good enough, smart enough, or fast enough to suit him.

After Cash's last awkward go at a bull, Hoot barked, "You're done. Hit the showers."

With a muffled groan, Harlie forced sore muscles to push her to her feet.

"No run tonight. Tomorrow's your first bucking. Spend some time getting to know each other, 'cuz you're in each other's hands tomorrow." He turned and took two steps.

Cash spoke. "Aren't you gonna say *one* good thing about today?"

Hoot kept walking. "You're alive, ain't you?"

"Goddamn old coot." Cash said under his breath. "I thought we did pretty good."

Harlie put a hand to her chest, blotting a runnel of sweat. "Maybe, but attaboy's aren't going to help us get better." Cash was always looking outside himself for validation. She watched a muscle jump in his jaw but he didn't say anything, just began his trudge to the bunkhouse. They all followed.

Not your problem.

What she'd give for a long bath. She rubbed the bruised underside of her arm. A bubble bath.

Ms. Leonard would let you take one, you know she would. She eyed the house. *Oh yeah, and what would the guys say then?*

A hot shower would be the next best thing. Lowering her head, she sped up. If she hurried, maybe she could get in the shower first.

***

"Angel, you should've seen. It was like this dangerous ballet. It was terrifying and beautiful and I can't wait for tomorrow, to do it again." She kicked a rock in the packed dirt drive and kept walking toward the road. "Hoot says part of our job is to entertain the crowd, so I'm gonna do freestyle. He showed us a video of a 'fighter who turned his back to the bull. When the bull's horn touched his butt, he used the bull's momentum to do a back flip and landed on his feet at the bull's shoulder. Man, it'd give you shivers." Her feet turned left at the end of the drive. "I think I did okay. I stumbled a couple of times, but I didn't get hurt." Would she be worrying Angel with the danger in her job? Did Angel even hear?

It made Harlie feel better to believe that inside the silence, somewhere, Angel did hear. The old Angel, the one who loved 'Harlie stories'.

She now wondered if Angel had lived through them, kind of like their mom did with the romance stories. A safe, vicarious thrill.

Except Angel's life hadn't turned out so safe, had it?

Harlie pushed on, ignoring the bull's-eye bullet of blame tearing through her heart. Safety had been Harlie's job, even before the PBR. And she'd failed to keep Angel safe. After all, when mom was alive, Angel had been a pretty normal kid.

"So tomorrow, we're learning rider protection. There'll be bull riders coming out and it's up to us to keep them safe."

As she did every night, she made the mistake of pausing, waiting for a response. She knew better. The silence on the line grew, expanding into a yawning black pit. And as she did every time, she fell into the emptiness, the roar of failure rushing past her ears, trying to hold in the scream that clawed her chest, trying to get out.

Angel.

"I gotta go, Littlest. I love you." She forced the rest out in a broken whisper. "Come back to me, okay? I'm not sure how long I can do this without you."

Like an idiot, again, she waited for a response.

She tripped and fell. Again.

***

She walked until sounds penetrated her darkness and the world around her came back to focus. The night birds sang their version of Marco Polo and the breeze whispered in the dried grasses. Harlie pulled the calming scent of sage through her nose.

The yellow squares of light from the bunkhouse windows onto the dooryard dirt welcomed her back. She stepped faster, wanting the distraction of human contact. The floppy screen door shushed over the wood planks and slapped closed behind her. The guys reclined on their bunks, pillows wadded up behind them, talking. All but Cash. His bunk was empty.

"I about filled my shorts when you went down, Deuce." Levi said. "I thought you were a goner."

Deuce's right leg lay propped on a bag of ice. "Actually, except for the hoof on the back of my leg, he missed me. Coulda' been lots worse."

Harlie crossed to her bunk, pulled back the shower curtain "Jonah and Levi, y'all have got bulls *down.* Where did you learn that?" She dropped onto the bed and lay back, hoping the guys wouldn't notice they were actually having a conversation.

"At home," Jonah said.

When it was clear Jonah was done, Levi supplied more detail. "We work bulls all day long at home. Exercise 'em, haul 'em to rodeos, practically live with 'em—it kinda just sinks in."

"You were the best out there today, Harlie."

The admission spread over her blistered ego like butter on a burn.

Deuce's melting ice crackled in the quiet. "But that doesn't mean you belong here."
He said as if it were simply a fact. "You're different, and you're always going to be."

Levi nodded. "You gotta admit, it's true."

She rolled her eyes. "So-the-hell-what? If I can do the job, what difference does it make?"

Levi's gaze slid away, to the wall, the floor, finally stopping on a rough-hewn ceiling beam.

"But I'm faster than *any* of you!"

Deuce's eyes were soft. Sad? "You heard Hoot. You're made of glass. You can act like we're the same, but that doesn't make it so. No offense meant, really. But you could put my life in jeopardy."

So much for acceptance. Having it offered, then snatched away hurt worse than their disregard. The concussion sparked a fuse that flared, hot and fast. "What about me? I'm putting my life in the hands of you inept oafs and you don't hear me whining!"

Her words bounced off them. They just looked at her from behind the wall they'd built.

And here she stood, as always, on the outside. But it only started bothering her since she'd come here. "Well screw you all." She hopped up and pulled the inadequate wall of bilious shower curtain. "I don't need any of you."

She opened the nightstand drawer, brought out the glass house, and lay back on her bunk, listening to the moth's wings humming at the screen. Running her finger over the design, a wave of homesickness scoured her chest hollow. Only two more days and she'd be flying home. She pictured herself walking into Angel's room . . . No. She shied away from yet more sadness. Instead, she dredged up a memory. A good memory.

The dairy wasn't so bad before mom died. After dinner on summer nights, she and Angel would sit on the rusty old glider on the front porch watching the stars, then the fireflies, come out. In that fairy-magic time of night, reality receded and anything was possible.

They decided that Harlie would be a large animal vet and Angel, a schoolteacher. They'd live together in a Victorian house, outside a charming small town somewhere . . . maybe Iowa. They made a pact that neither would marry, and instead of children they'd have a menagerie of animals that changed depending on the night: camels, ferrets, possums, skunks, and one crazy night, a giraffe.

Harlie sighed. They'd been so young, and those nights had been so simple-so innocent. She swallowed the bittersweet taste on the back of her tongue. Those days seemed as far from now as the unfamiliar scattering of stars outside her window.

"Where is she?" The screen door slapped behind the angry voice and boots tromped across the boards, getting closer.

Alarm skittering across her nerves, Harlie sat up, dropped her feet to the floor and set the glass house on the scarred nightstand.

The curtain whipped back, revealing Cash, jaw tight, lip lifted in disgust.

"What's going on?" Deuce sat up. The twins did too.

"*She's* got a job with the PBR." He said it like she was some kind of puppy-killer.

Of course the word got out. And of course Cash was the first to hear it.

"How do you know?" Levi asked.

Cash's razor sharp glare didn't waver from her face. "I heard two of the hands talking."

Without a command, her muscles snatched her body to her feet. "So what if I do? Is that your business?"

"So *what*?" His red face darkened a shade. "You come in here, all pushy, acting like you're 'one of the guys'," His air quotes punctured air thick with antipathy. "And you've got a full ride! Little Princess with her crown—you've already waltzed into a spot that one of us could have had. Should have had." He turned to the other guys. "They paid her tuition, flew her ass in here, and she's got a job just waiting for her!" He turned back to her, his face painted in lines of disgust. "This is bullshit."

Princess? She remembered the days she spent sweating in the sticky summer heat, mucking out Ohio barns to make money. Remembered walking the half mile to the bus stop, the wind-chill below zero and the wind howling through her last-year's-too-small winter coat. The look on the director's face that told her she was little more than a prop, the slack-jawed lust on that actress's boyfriend's face.

A glass-strewn, blood-splashed kitchen.

"Fuck you, Cash." She spit out, fists clenched at her sides. "You know nothing about me." She stood on her toes, putting her face within millimeters of his. "Do you know how many times being a woman *kept* me from things? How many jobs? Opportunities? Stuff you men take for granted. You know, little stuff—like a living wage."

The more she talked, the more pent up outrage boiled from her gut. "So yeah, I agreed to be the PBR's dancing chicken. I don't delude myself that I'm special—any woman desperate enough to risk her life would do." She panted a second, to be able go on. "See, that's the way the world works when you're not a 'big-time everything' like you." A sound of disgust came from the back of her throat. "Maybe if you worried more about you instead of me, you'd make a better bullfighter." She stepped around him. "Not to mention a better human being."

Face purple, Cash raised his hand. "You bitch!"

She took a flinching half-step back.

He took a handful of shower curtain in his shaking fist.

She opened her mouth but before she could yell, his fist descended.

With a ripping sound and the jingle of shower hooks, the rod came down.

She covered her head with her arms, but the rod never touched her. It bonged off the nightstand.

She didn't have to look to know what happened — she felt the glass shatter in her chest.

Ruby shards scattered across the floor. The leaded framework lay twisted in the middle of the debris.

The air went out of her like a punctured Macy's parade balloon and her knees made a hollow boom as they hit the floor. Moving her arms in broad sweeps, she pulled the shards to her chest, sheltering them like a mother bird with her chicks.

Her ears rang with the internal silence that followed a bomb blast. She cherished the silence, because she had already begun to dread whatever lay beyond. She turned her face, and spying a slash of red under the nightstand, swept it from a dust bunny nest into the pile. Ignoring the trees of denim that circled her, she huddled, arms around the mess, forehead touching the floor.

"Ah Jesus, Harlie. I'm sorry."

"There's blood. She's cut her hand."

"Should we call Hoot?"

A hand touched her back.

Her back shivered from under the touch. "Don't call anyone. Leave. Me. Alone."

"Maybe we should just leave her for a bit. Let her get herself together. Okay?"

The denim forest shuffled away. A small part of her brain registered the sounds of them gathering their things for a shower. The rest of her watched the light of the train, getting bigger as it approached. The Reality Express slammed into her.

Angel is gone.

It doesn't matter. It doesn't matter.

She forced her will down her extremities, commanding them to move. She opened the bottom drawer of the nightstand, pulled out a plastic bag, and carefully lowered the pieces in. Any imagined magic inside the little house was gone. Still, she tucked the bag into the drawer. She struggled onto pins-and-needle feet, fell onto the bed, and holding her bleeding hand off the edge, rolled with her back to the rest of the room.

You still need to call Angel. She'll wonder . . .

No. The Reality Express left no survivors. The glass house wasn't some magical talisman that held Angel safe inside. It was just a cheap trinket. Meaningless. Wherever Angel was, it was beyond the sound of her big sister's voice. It didn't matter if Harlie called or not.

She stared out of the window at the stars' cold light, recalling a fact from her high school science teacher.

Most of those stars were already dead.

Chapter 10

Harlie made it a point of being out of the bunkhouse before the guys woke. It wasn't hard; she was awake anyway. She leaned on the fence of the corral behind the bucking chutes, watching the sun come up over the bulls' backs.

She felt the weight of fatigue in her muscles and her mind. The same thoughts raced around the same worn track, like mice on crack: Angel. Bullfighting. Otherness. Failure. Angel, bullfighting, other—

"Baaaahhh."

She turned, shielding the target on her ass. "I am *not* in the mood. Go. Away."

The dirty goat hesitated, surveying her with those deviant eyes.

She glared back. "I have a recipe for goat stew. I'm not afraid to use it."

He must have decided she meant it because he turned and sauntered away.

When she was sure he was really gone, she turned back and rested her chin on her hand on the cold metal bar. Some of the bulls were awake, standing chewing cud, others lay with their legs tucked under them, nodding off.

A few birds were awake as well, cheeping at the sunrise.

The peaceful scene seeped into her cracks, calming her worries. Hanging out with animals usually did that. Besides, moping wasn't going to help.

Reality is what it is. All you can do is move forward. It doesn't help, wanting.

All her usual rallying cries fell into the black hole of a future without Angel, screaming on the way down. She rolled her shoulders, trying to shrug it off. She could whine and moan all she wanted. Ahead of her stood the whole rest of a life to fill up.

A bull rubbed his butt on the fence and the bar under her hand vibrated. Bullfighting would be a good career - if only she could do it solo. She remembered the thrill of freestyling – moving with the bull in perfect synchronicity. Well, at least she'd get to do that some of the time. Providing she got through the next two days.

Snatches of deep timbre voices drifted on the still air. Time for breakfast. She pushed away from the fence, tightened the baling twine around the waistband of her shorts and took on the day.

For once, she'd gotten the timing right—Deuce was the only one at the table when she rounded the corner. She grabbed a mug from the table beside the door, dispensed coffee from the industrial coffee maker, then walked to her normal seat beside him. She stepped over the bench and sat, listening to the bird calls and taking comfort in the domestic sound of clanking pots and running water from the kitchen behind her.

The rest of the men came around the corner and sat in their usual places.

She sipped, avoiding all eyes. *If I'd have turned faster, my ass wouldn't have been in biting distance . . .*

"Harlie, I'm sorry about last night." Deuce set down his mug with a clunk. "We're *all* sorry about last night."

She studied the surface of her coffee like it foretold the future, hoping the clothes dryer tumbling emotions inside didn't reflect on the outside. She'd shown way too much last night.

"I'll replace that . . . thing I broke."

Her head snapped up and she gave him what Angel called her 'Cooper Kiss of Death' look.

It didn't strike him dead, but he did flinch.

"That *thing* can't be replaced."

The screen door squealed. "What's going on here?" Hoot took the step down from the kitchen, his voice rasping the quiet.

Afraid of what she'd reveal—be it by words or emotion, she ground her teeth together. She was done talking.

Hoot walked over, gaze scanning the cowboys at the table, to land on her. "Y'all have a problem?"

She shook her head.

His frown told her he wasn't buying it. "Well, you don't want to talk about it, fine. I'll talk, y'all listen."

The screen door opened. Miz Leonard carried a platter of waffles in one hand, one of crispy bacon in the other.

The men rose around Harlie, as they did every morning when she came through the door.

"Good morning."

"Mornin' Ma'am," they chorused, then sat.

Oh yeah, they have manners for Ms. Leonard. Harlie just managed not to snort.

You'd better focus on today. What happened last night didn't kill you, but today could.

Through grace, to ignore the hands that clasped hers on both sides, she visualized herself doing fake after perfect fake, her feet moving fast and graceful.

They dug in, and Hoot picked up the TV remote. "You can eat and watch at the same time. It's gonna be a long day. If you want to be on your feet at the end of it, pay attention." He clicked on the TV, freezing the tape at the beginning of a ride. "You know how to turn a bull into a spin and what to do during a ride. But after's when you really go to work."

"The bull's probably still gonna be spinning – takes him a bit to stop. But when he does, he's gonna be lookin' for somebody to run over." He advanced the tape a few seconds. The bull sighted on the rider, on his butt in the dirt. He'd taken two plunging steps before the bullfighter ran between them. The space was tight, tight enough that he had to turn sideways on his way by.

Harlie swallowed the wad of syrup-covered cardboard in

her mouth.

"We call that shootin' the gap. Now, watch the bull's head." He advanced the scene, slow motion. "He picks his head up, you got his attention. When his head turns, you got him."

 The bull lifted his head and ran after the bullfighter.

"You work in a circle. That bull's spinning. Your first move may not pick him up. The next guy tries, then you again. See?"

The rider hopped up and ran for the fence. "That's the best that can happen if everything goes right."

She gave up on eating and put her fork down.

"But you better have your shoes tied tight if there's a wreck." He advanced to the next ride. The bull came out of the chute in a huge rearing leap that left the helmeted rider behind, on his pockets, arm stretched straight. When the bull kicked, the centrifugal force pulled the rider forward and his head cracked down right between the bull's horns. The helmet flew off and by his rag-doll flop, he was out cold. Hoot froze the picture.

"Every wreck is different. I can give you basics but you have to have an instinct, bull savvy, and awareness of what's goin' on. I can't teach you that."

"Always walk to a wreck, not run. It gives you the chance to see what's what, and make a plan. You run in too fast when the bull's spinnin' and the rider's hung, you're gonna get kicked, or the rider's legs are gonna hit you. A friend of mine got his cheek laid open by a spur flyin' by. Saw his teeth, right through his cheek."

"Jesus." Cash's fork clattered to his plate. Levi swallowed. Audibly.

Waffles abandoned, the students leaned toward the TV.

Hoot advanced the tape. The cowboy was tied to the bull by his hand, flying like a helicopter blade around the spinning animal. "Nothin' you can do for the rider til the bull stops spinnin'. So you gotta get the bull lined out."

One of the bullfighters ran in, slow. The bull's head came up and he zeroed in on the man in front of him. Hoot paused the tape.

"Once he's straight, the other fighter moves in an' frees the rider." He clicked a button and the film rolled.

The rider was now being dragged, his legs bouncing around the bull's rear hooves.

Harlie sucked in a breath. Sixteen hundred pounds on a knee could end a man's walking career, let alone his riding one.

The second bullfighter ran in on the opposite side of the bull, caught the tail of the rope and jerked it. The unconscious man's hand popped free and the bullfighter moved in, standing over him in a protective stance.

Hoot stopped the tape.

"Wait." Deuce pointed to the set. "Was the rider okay?"

"Huh?" Hoot checked the TV. "Oh, yeah. He walked away." He held up his hand, spreading his five fingers. Well, four and a half, technically.

"First. You stay back til you can get in safely. You get knocked out, you're just one more disaster in the middle of a calamity." He folded down a finger. "Second, line out the bull." He folded the half finger. "Then you free the rider. Don't touch him or try to help. Just keep him safe until the medics show. Stand back and let 'em do their job."

Harlie nodded, repeating the steps in her head.

"The fighters got to work together, as a team, or it turns into a rolling ball of butcher knives out there."

She glanced around the table.

The guys looked only at each other.

I'm screwed. Her molars ached. She forced her jaw muscles to loosen. Wouldn't you know the perfect career she'd lucked upon would have a huge fault. Or maybe the flaw was hers. Either way, she was just as screwed.

Hoot turned off the TV. "We'll go over bad wrecks tomorrow."

"Holy shit," Cash said, "You saying that wasn't a bad wreck?"

"Nah. But don't you worry about that now. A bad wreck happens today, somebody gets hung up, you let Bubba do the hard stuff. You jest line out the bull." He frowned at them in turn.

"No heroes today. You got that?"

"Yessir." They acknowledged in dead-serious tones.

The responsibility of the job weighed heavier than the waffles that sat like an anvil in Harlie's stomach. She tried to shake it off. No way to do the job if she was worrying about not being able to do the job.

Hoot took a last sip of coffee and the hollow thump of the mug on the table sounded loud on the quiet porch. "Well then, let's go save somebody."

Fear of failure was only one of the ingredients of the noxious stew sloshing with the undigested waffles and coffee in her stomach.

She stood and followed the others to the arena.

Teamwork.

Hoot had said they'd have to put their lives in each other's hands. She wouldn't trust these guys with her dirty laundry, much less her life. Or Angel's future.

She shifted her hat to blot the tickles of sweat. Screw that. She was watching two asses in the arena—her own, and her rider's. The other asses were on their own.

You'll just have to work harder, that's all.

She shoved her hands in her front pockets. That work-harder part, she had down.

Funny, how the guys walked around her, hovering, keeping her in the center of their circle.

Did they really feel bad about last night? She shot quick glances from under her lashes, but she couldn't tell. She'd never learned to see behind the masks of people's faces.

A better question was; why did she want to see this time?

At the arena, the high school cowboys already straddled bull-loaded chutes. Bubba, the bullfighter's safety net, jogged in circles in front of them, warming up.

"Okay." Hoot turned to them. "You, smartass. You pair up with him." He pointed to Deuce. "Get on in there."

Cash and Deuce looked at each other for the space of a heartbeat, then nodded as if they both understood something unspoken before ducking under the fence to the arena.

Harlie put a heel on the fence and stretched her hamstrings, but she kept her focus on the arena.

A pimply-faced kid lowered himself onto a black bull and prepped his rope. Manuel tightened the bull's flank strap. "This is a mean 'un, boss!"

"That's good for their first one." Hoot yelled back.

Cash and Deuce shot him are-you-out-of-your-mind looks.

"Don't you evil-eye me. The mean ones are easy. They're lookin' for a target, so it's easy to get their heads up. It's the smart ones you have to watch for. They know which one was on their back, and they're gonna go for the rider no matter what." He spit a stream of brown juice in the dirt. "Y'all better be watchin' the gate – not me. Smartass, move up near the chutes."

Cash took two steps toward the chute.

The gate swung open, effectively trapping Cash behind it.

The bull bucked straight out of the chute. By the time Deuce leapt into action the bull was well past, bucking straight down the fence. He ran after, yelling.

By the time Cash got around the gate, it was over. The whistle blew and the rider pulled his hand out of the rope. The bull's last buck launched him onto the fence. His feet never hit the ground. The bull ran the perimeter of the arena to the open out-gate.

"Get your useless butts over here!"

The guys walked over, heads down. Harlie almost felt sorry for them.

Almost.

"'Member the part about you can't outrun a bull?" He glared at Deuce.

"Yessir."

"You better be off your heels and in position when that gate opens. Lucky for you the rider kept hisself outta trouble." He turned to Cash who toed the dirt. His face had to be crimson, but she couldn't see through his hat brim.

"You can't outrun a bull on a good day but you got no

shot tryin' to do it from behind a gate." He shook his head. "I'm not real sure y'all ain't hopeless. Sit."

He surveyed his remaining candidates. "You, girl. And the quiet one. You're next."

Harlie ducked under the fence and bent to tighten the laces of her Walmart tennies, her heart throwing fast, staccato beats.

Jonah seemed like a nice guy, as much as she could tell from the couple of words she'd heard him speak. She hoped she could trust him to step in if she were in trouble. She took her position by the latch of the gate. Jonah stood far enough out from the hinge side not to get trapped behind it.

A big kid with his hat shoved down so far his ears stuck out, sat astride the bull, prepping his rope.

A short black and gray mottled bull with small horns stood in the chute. He didn't buck. He didn't throw his horns around. He stood gazing out at the arena like an old hand, waiting to do his job.

But Harlie recognized the malicious intent in the white-rimmed eye that gazed through the chute slats.

Wouldn't you know, we'd get a smart one. That one was looking to hook someone. She glanced at Jonah, who looked as determined as the bull, but with a bucket of scared mixed in. "Watch him." She rubbed the silk of her shorts. Just for now, she'd believe in their magic.

Jonah nodded.

The rider pounded his fingers closed and slid up on his rope.

Harlie went up on the balls of her feet.

The gate swung.

The wreck was like one of Hoot's tapes, only in fast-mo. The bull took a huge, rearing leap, which the rider handled. But he wasn't prepared for the steep drop. Tied to the bull, his hand was jerked down, followed by the rest of him.

His feet flew up behind and the rider somersaulted with a half flip to land, butt in the dirt, facing the bull.

The tape switched to slo-mo. The kid's eyes were

103

cartoon-character-wide in stunned anticipation of a bone snapping impact. He froze.

The bull, sighting the easy target that had fallen from the sky like a gift from the bovine God, lowered his head and charged.

Harlie took two running steps and leapt between them, stretched out like Michael Jordan going for a layup. Her fingers brushed the bull's face on the way by.

As soon as she landed, she spun. The bull wasn't buying it.

Horns aimed at the pockets of the scrambling cowboy's Levi's, the animal closed the gap.

Jonah ran in on the bull's other side.

"Hey bull!" She grabbed the bull's horn, trying to turn his head. She might as well have tried to pull a locomotive off a track.

But the tug broke his concentration. He swung his head.

Bouncing on her toes, Harlie waved her arms. "Hey-hey-hey, bull!"

Jonah stepped between the bull and the rider, who'd finally managed to gain his feet and run for the fence.

The incensed animal charged.

Chutes at her back, Harlie threw a fake right and went left. And kept going, leaping onto the fence beside the cowboy. The beat of the bull's hooves thundered in her chest as it passed beneath them.

Her grin was reflected in the rider's laughing eyes. She saw that he felt it too – the thrill singing in his blood.

He clapped her on the back. "Thank you, Ma'am. Saved my bacon for sure!"

"That was my pleasure." Still smiling, she hopped from the fence.

You did it — you saved your first cowboy!

That kid would go safe home to his parents, mostly because of her. The rare rich taste of success filled her mouth. The sweetest taste on earth.

God, she loved this job.

Jonah handed over her hat, which she hadn't even realized she'd lost in the scramble. "You did awesome."

"Get over here!" Hoot's gravel voice pelted them.

Here we go.

"Girl, you missed the 'team' part in 'teamwork'."

She stepped through the fence, shielding the small nugget of pride in her chest. He couldn't take that away.

"He was standin' right there, ready to come in, and you cut him off. If a rodeo could make do with one bullfighter, they suren' shit wouldn't pay for two."

Had she? She hadn't been aware of Jonah, hadn't seen him until the very end.

She glanced to him. "So sorry."

He ducked his head. "I'm slow. You did good."

"And you. You gotta get in there. If that bull had hooked her, you'da been too far away to help."

"Yessir."

"Sit. Twin and Smartass. You're up."

Harlie sat at the end of the bleacher, trying to calm her banging pulse. *You did it!*

When Hoot turned to shout instructions at the arena, Deuce put his palm out, bench-level for a low-five. "Nice save."

She squinted at him. Then deciding to chance that he meant it, she tapped his palm with her fingers. "Thanks."

An hour later, Hoot called for a break. "Here's what I think, so far." Hoot stood in front of the bleachers and looked at the twins. "You two work okay together. You got bull savvy, and you seem to know what the other's gonna do before he does it."

A compliment? Harlie locked her jaw so it didn't flop open. *Has the world stopped turning?*

"That helps make up for the fact that you're slowrn' a turd in the sun and just about as graceful."

The twin's faces turned a matching tomato-red.

"You gotta learn to work with anybody. So you don't work together. And *try* to pick up your feet at least once today."

He turned to Cash. "You got no awareness of where you are, and where you needta be. You're always late. You're gonna get somebody hurt. We'll see how you do, but ifn' you don't get better today, you're goin' home."

Cash's face passed tomato and hovered at eggplant, a muscle in his jaw jumping as he shot death-rays at Hoot.

But Hoot had already moved on to Harlie. "You. You got the best reflexes, speed and some bull-savvy. But bullfightin' is teamwork. You can't learn that, you can't do this job. Period."

Panic zipping over her nerves, she waited for the whiz of a falling guillotine blade.

A glacial glare from under his gray wired brows. "You work on that."

"Yessir." The word slipped out on her grateful exhale.

Deuce was last. "You. You cain't save everbody." He threw his hands up to flop around his ears. "You're runnin' around, tryin' to help the rider, the other bullfighter, I half expect you to jump up on the horse and try'n help the safety roper."

It was Deuce's turn to pull a chameleon — his face blended with his red t-shirt.

"You jest worry about turnin' the bull into a spin, and keepin' the rider safe. That's what you're paid to do. Got it?"

Deuce nodded.

"Okay, let's try not to kill anybody the rest of the day."

They stood.

She didn't want the attention but needed to know. "Hoot sir? Tomorrow, will we get to practice freestyle?"

"Don't you hear? You need to focus on workin' with a partner."

Hope shredded, she stepped down from the bleacher. "Yessir."

***

The guys chatted in the bunkhouse after dinner. Harlie lay on her cot, massaging her calves to work out the cramps.

Teamwork. Hoot had made his point; she had to learn to work with these guys, or go home. And she was beginning to understand that meant she *had* to connect with them, on some level. She dug a knuckle into the belly of the muscle, biting her lip only partially due to the physical pain. She was alone in a

106

roomful of people, and had to admit lots of that was her own fault.

Where to start? People made small talk seem so easy but it never had been for her. Hell, she'd never seen the need for it, until now.

Failure was a powerful incentive.

"Damned old man. Nothing makes him happy." Cash lay, stocking feet crossed, looking up at the ceiling. "How do we know he was any good to begin with? Never seen clips of *him* working bulls."

"Probably weren't cameras back then." Levi said, and they chuckled.

Deuce rolled the toothpick to the other side of his mouth. "I know he's trying to make us do better, but at some point—"

"You're wrong." The words were loud and flat, from being pushed from her diaphragm and through her clenched teeth. "He was good. I saw photos."

Heads swiveled. Seconds ticked.

She should have known that correcting Cash was the exact wrong thing to say. She barreled on in spite of the heat pounding up her neck. "It's true. He's got a tack room full of stuff he's won in rodeos. There's even a photo of him and Lane Frost together."

"Lane Frost, really?" Jonah breathed.

"Yep."

Silence fell.

Just say something. Even if you say the wrong thing, at least they'll be talking to you.

That is, if they would.

She just proved she sucked at small talk, so it was time to try some big talk.

"Oh hell." She sat up and leaned her elbows on her knees. "Look. I don't know how to do this bonding thing, okay? All I know is that we have to work together to get through this and get our PRCA cards. I know you guys don't like me. That's okay, because I don't—"

"Who says we don't like you?" Deuce sat up and dropped his feet to the floor.

She rolled her eyes. "Oh, come on. You think I should be in some farm house, birthing babies and cooking up hearty meals for the menfolk."

"Don't put words in my mouth or try to make me sound like some mouth-breathing caveman." His words were tough, but his expression was harmless. "I think there should be equal rights, and pay, for women. It's just that I was raised to think of women as ladies. They should be treated well, and protected. You can fight bulls. Hell, you have the right to *ride* the damned bull if you want to." He shrugged. "I just don't get why you'd want to."

All of them were looking at her. Panicky, she looked back, caught. This is where she always said something snarky and walked away. The words piled into her mouth. She swallowed them. They were reacting better than she'd expected. She couldn't blow it now.

Deuce tipped his head. "Hey, I really would like to know."

She clasped her hands, studied her ragged cuticles and tried to find a middle ground between telling and snarky. Say *something*. "Look, I'm no different than you. I may be glass but I have skills to make up for it. Oh okay, I have boobs, and I sit down to pee, but that's where the difference ends. I take care of myself. If I don't work, I don't eat." She met Cash's stare. "I'm not trying to put anybody down, or show them up. I just want a place. I'm not asking—I've earned it, and you know it."

Deuce nodded. "She has a point."

The tension broke in her shoulders when she shrugged. "So what's the problem?"

***

It was almost lunch when the last bull cleared the out-gate. Harlie trudged to the fence, wiping sweat and chewing grit.

"I'd love to give that old man a whistle enema." Cash grumbled, snatched his cap from the dirt, slapped it against his knee and trudged after her.

"Ever' single one all y'all are as worthless as a bucket of spit today." Hoot added a stream to the dust to demonstrate. "You stunk yesterday, but today you'd have to take lessons to be fools."

Harlie plopped on the bleacher and tried to suck the heavy air into her lungs.

Hoot hadn't let up a second on them this morning. She could almost see the belligerence radiating off the other students. Maybe it was just a heat-shimmer.

"Pack it in. Y'all're done for the day."

All five heads whipped up.

Harlie's stomach withered to an acorn-sized lump. *Is he going to send us home?* "Hoot, Sir, let me try again. I can —"

"Nope. You keep goin' an somebody's gonna get hurt. Go get a shower. Manuel will take y'all into town for the afternoon." He turned and walked away.

The students exchanged confused looks.

"Is he giving up on us?"

"Did he just give us the day off?"

"I don't know." Harlie stood. "But I call first dibs on the shower." She took off, sprinting for the bunkhouse. Outraged yells and the pounding of boots followed her.

Texas must trust their citizens more than California; they rode in the ranch truck's bed the fifteen miles to town.

In the two-block 'downtown', Manuel pulled over and yelled out the window. "If you eat at the Lunch Pail, just tell them you're Hoot's students and they'll put it on his tab. You're on your own until four-thirty. I'll meet you here. You don't show, you hike back. And Hoot told me he's not putting up bail money, so stay outta' the bar."

When they'd piled out onto the sizzling sidewalk, the truck pulled away in a cloud of motor oil.

Cash brushed off his Wranglers and looked up and down the sleepy street. "What the hell is there to do in Chilly, Texas, for six hours?"

Harlie said, "I don't care, as long as there's A/C."

Deuce pointed. "We didn't get lunch. Let's start there."

109

The Lunch Pail was a once-white, greasy-spoon diner with gas pumps out front. One of those 'Eat here and get gas' places.

A cowbell clanked the glass door as they walked in and the room pushed a bacon-scented, cool breath against her face. "I may stay here all day."

She strode to the bar stools at the counter but when the guys piled into a cracked red vinyl booth and tossed their hats on the window sill, she reconsidered. Sitting cheek to jowl with those magpies was the last thing she wanted but she should probably put out the effort.

Two steps brought her to the table. "Scoot over." She told Jonah. When he did, she slid onto the cracked vinyl seat.

Deuce pulled plastic-clad menu boards from behind the napkin dispenser and passed them around. Harlie declined. She knew what she wanted.

A teenage waitress in short shorts walked up, a pink kerchief over her hair. "What can I get y'all?" She pulled a pad out of her white apron, and a pencil from behind her ear. She was pretty, the way all teens were pretty. But underneath, Harlie could see the big hipped, world-weary wife and mother she would become.

Cash shot her a bad-wolf grin. "Shouldn't you be in school, Darlin'?"

She rolled her eyes but her smile brought out a dimple. "I graduated last year, Cowboy."

Do girls really fall for that cheese? "Rein in the hormones at least until I get my food ordered. I'm hungry."

The girl finally pulled her attention from Cash. Harlie ordered a BLT, fries and a diet Cola.

Cash looked her over. "You should order a milkshake. You could stand to put some curves on those bones."

"Dude, the day I need your advice will be the day after my lobotomy."

The guys laughed.

When they'd ordered, the waitress sauntered away with a hip-roll that proved she knew the men were watching.

110

Harlie cleared her throat. "Can we talk?" Once the door swung behind the girl, their heads swiveled to her. She huffed out a breath, but managed to bite back a retort. "We have one more day to impress Hoot. I don't know about you, but I *have* to graduate."

Deuce said, "I've got to get my PRCA card out of this. I can't work rodeos without it. Hoot's recommendation will really help. I hear they think highly of his school."

"Damned if I can see why." Cash tore the paper wrapper off a straw. "It's like Boot Camp. Only I didn't sign up for the Marines."

"Yeah, but you gotta admit you've learned a lot. You look lots better than when you started." Levi blushed, as if realizing the compliment came out backhanded.

Harlie dropped a napkin in her lap. "We all have strengths and weaknesses. We all know what they are so we should be able to help each other out." She pointed across the table. "Jonah, you know what the bull is going to do. Talk to us. We can get there faster than you. See?"

They strategized and passed information through lunch. She was never going to be buds with these guys, but this was what her high school biology teacher would have called a 'symbiotic relationship'. They needed each other.

For another day, anyway.

By the time they spilled out of the diner, the hot, damp air hit like a cudgel. The sun seared her through her t-shirt.

"Where to now?" Deuce asked.

She scanned the shade granted by the awnings jutting from the old brick buildings. "I'm going to check out downtown. All two blocks of it. I might catch the movie."

The old-fashioned movie house was obvious, thanks to a two-story bulb-lit arrow sign, pointing to a cracked marquee.

"Sleepless in Seattle?" Cash mock-gagged. "I'll pass."

"Hey, it's got air conditioning. That's all I care about." Levi said. "I'll sleep through the movie anyway."

She walked to the sidewalk and turned left.

"Hey, Coop, wait up." A chorus of trotting boot falls

sounded behind her.

She stopped. "Coop?"

Deuce came even with her. "I think it fits you. Your last name's Cooper, right?"

Shaking her head, she walked on. She'd never had a nickname. She kinda liked it, though. Sounded like she belonged to a gang or something.

The rest followed. The stores leaned toward seedy: a used bookstore, second-hand clothing, a realtor's window displaying dusty faded photographs of dusty land for sale. Several of the windows were shuttered with tan butcher-paper. "Chilly isn't exactly thriving, is it?"

"Hey, look at that." Cash pointed across the street. "This town is a dump but they got an ink pusher."

The sign above the door announced the 'Inkslinger Tattoo Parlor'.

"You know what? We should all get tats." Cash turned to them, his face lit like a little boy at an arcade.

Harlie eyed the building. "I don't have money for stuff like that."

But it would be cool.

Levi shook his head. Jonah said, "Our dad would tan our hides."

"Hell, all the more reason to do it. Look, this week is the start of your career as a bullfighter. Don't you want something to commemorate it?"

Deuce pushed his cowboy hat back on his head. "I want one."

Cash punched his bicep. "Now you're talkin'." The two checked for traffic then stepped off the curb.

"Wouldn't hurt to watch," Levi said.

Harlie shrugged. "They're bound to have A/C, anyway." *And I won't have to pay a movie house for it.*

The place must've been a barbershop in a former life; four red padded swivel chairs faced the street, all of them empty. A man in a leather vest and tight-legged black jeans stepped from a back room. His gray-laced black hair was pulled into a ponytail,

112

and a handlebar mustache drooped past his chin. As he got closer, Harlie realized what she took as a tight, multi-colored shirt was skin. Every visible square inch was 'inked'—and more, judging by the hissing snake head peeking from the collar of the vest. "Can I help you?"

"Dude!" Cash scanned the guy's impressive billboard expanse of skin.

One corner of the man's mustache kicked up. "Name's Daryl."

"We're all thinking of getting tats." Cash strolled to the photo-covered wall opposite the chairs.

"Some of us are." Harlie added.

"I've got flash sheets." Daryl lifted a thick binder from the counter. "What were you thinking of?"

Deuce stepped over and flipped pages. "We're all in a bullfighting school, and —"

"Ah, Hoot's students." Daryl flipped to the back of the binder. "You might want to look at these then."

They stepped and looked over Deuce's shoulder.

Real-to-life bulls and cartooned smoke-snorters filled the pages.

"It'd be cool if we all got the same one." Deuce said.

Pages flipped.

"That one." Deuce poked a finger in the middle of the last page.

"That is epic." Cash breathed.

Men turn into little boys so easy. Harlie leaned in to see.

It was in the tribal style, a few slashed lines giving the feel of a bull skull. On second look, there was a man's body in the middle.

"Wow. That *is* cool." Admiration pried the words from Jonah.

"I'm in." Cash said.

"It's perfect." Deuce traced the lines with his finger.

113

"Love the symbolism. We're protecting men from the bulls. The riders are at the heart of what we do."

"How much?" Jonah asked.

"Depends on how large you want it." Daryl walked to the counter and fiddled with equipment.

The herd followed. Cash thought a moment. "About three inches. And I want it right here." He pointed to the left side of his chest. "Right over the bulge of my pec."

"Oh, yeah." Deuce said.

Alone at the counter, Harlie flipped pages. If she had the money . . .

Daryl smiled. "Eighty bucks. Each."

The twins looked at each other for two seconds, then nodded. "We're in." Levi said.

Deuce turned to her. "What about you, Coop? This one may not be right for you but you've got to get one."

"Yeah." The others chorused.

"Oh." She stopped on a page of symbols: ankhs, peace signs, Celtic crosses, and at the bottom, a black and white Yin/Yang. She stroked the photo, feeling the edges of the carved-out place in her.

Cash walked over. "Isn't that the thing on the lid of that box I broke?"

She slammed the book closed. "Never mind."

Cash winced. She hadn't realized she'd slammed his finger in the binder. He pulled it open to the correct page, held it up and pointed. "Hey, Daryl, how much for this one?"

Harlie grabbed for the binder. "Quit. I told you I don't have money for that."

Cash held it out of reach.

"It's simpler. Forty." Daryl had Deuce in the chair, taking off his shirt.

Cash turned and speared her with a look. "I owe you." He whispered. "I know you don't think much of me, but I pay my debts."

She crossed her arms. "I'm not doing it." She wasn't having anything on her body because he felt an obligation. It

114

would taint the meaning and that symbol was far too precious to be stained.

A muscle in his jaw jumped as he studied her.

"I've got an idea. Wait here." He walked to Daryl, and began a whispered conversation. Soon, all the guys were whispering.

It doesn't matter. But she couldn't help running her finger over the curled figures, couldn't help the echo of loss that tolled in her chest. *Angel.*

"Okay, it's settled." Cash stepped in front of her.

She snatched her hand away from the sheet, put it behind her and took a step back. "I'm not taking your money."

"You don't need to. We negotiated. Since we're all getting tats, Daryl's throwing yours in free."

She shot a look across the room. Daryl was prepping Deuce's chest. The twins stood watching. "Is that the truth?"

"Hey, doesn't this guy look like he needs the business?" Sincere eyes held hers as he extended a crooked baby finger. "Pinkie-swear."

A tattoo wouldn't bring Angel back, or keep her safe, any more than the glass house had. It wouldn't hold Harlie safe in the arena, either. It had no power. She knew that.

But something about it would make her feel a bit less alone. It would seal the bond with Angel, even if it was only on her part. "Okay."

"Awesome. Come on. Last chair has your name on it."

Chapter 11

The next day, following a celebratory chicken fried steak and mashed potato dinner, the students leaned over the picnic table watching Hoot sign their completion certificates with a dragging, left-handed scrawl. Harlie sat among them, a part of them in a way that was different than the last time she sat here.

Getting a tat with them wasn't some kind of little boy blood-brother ceremony.

"Y'all did okay today. You worked together, and nobody died."

High praise, considering. But Harlie didn't need Hoot to tell her. Once they decided to help each other instead of compete, they'd fallen together as a team easier than she'd have thought possible. She was both grateful, and glad, she didn't have to do that anymore. Trusting another in the arena felt foreign; like she was dancing in too tight shoes. On the wrong feet.

She reached for the plain document that was her passport to her next life. Joy must be made of Helium, because it rose in her, expanding her chest, making her head swim with rarefied air.

She grasped the certificate but Hoot didn't let go. "This doesn't mean you're done. You gotta keep getting better. Remember, you don't bounce; you break." His stare reminded her of a bull's in the arena. Testing. Challenging.

"I will, Sir. I promise."

He had comments for each of the others, but the voices

faded to white noise. Her eyes scanned the certificate, stop-action snippets flashed in her mind of her future - throwing fake after pirouetting fake, leaping in brilliant pass-throughs, saving countless bull riders over the years of a storied career.

She'd already done more than any other woman had managed. The small coal of pride that she'd sheltered deep in her chest all week burst into flame, spreading warmth, melting iceberg chunks of doubt.

You can do this.

"We're done. The truck leaves for the airport in the mornin' at six. Y'all be on it." Hoot rose. "I done raised my kids. Don't need more runnin' around, tearin' up the place."

Deuce's grin matched hers. "Aw, come on, Hoot. You're gonna miss us. You know you are."

"Bah. There'll be more where you came from in a couple weeks." He flapped a hand at them and walked to the house.

Joy hung thick as the humidity in the air. In some kind of testosterone mind-meld, the guys huddled, arms on each other's shoulders and yelled some nonsense. Harlie shook her head and walked back to the bunkhouse.

I'll be home tomorrow.

Anticipation crested in a rolling, sparkling wave . . . that crashed on the rocks of reality.

The Angel she returned to wouldn't be the innocent sprite that flitted through childhood. While Harlie was out having fun, Angel had been staring out that window. Skewered on the double-edged sword of homecoming, her feet stopped. She put a hand to her chest.

The guys flowed past her.

"Come on, Coop, we're going to celebrate." Deuce threw over his shoulder. "Cash has a flask stashed."

"You go on. I'll be there in a few." She headed for the corrals and quiet comfort of bovine company.

Leaning on the fence, she ran her fingers over the swelling on the inside of her forearm, tracing the Yin/Yang scar she'd had inked in the same place Angel had carved hers.

The past week's fear and anxiety was a whisper compared

to the heavy, mouth-breathing panic that prickled the hairs on the back of her neck at the thought of going home.

Drumming her fingers on the top rail, she watched the bulls standing in the paddock and tried to soak in their disinterest. Given her life so far, she should be good at accepting.

But dammit, she wasn't. Bovine therapy wasn't working. She had to move. Had to *do* something. She walked down the fence to the next corral where a lone blond bull stood chewing cud and swishing flies.

She imagined taking him on. Holding until his nose was a foot from her chest. Her feet moving light and fast as she spun away, perfectly balanced.

Her feet stirred dust, practicing the moves she'd learned this past week.

If I could just have one more freestyle practice . . .

She glanced around, thumbs beating a drumroll on the top pipe. This corral was farthest from the barn, and the arena. She was alone.

Except for the bull. He was short squat and polled; no horns to dodge. He didn't look so tough.

Fear zinged under her skin, but it was the light, intoxicating kind. *This* was something she could do. Something she was good at.

Still, she hesitated, resisting the magnetic pull of thrill.

Hoot would kill her if he knew.

Thirty, forty seconds tops. You could be in and out and no one the wiser.

Besides, if she could do *this,* then maybe it would give her courage to walk back into that room in Southern California and face reality.

One last look around, then she ducked under the middle pipe and stepped away from the fence.

The bull just looked at her.

She wiped her sweaty palms on the back pockets of her jeans, then waved her arms.

The bull threw its head up.

Afraid her voice might summon someone, she snatched

off her straw hat and waved it.

The bull didn't lower its head, or paw the ground. By the time she saw movement, it was on her, faster than she'd thought possible.

Jesus!

She threw a fake at the last second, but before she could turn away, the bull stepped on her foot, throwing her off-balance. A white flash of pain shot up her leg but she managed to catch her balance, and spun.

The bull must have wheeled on its haunches because his head was right there, a foot from her face, coming on.

Too close!

Panic sharpened her focus: the wild in the white-rimmed eye, the arcing string of saliva from its lips, the curly tuft of blonde hair between its ears.

She only had time to throw an arm up before the impact.

The head hit her in the armpit, driving her air out in a whoosh. Her feet left the ground and she was flying. Dirt passed under her, the small stones getting bigger and bigger . . .

A land mine went off. An explosion of pain in her left shoulder shot sparklers of white across her vision. Screaming, I-can't-live-with-this agony coursed through her, blocking coherent thought.

Instinct screamed in her head.

Get up! Get up! Get up and run!

Somehow she was on one hand and her knees, scrabbling. The other arm tilted to the side, useless except for the iron-sided agony throbbing and surging with her heartbeat. The fence was miles away, at the end of a dark tunnel. She should try to get to her feet, but that would take time—time she didn't have.

The ground shook as the hooves got closer.

Fighting the urge to roll into a ball, she forced her knees faster. Black spots bloomed across her vision.

"Hey, hey, hey!" A familiar voice crossed behind her and something bumped her butt.

She heard a thud and slammed her eyes shut before realizing it wasn't her that was hit.

Pain roared in her ears before blackness filled her vision and took her down.

***

She came awake to orange light on the back of her eyelids and the sound of retreating shoe squeaks. When she shifted, testing for pain, paper crinkled under her. Her shoulder telegraphed a dull throb, her foot, a lesser one. She touched her right shoulder and found her forearm Velcroed to a band strapped on around her chest over the t-shirt. Maybe she'd just lay here for a few minutes and pull her scattered chickens together.

"So I have to ask," The scruffy growl snapped her eyes open, "did you learn anything?" Hoot sat leaning forward, elbows on the arms of a plastic chair.

She lay on an exam table in a tiny, curtain-walled area of what she guessed was an Emergency Room. Awareness rushed back, along with the memory of her epic stupidity. "Who drew the bull off me?" She groaned.

"The Oklahoma kid."

"Deuce? How did he know —"

"You kin ask him yourself. He's down the hall."

She winced. "He got hurt?" Her voice came out skinny.

Hoot tented his fingers. "Yep."

She closed her eyes and tensed her stomach muscles to sit up.

A heavy hand fell on her good shoulder. "Doc says to lay here until he clears you."

She kept her eyes closed. "How bad?"

"You got a dislocated shoulder. EMT put it back in and gave you a shot of painkillers. Foot's not broke. Other'n that, just bruises—"

"Not me. Deuce."

"Ah, he'll be okay. Bull popped him under the chin. He took a little dirt nap."

Guilt burned like salt in an open cut. "Shit. Who saved Deuce?"

Hoot sat up and pushed out his bony chest. "You're looking at him."

120

She groaned. In one fell swoop, she'd not only managed to hurt herself and Deuce, but put her teacher in danger as well.

"Was you behind the door when brains was passed out? What in tarnation was you thinkin'?"

"I saw that bull all alone, and I thought . . ." She tried to remember but that part of her brain was still dark.

"Didja ever think that bull was on his lonesome for a reason? Jesus, girl, that's the meanest bull on the place. He'd as soon hook you as eat."

She wanted to pass out again, so as not to face this. Instead, she turned her head and looked Hoot in the eye. "I'm sorry, Hoot. I'm so sorry."

He made a disgusted sound in the back of his throat and with effort, pushed himself to his feet. "You're a loner. And loners don't make bullfighters. You'd best set your sights on somethin' else afore you kill somebody." He hobbled out of the room. The look of disappointment on his creased-leather face hurt more than his blunt-force words.

Just because she had the guts to try bullfighting didn't mean she had the brains, or the temperament. Good judgment was paramount and she'd just displayed the opposite.

She'd known accidents were bound to happen and had been ready to pay the price. In theory.

Reality was different.

She could handle her injury, when it came. But could she handle her responsibility for the injury of others? In this job, her mistakes wouldn't just be hers.

And being responsible for other's lives would connect her to them in a way she hadn't realized.

Her perfect job came with an ugly side.

"Oh, there you are." Hoot's wife brushed aside the curtain and stepped in.

Harlie rolled onto her good side and sat up. "Ms. Leonard, you didn't need to come down." A wave of dizziness hit and she swayed.

"Here." She put her hand on Harlie's neck and pushed her head down onto her knees.

The hand was smooth and cool. It felt good. "I'm okay." She said into her jeans.

Ms. Leonard's hand circled Harlie's arm. "Try it again."

She sat up slowly. "Better. Thanks, Ma'am."

"Call me Clarice." She dropped her handbag in the chair. "Be grateful that you were out for most of it. I've seen men with dislocations cry like babies for their mommas." She had a wobbly voice, like an old Katherine Hepburn.

"Yes'm." Clarice may look and sound like a grandma out of a picture book, but as the wife of a bullfighter she must have seen more than her share of blood and pain. But that didn't make Harlie's sin any less. "I'm so sorry I put your husband at risk." The words caught on the barbs in her throat, coming out ragged.

"Oh posh. We know you didn't mean to. This is a dangerous business and things happen. He may look old to you, but Hoot Leonard still can handle any bull on the place."

Harlie's weighted-down gaze slid to the floor. Ms. Leonard's understanding hurt more than a tongue-lashing would. She put her face in her hands. "I've ruined everything."

"Only if you give up." There was no wobble in that steel-tipped voice.

She lifted her head. "You didn't see how Hoot looked at me. No way he's going to recommend me to the PRCA after this."

"Hoot's been cheering you on the whole time."

"Are you delusional?" Harlie slapped a hand over her mouth but it was too late. *Must be the painkillers.*

"Oh Hon, the look on your face!" Ms. Leonard giggled. "My husband's bark may be legendary, but under that he's a pussycat."

Harlie left her hand where it was, just in case something else inappropriate tried to slip out.

"From the minute you had the spunk to tell him you were bunking with the boys, you had him on your side. He's been hoping you'd make the cut."

She lowered her hand. "Ma'am, I don't mean to argue with you, but you weren't –"

"Do you think Hoot Leonard would lend his bullfighting shorts to just anyone?" She crossed her arms over her chest. "He wore those shorts every event of his last three seasons as a bullfighter." She looked over her cheater glasses. "And three world finals."

Harlie tried to process the information, but her mind ground gears as if there was a student driver at the wheel. Hoot *wanted* her to succeed? She shook her head. If that was true, she felt even worse. "If you say so, Ma'am. But that was before today."

"I've been married to the man for nigh onto fifty years, you can trust me. He's still proud of you." Her lips pulled to a tight line and her bright blue Mrs. Claus eyes narrowed. "Unless you're going to let one mistake run you off, that is."

Hoot is proud? Of me? The lady seemed sure though, and she should know. Harlie scrubbed her good hand down the leg of her jeans, wincing when she hit a bruised spot. There really wasn't any way but forward, regardless. This job paid way better than any other job she was qualified for. And Angel's care would take every bit of it.

Besides, being able to save men in the arena, and maybe even get to dance with bulls now and again . . . She loved it. Might as well admit it, she was hooked; a full-blown thrill junkie, antsy for her next fix. Even after getting run over today. Even after knowing how awful it was, living her secret wish, when Angel was living a nightmare.

She sighed. "No'm. It won't run me off."

"Didn't think it would. Any woman strong enough to step into a man's world is tough enough to stare down her own mistakes." The old lady's hard look melted to a smug grin.

The curtain was pulled back by a tired-looking man in a white lab coat, too young to be a doctor. "Now, let's see how our lady bullfighter is doing." He tossed her chart on the counter and stepped to the table.

"Hoot and I will be in the waiting room. We'll drive you back when you and that cute Okie are ready to go." She winked and ducked out of the curtain.

"How are you feeling?" The baby face fiddled with the Velcro setup.

"Like a bull ran me over."

He probed her shoulder then stepped behind her. There was the shush-snick sound of Velcro letting go, then the elastic band that stretched from below her breasts to her waist tightened, like a corset. "You're going to need help getting this on and off, but it's the best way to keep your shoulder stable and supported."

Great, she'd have to ask for help. This day just kept getting better. "How long until I can take it off?"

"The tendons are going to need three to twelve weeks to heal. Then there's ten weeks of physical therapy." He walked back around the table to adjust the arm Velcroed on the front of the contraption.

She was due to talk to Steve Rawlings next week. It would take him at least a couple of weeks to get her booked on the rodeo circuit. "I can probably live with three weeks. Can you give me exercises to do after that?"

He sighed. "You rodeo people are all the same. Your bodies are essential for the job but you refuse to take care of them. How do you expect to heal?"

She slid off the table easy, to be sure her knees held. When they did, she glanced around for her hat. After wearing it nonstop for a week, she felt a bit naked without it. "I heal fast."

"That's what they all say." He tsked, scribbling on a pad. "Here's a script for pain, and one for inflammation. You can have them filled at the Pharmacy off the lobby." He stepped to the counter, retrieved her chart and pulled a few sheets from it. "Here's some exercises, for *after* the brace comes off. But if it hurts to do them, don't. If you force the tendons before they're healed, you're going to do more damage."

"Got it." Man, she missed her hat. "Can you tell me where to find the other guy who came in from Hoot's school?"

"Two curtains down."

"Is he okay?" She held her stomach muscles taut, to take the blow.

"A concussion. He's free to go. Lucky that all you rodeo

124

people have hard heads."

"Thanks." She stepped out to the hall.

"Empty ones, too." The doctor's mutter came from behind the curtain.

What the heck was she going to say? How do you apologize for almost getting someone killed?

Like Ms. Leonard said, you gotta stare down your own mistakes.

The second curtain down came up way too fast. Afraid she'd chicken out if she hesitated, she pulled the curtain aside and walked in.

Deuce was buckling his belt. He glanced at her then quickly pulled up the zipper on his jeans.

"I'm so sorry my stupidity got you hurt." In spite of the burning in her face, she held her chin up and looked him in the eye. "Are you going to be okay?"

He finished tucking in his shirt. "Yeah. Just a headache. Looks like you got the worst of it."

"What made you come to that back paddock?"

He lifted his hat from the chair. "You said you'd be right behind us. You weren't. So I went looking." He scrubbed a hand over his face. "I'm going to see that hit you took in my dreams for a long time."

"I'm sorry, Deuce. Sincerely." You'd think that saying that would get easier, as often as she'd said it today.

He worked the straw brim that had gotten creased in the wreck. "I'm used to bailing out women. Don't worry about it."

Her 'asshole radar' pinged. "What does being a woman have to do with it?"

He sighed. "In my experience, women just seem to get into messes they need help out of. That's just the way of it."

"That's bullshit."

He glanced at her, eyebrows raised. "The one thing I've learned this week is that it's a team effort. We need to help each other." He settled the hat on his head. "You could stand to work on that."

Her mouth opened and closed as if that would siphon

words from her brain. He was right. They both knew it. So why couldn't she say it?

"You're welcome." He tipped his hat at her and walked out.

Chapter 12

It was late afternoon by the time Harlie retrieved Yolanda from LAX's long-term parking lot. It had only been parked a week, but it took a bite from what was left of her cash. After a bus ride and a quarter mile trudge, she managed to start the car with one prolonged grinding.

Twenty minutes later she pulled into the cracked asphalt parking lot and parked at the squat stucco building—Compadres Mental Health Center. The last rays of sunset hit the façade whose style tried for Sedona, but only made it to Tijuana. She sat watching the lights come on inside, joy, hope and dread warring in her chest. Angel had been here less than a month. It was way too early to be hoping for a huge improvement.

But Harlie's heart wasn't listening. She wanted her sister back. The one so bursting with life that every third step was a skip. The one with the mischievous giggle that would bring Harlie running, knowing Angel was into something. The one whose eyes trusted that Harlie would keep her safe.

Through the windshield, watching bits of trash shift in the dusky breeze, her aloneness blew away. She was home. This may be a new place, but it was home because this was where Angel was.

A stomach snarl brought her back to the present. Well, it was going to have to be content with the peanuts she'd gotten on the plane — no work meant no pay. With her left hand, she made the awkward reach to turn off the ignition. She fumbled pulling the keys out and dropped them.

"Shit." This was going to hurt.

Given the prices at the pharmacy, she could only afford one of the prescriptions. She'd chosen the anti-inflammatories over the pain-killers. They'd get her back to work faster. Holding her breath, she reached across her body and bent. Her back muscles screamed. Her Velcroed arm shifted and her shoulder breathed fire. Her fingers scrabbled, brushing the floor.

Hurry, hurry, hurry —there!

She snagged the ring, sat up, and spent a moment just breathing. Surely not every muscle hurt, but naming the ones that didn't would take lots less time. They'd loosen once she got moving, but damn, she dreaded the climbing out of the car part.

Seeing the light from the second to the last window on the left, the tug of Harlie's missing half got her moving.

Chrissie, the night nursing supervisor looked up from the reception desk. "Wow. What happened to you?"

"A freak accident." Harlie had given the details of her trip to the supervising staff before she left, in case they needed to reach her. Limping only a little, she shuffled to the desk.

Chrissie looked over her glasses. "You know what they say, you mess with the bull, you're gonna get the horn."

"This one didn't have horns."

Chrissie gave Harlie a head-to-toe look-over. "Well aren't you lucky." She'd made it clear before Harlie left that she thought Harlie's choice of career was insane.

Easy for her to say. *She* had an education. "How is she? Any better?"

The nurse removed her glasses and stood. "You'll see a change from the last time you saw her."

Harlie read the reserve on Chrissie's face. "There's a 'but' in there, somewhere."

"The drugs appear to be having an effect, but don't expect too much." She walked from around the desk and touched Harlie's good shoulder. "She's moving now, mostly rocking. She is still non-verbal and avoids eye contact. Come. I'll walk you down."

"But the doctor thinks she's improving?" Dread and joy danced in an uneasy alliance in her chest. Harlie studied the nurse for any nuance of expression that would help her prepare.

"When she's fully cognizant, the real work begins. Here we are." She walked into the room. "Angel, look who's here. I told you Harlie would be back soon!"

Heart beating like a brass band playing a Sousa march, Harlie stepped in. Angel sat on the edge of the bed in pj's, head down, rocking. Her hair fell forward in a brown curtain, hiding her face. Her hands rubbed over each other in repetitive movement — not hand-wringing exactly — more like she was washing her hands, over and over.

"Hey, Littlest." Harlie stepped to the bed.

Angel stared at the floor, lips pursed, as if she were thinking – hard.

Harlie put a hand on her sister's knee. "Angel. It's me."

Her sister gave no indication that she saw or heard. She just rocked. Harlie's heartbeat slackened to a sadder, bluesy beat.

"I'll leave you two to visit." The nurse's shoes squeaked down the hall.

Her sister was in there somewhere. Harlie had to believe it.

Denying reality again?

Maybe. But it worked. When faced with the incomprehensible, it was the only other choice. As long as her denial was conscious, reality, when it hit, wouldn't hit so frigging *hard.*

At least that was the theory.

She knelt on the tile to better to see Angel's face, and rubbed her fingers over her sister's flannel covered thigh. "I know you're doing your best, Littlest. You always do." She pushed down the sadness that rose in a liquid wall, threatening to swamp her. "Just don't stay away any longer than you have to, okay? I'm out here all alone. I need you."

She sat telling Angel stories about the past week and drinking in the sight of her sister until her legs threatened cramps and a glance outside showed it was full dark. Harlie struggled to her feet. "Let's get you into bed."

It wasn't easy one-handed, but she worked the covers down and eventually got Angel tucked under them. Lying on her side, eyes closed, Angel's head still rocked on the pillow and her hands still moved under the blanket.

Her restlessness wore at Harlie's ragged edges. Was Angel worried? Afraid? It hurt her heart to think so.

She should bed down in the car, but she couldn't make herself leave. She'd been too long lonely, aching for her sister's soft back at hers. Stepping to the door, Harlie eased it closed, snapped off the light, then walked over and carefully lowered herself beside Angel. Once her body stopped singing a pain chorus, she relaxed and reached up with her good hand to cup the vulnerable nape of her sister's neck, the way she used to when Angel was little.

Angel's body ceased its restless rocking.

The scent of shampoo, soap, and her sister washed over her. Harlie's mind unwound.

I'll just stay a few minutes, until I'm sure she's asleep.

A bolt of pain jolted her awake. Something shook her shoulder.

"Harlie." Annette, the daytime nurse supervisor bent over her, whispering. "Chrissie told me you were here. I let you sleep but you can't be here when shift changes."

Harlie sat up in one fluid motion, having learned the hard way that it hurt less that way. Sun poured in the windows. "Holy crap, it's morning." She swiped drool off her cheek. No bad dreams. No pain. She hadn't slept that well since . . . since the last time she and Angel had slept together, a hundred years ago. "Thanks for letting me sleep."

The woman's teeth flashed white against her brown skin. "How could I not? We haven't been able to get her into bed since she came here. She just naps, sitting up." She stepped around the opposite side of the bed and tucked Angel's hair behind her ear. "I'll get her up and dressed. Why don't you catch a shower before everyone gets here?" She nodded to the bathroom in the corner of the tiny room.

"I'm good." She stood, testing her bad foot and wincing, adjusted the brace on her shoulder.

Annette's thick brows came together. "You'll need help undressing. Come here."

Allowing help was worse than having a stranger's hands touching her skin. "No, really. I'm okay." She finger-combed her hair. Maybe if she stuck her head under the faucet . . .

The woman put a hand on her ample hip. "Don't be so stubborn. You need help. I'm a nurse."

"But you have patients to care for." Something thick and soft in her throat made the words come out soggy. "I'm just —"

"You're just wasting time." She bustled to the bathroom and waved Harlie over. "Hurry now."

***

Five hours later, Harlie pushed open the door of the diner where Steve Rawling had suggested they meet. She'd lucked out; he was in town today to meet with a network.

He waved from a booth by the window and stood as she approached, brows knit. "How long are you going to be out?"

She shrugged, then to hide her wince, ducked her head and settled in the booth. "Three weeks, tops, but—"

"What the hell were you thinking?"

She sat still, as the knife slid in. She shouldn't feel betrayed by Hoot. Rawlings had paid her tuition. In her experience, allegiance followed money like flies followed a herd.

And besides, it was her own damned fault.

"You got in the ring with no backup? You got mental issues I don't know about?"

Mental issues? A snapshot memory went off in her brain like a flashbulb. Angel, face blank save a single rolling tear, stood taking the school bully's taunts— 'Crazy lady, times *two!* First your mother, now *you!*' The hackles of her guard dog temper went up. She growled, "Now wait just a damned minute."

"No, you wait. I'm not telling anyone up the food chain. But I laid my reputation on the line for you. If you don't make it after giving it your best shot, fine. But you try to throw it away

131

without a good reason, I gotta right to say something."

She saw the edge of the cliff in his eyes. Heard it in his tone. Trying to catch her runaway tongue, she studied him: the tan line that ended where his cowboy hat would start, the string tie, the sincere expression. The power suit didn't cover the fact that he was also a country boy. One who was taking a big chance on her. He had no way of knowing he'd just hit a trip wire. She took a deep breath. If she stepped off that cliff, Angel would go down with her.

The hair on her neck went down. She hadn't planned on eating a shit sandwich for lunch but after all, she'd made the damned thing. "Trust me. I only make mistakes once." She slid the certificate of completion across the table. "I did manage to get this."

"Good." He fingered the paper as if judging its authenticity. "Gotta tell you, I'm impressed; I didn't think you'd make it."

Her head snapped up. "Then why the hell did you send me?"

"Hey, a girl has never attempted this. You have to admit the odds were against you finishing." The storm had passed as quickly as it came. "Good job. You're one step closer. Today we'll go over the next step." He signaled for the waitress. "You know what you want? I'm buying."

In spite of the jumpy nerves, Harlie's stomach demanded one of everything on the menu. She ordered a chicken dinner, instead.

They talked about bullfighting school until the food came, but then her hunger commanded her full attention until nothing was left but bones and butter smears, and her stomach hummed with happiness.

"Better?" From his over-the-coffee-cup stare, Steve saw too much.

She nodded, then ducked her head to wipe her lips with her napkin. "Okay, boss. What's next?"

While a busboy had cleared their table, Steve put down his cup and lifted a file folder from the seat beside him. "First, you need some experience. I called some people I know and got you work. Small rodeos mostly, scattered across the western states. It should help get your name out there." He thumbed through paper, then passed her a full-page list. "You'll be on the circuit. A different rodeo every weekend."

Arizona, New Mexico, Texas, Oklahoma, Nevada . . . "Nothing in California?"

"California isn't exactly a hotbed for rodeo. You'll get better exposure elsewhere." He waved his empty cup at a waitress. "I warned you that this career would involve a lot of travel. You said you had no ties."

"Yeah, yeah, I'm good with that." She scanned the list. All those miles. How long would Yolanda hold up?

How are you going to leave Angel—again?

A waitress with a coffee pot hovered only long enough for an in-flight refueling, then was gone.

"This next step is really important. You've got the advantage — all eyes will be on the female bullfighter. But I can't just shoehorn you into Touring Pro events. You have to earn your way there. The rodeo organizers will appreciate that you can put butts in seats but you'll have to impress the stock contractors as well."

She sat up straight. "I can do that."

"But that's not all." He pulled in a breath. "This is a man's sport. Not everyone is going to take to a woman bullfighter."

Remembering the faces of her fellow students the first time she walked into the bunkhouse, she snorted. "You think?"

"It's not enough that you do the job." He looked at the ceiling, as if the perfect words were etched there. "The organizers are going to catch crap for hiring a girl bullfighter. To surmount that, you've got to get them to *like* you. You know, to root for the plucky little gal."

She rested her good arm on the table and stuck out her chin. Oh, she knew what he wanted. He wanted her to show weakness so the rodeo guys would like her.

It had been on all those Lifetime movies that Angel loved.

The pretty ladies who acted brave until the hero showed up, then they 'dissolved into tears'. She'd even read it the one time she picked up one of mom's romances. *'He cradled her in his strong arms, as she dissolved into tears.'* That only happened in fiction.

In Harlie's experience, when you showed weakness people either skedaddled or screwed you.

He set his cup down, slow. "You've got to admit you're a bit . . ." He raised his shoulders in a don't-kill-the-messenger shrug, "rough around the edges."

Her fingers clenched all on their own. "Should I wear heels and a tight, short skirt in the arena too?"

"I thought about that." He waved a hand in dismissal. "But they'd never take you seriously."

Cliff or no, she opened her mouth to let him have it.

He put up a hand. "I'm kidding. I'm kidding, okay?" He fingered the handle of his coffee cup. "Look, all I'm saying is, you'll get farther with a little sugar than lemons. You know, that kinder, gentler thing."

"You mean while I'm putting my ass on the line, saving men's lives." She'd love to tell him where to put his kinder and gentler.

"Not at the same time." His bantering smile slid away. He huffed a sigh. "I'm not telling you to bat your eyelashes at them. I'm just suggesting you leave a small bit of that hardass attitude in California." His soft brown eyes were steady, serious.

She forced her muscles to relax. As much as it chapped, he was probably right. She knew she had a smaller hoop to jump through than anyone else in the arena. And her hoop had a blazing ring of fire around it.

But being a woman was what had gotten her this opportunity. She'd known there would be disadvantages and advantages to being a dancing chicken.

She remembered shooting the gap between the downed rider and the bull, the rush of air, the rush of adrenaline. The flush of victory.

This chicken was going to have to learn a new dance.

"Okay. Message received."

134

"Great." His salesman smile was back. "Let's see where we are at summer's end. If you do well, we'll see about getting you booked into the PBR Touring Pro events in the fall."

Touring Pro – the minor leagues of the PBR. A zip of happiness shot through her.

"When can you be ready?" He tipped a chin to her arm.

"The first rodeo you listed is Flagstaff, in three weeks. I'll be there, ready to go."

"Okay. I'll complete the paperwork, and you'll have your PRCA card before then." He lifted an additional sheet from the file folder and passed it across the table. "Now, for the good news."

It was a contract. A smile spread through her as she read. A full-time contract. With a raise.

Steve uncapped a pen and handed it across the table. "Welcome to the PBR family, Harlie Cooper."

***

In deference to her shoulder, Harlie kept her feet to a sedate walk through the doors of Compadres, but if she could, she'd skip every third step, just like Angel had when she was little.

A raise!

She hadn't expected that. And sure, Yolanda was going to need tires, and she'd have to build some shit-happens-savings, but to have a little change in her pocket . . .

"Harlie, hold up a minute." Annette stepped from behind the reception desk. "Doctor Nguyen is in and he wanted to meet with you."

"Okay. Just let me stop and tell Angel —"

"Now, please."

Seeing the nurse's serious expression, Harlie sucked in a breath. "Is Angel okay?"

"She's the same. But the doctor is only here on Mondays and he's leaving in a few minutes. Come."

Harlie followed the nurse down the hall behind the desk, elation dissipating with every step. She had a bad feeling.

The tank-bodied nurse stopped at a closed door and knocked.

"Harlie Cooper is here, Doctor."

"Come in." A soft voice drifted through the door.

An Asian man in glasses with a port-wine stain covering a quarter of his face sat behind a massive wood desk, crowded bookshelves flanking the walls behind it. When he stood, he didn't get much taller. He stepped forward and offered her a pudgy hand to shake. "Ms. Cooper. I've been looking forward to meeting you. I'm Doctor Nguyen." He gestured to the rest of the room where a leather couch and chair sat bathed in sunlight from a huge window. "If you would." He lifted a chart from the pile on his desk, walked to the sitting area and took the leather chair. His feet just touched the floor.

Harlie perched on the edge of the couch and tried to ignore the stain that crept from his hairline to cover his right eye. It made him look a little like that dog from the Little Rascals with the black eye. Only that was funny. There was nothing funny about this man. The power he held scared the spit out of her.

Doctor Nguyen was *the* doctor here, though she'd never met him because he was vacationing in Vietnam when she'd had Angel transferred. He supervised all the residents here, as well as the three other facilities he owned. Like it or not, this man held Angel in his hands.

He sat for a tortuous time, riffing pages in the folder in his lap.

She waited, her foot bouncing, until she could no longer stand the silence pushing against her eardrums. "Angel's getting better, right? I mean, she wasn't moving when she got here, and now she —"

"Since your sister is uncommunicative, I have just a few questions for you."

She sat forward on her seat, clasped her hands and nodded.

"The notes from the hospital are spotty. Did you say this was her first suicide attempt?"

Suicide attempt. The two words Harlie had been avoiding hung ugly, in the air. "She was having problems before. She was either her normal self, or she wasn't." How could she explain?

This man never met the real Angel, her lighthearted fairy. "Angel's like . . . you know, the first warm day of spring, when someone has cut the grass and the smell is rich, and the sun warms your bones. You know what I mean?"

He just nodded.

Heat rose to her face. She sounded like some new-age woo-woo hippie. But this man needed to know. "That's the real Angel. Around nine or ten, the other Angel showed up. Dark, quiet, depressed."

"How long did this go on before—"

"About two years." She didn't want to hear those hideous words again. "The bad times happened more often, and they got worse."

"Worse how?"

She squinted, sorting through words to find the right ones. "I could see it on her face. Like the sun was blotted out by the clouds, you know? Then she'd go away in her head." She shook her head. "I mean, I could rouse her, but it was like she was listening to something no one could hear. Like that was more interesting, more real than what was happening in this world." She shrugged. "I'm not very good at this. That's just what it seemed like."

"No, that helps."

"But doctor, what *caused* it? Whose fault is this? Did something happen to her?"

"I was hoping you could illuminate me on that. Was there a traumatic event around the time that these episodes began?"

Harlie remembered the broken glass. At the dairy. At the apartment. She shook her head. "I didn't see anything and Angel wouldn't say anything, though I asked and asked." She bit back more words. It had been a long time since the fire. Maybe a statute of limitation had passed since their escape. Maybe there was some kind of patient/doctor privilege thing. But why take the chance? If it would help, she'd spill in a minute. But dammit, that was the problem. She didn't *know* anything!

"Your sister's Dysthymia, coupled with double depression, put her in a catatonic state."

Like one depression wasn't enough? When her fingers tingled, she loosened her grip. "But she's just having a bad patch, right? When she wakes up, she'll just pull herself up by her bootstraps, same as—"

"Early onset usually takes place during the teens. Your sister had an earlier onset than that."

The full chicken lunch rolled over in her stomach. "You say that like it's not a good thing."

"Early onset cases are harder to treat, and tend to last longer."

"But you can treat it, right?" Maybe she needed to get a second opinion? But the raise she'd gotten wouldn't come close to paying for that. Even if she could wrangle it, what if this doctor was offended? Would it effect his treatment solution?

Goddamn it, she hated leaving Angel in the hands of someone else. That was Harlie's job.

He drew a deep breath and leaned against the chair back. "I wanted to discuss a treatment option with you." He closed the folder and leaned back. "Your sister doesn't seem to be responding to Depakote, and the longer she remains in this state, the longer and more complicated the recovery. We can't move forward with therapy until she's lucid and verbal."

"So, do you want to try another drug?" She wiped her damp hand on her jeans.

"I believe electroconvulsive therapy to be a good solution."

Electro . . . conv— His meaning jolted her brain. *"Shock* treatments?"

His nose didn't wrinkle, but it twitched, just a bit. "That is the old term for it, yes."

Oh yeah, slather lipstick on *that* pig. Her neck spasm pulled her head right and left. "Nuhuh. No."

"Allow me to explain." He put up a hand as if it could stop the horrific picture forming in her mind. "The APA favors early ECT intervention in cases similar to your sister's. I assure you, all treatment is done under anesthesia with muscle relaxants."

His Kindergarten teacher tone raised the fine hair on the back of her neck.

"Ms. Cooper, I assure you. The patients have no knowledge or memory of the—"

"Really? How do you know?"

"Pardon?" The one word came out prickly. This man was not used to being questioned.

"Have you ever had it done to you?"

He drew himself up at least a quarter of an inch. "Of course not."

"Well, you're not doing that to Angel."

"Ms. Cooper, the Surgeon General report found that —"

"Did the Surgeon General ever have it done to *him*?"

"I wouldn't know. I assume not." An irritated frown flickered over his features before the aloof doctor mask fell back into place. "If you won't allow me to treat your sister in a way that is medically indicated, I see no reason to keep her here. I have patients waiting for beds."

It took a major effort, but Harlie leashed her temper. Being at odds with him could influence the effort he put out to get her sister well. Besides, who was she to know this wasn't best for Angel? What was her GED against his degrees slathering the walls?

But . . . She remembered Angel's bright-eyed smile.

No. This man may know a lot more, but he didn't know Angel. He didn't love Angel. Anesthesia or not, this wasn't happening.

She remembered Steve's 'kinder and gentler' pitch. Maybe it was time she practiced.

"Dr. Nguyen, I'm sorry. This is a lot, coming at me all at once." She put her fingers to her temple, like she had a headache. "Couldn't we give the drugs a while longer to work?" She tried the pound-puppy look that Patrice, the movie star, used with such devastating success.

His lips relaxed. "That could be an option, but I wouldn't want to delay treatment—"

"See, I love my sister, and the thought of her being . . ."

She didn't have to fake the shudder that rattled through her, jerking a bolt of pain from her shoulder. "I'll be in town for two more weeks. I'll talk to Angel. I'll work with her every day."

He referred back to the file in his lap and flipped more pages. "All right. We'll give it a bit more time."

Her held breath came out in a whoosh. "Thank you." Anxious to leave before he changed his mind, she hopped up like the couch was on fire.

Her hand was on the door knob when his voice stopped her.

"And Ms. Cooper?"

She turned.

He looked over his glasses at her. "You may want to work on your acting skills. You're really not very good at it."

Her role as a stunt double never had included lines. "Yessir, I will." She turned the knob and escaped.

Rodeo Days

"Courage is being scared to death and saddling up anyway."

– John Wayne

Chapter 13

Though it was hot in the car, Harlie took her time with the needle, making sure the stitches in the silk were even and perfect. Just a few more inches and she'd be done.

"Shit." She stuck her punctured finger in her mouth to avoid getting blood on Hoot's green silk shorts. She'd tried to return them the morning she'd left the ranch, but he'd scowled and said if she didn't take them, he was throwing them out. But thanks to Ms. Leonard, she was onto him; he may bark like a junkyard dog, but he wouldn't bite. She checked her finger to be sure it was done bleeding, then pushed the needle through the material again. Once the side seams were taken in, and the long shoelace she'd threaded through the waistband was tied tight, the shorts should fit great.

A dented, sun-faded red truck towing a new horse trailer pulled alongside her in the grass and parked. The fields behind the Coconino County, Arizona, fairgrounds were filling fast.

Anticipation bubbled into her blood and her heartbeat picked up to a fast trot. The first Friday night of her debut rodeo would begin in four hours. The summer stretched ahead of her like a golden dream—a string of rodeos forming a yellow brick road she'd follow to the PBR. She took in a deep whiff of her future: grass, horses, manure, and adrenaline. The smell of success. She smiled, tied the last knot and bit off the thread, remembering another emergency repair.

Angel's worried eyes were barely higher than the card table where Harlie had sat, sewing Aunt Beasley's dress. Aunt Beasley was Angel's only doll, and she had been late for a romantic tea with a teddy bear.

Harlie ached for those simple days. How had life gotten so screwed up?

She'd spent every waking minute with Angel the past week, touching, talking, reminiscing—trying to get her sister to return from wandering the twisted, lonely halls of her mind.

Harlie'd caught a glimpse of Angel a couple of times. Passing in front of her, Angel's eyes flicked a bit, before staring blindly forward once more. But since the nurses never saw it, Doctor Nguyen didn't count it as progress.

This time, it wasn't denial. Angel was in there.

But would she come out for strangers?

Harlie stared at the dusty truck, seeing Angel, sitting on that hospital bed.

Stop it. You can't be two places at once. You're earning money for her care. That's most important right now.

She knew that. *Knew* it.

So why did her happiness feel so damned disloyal?

She had to move. Had to walk off some nerves. Once the thread and needle were stowed in her kit bag, she grabbed her wallet, donned her straw cowboy hat, climbed out of the car and locked it. Yolanda would be her hotel for the night, and every night this summer. The advance she'd wrangled out of Steve was already spent on hip pads, a bullfighting vest and gas to get to Flagstaff. Maybe in a few weeks, if Yolanda held together, she could get a real pair of shoes with cleats, for the arena.

She took bouncy steps toward the two story white building skirting the arena. The top floor was grandstand seating, but what she sought was on the ground floor. She dodged a cowboy leading a horse and a tractor hauling a flatbed of hay, to open the door marked 'Administration'. A line of cowboys snaked down the narrow linoleumed hall, all of them talking at once. The cinderblock walls amplified the sound to shout-level. She stepped to the last man in line and tapped him on the shoulder.

"Excuse me. Is this the line for check-in?"

He turned, and the hallway was obscured by acres of plaid shirt. "Well, Darlin', you're in the right place." He looked her over. "You a new can chaser?" He took off his hat and extended his hand. "Don't believe we've met. I'm Donny Peets, professional bulldogger."

She gave his hand a two-pump shake and let go. "Harlie Cooper. What's a can chaser?" He kept her limp hand hostage until she snatched it back.

He cocked his head. "You're a barrel racer, right?"

"Bullfighter." Her hands slipped into her back pockets, pushing out her chest. Her chin jutted, without orders from her.

He chuckled. "Get out."

She rolled her eyes at the echo of Deuce's first words to her. "Why is that funny?"

He looked down on her from the corner of his eye. "You're not serious. Little thing like you?"

"News flash, Mr. Flintstone. The 'little woman' is doing *lots* of things nowadays."

"No need to puff up your tail, Darlin." He put his hands up in mock surrender.

Derision she could take. Condescension made her want to grab a two by four. "I'm not your Darlin'. And I've got my PRCA card; I can do anything I want."

He grinned big. "Not thinkin' of trying bulldoggin' though, are ya?"

She opened her mouth to explain that she'd leave that to the brainless, but stopped herself in time.

Kinder. Gentler. Steve had warned her that rodeo was a small world. No telling who this guy knew. She swallowed what she longed to spit out. It was bitter. "Nope. I'll leave bulldogging to big strong guys like you."

Luckily, he was prideful enough to miss the sarcasm on his way to the compliment. Doctor Nguyen was right; she sucked at manipulation. Yet one more skill she'd have to learn to survive.

"Hey, Boog!" He shouted over the cowboy hats to where the line disappeared into the rodeo office door.

A burly dude in a t-shirt showcasing serious muscles turned. "What?"

Donny pointed to the top of her head. "This little lady here says she's a bullfighter!"

In slow-motion, the entire line about-faced in her direction.

She slapped a smile on her flaming face and tried to look like a professional.

Given the whispers, the slack jaws and the chuckles, it didn't work. The line advanced, a welcome distraction. She shooed Donny forward. "Move up. You're holding up the line."

Ten minutes later, a bored rodeo secretary scrutinized her PRCA card, then handed it back. "Cooper. Bullfighter." She checked a line on the roster in front of her, then looked to the next guy in line.

Harlie walked down the crowded hall against traffic.

"They told me that bull was a Bufford, but he blew up, and ducked off right from under me."

". . . so we all got ground money, but it wasn't even enough to repair my kack."

"Yeah, Slack was a money horse, but Cochise, now there was a rank spinner. I saw him once —"

"Hey, there's that girl 'fighter. I'm catchin' the bull riding for sure."

Harlie let the drawl and dialect flow over her and smiled. Part of her job was to put butts in the seats. At least she'd be successful at that.

She stepped into the laser sunrays of the half-circle orange ball on the horizon. Her stomach growled. Best grab something light before she got too jumpy to eat. The lunch truck was doing a brisk business with the competitors, but it was probably just a warm-up for when the spectators showed up. She fell into line and scanned the prices on the menu board.

"Don't eat the chili." A deep voice came from behind her. "The rodeo dogs are good, but you put chili on it, you're gonna be up with the trots all night."

She turned to the cowboy behind her. He was tall, thin, and almost comically ugly, with a prominent Adam's apple and a crooked nose. He tipped his hat. His smile was missing a front tooth. It gave him a goofy, happy-go-lucky look.

You just had to smile back at a grin like that. "Thanks for the tip."

"If I recollect right, the burgers are good, and the fries too." He scanned the board. "But the frijoles? I think they use them in the chili. I wouldn't go there."

"I won't." He looked as harmless as a puppy. "I'm Harlie."

"Oh." He snatched his hat off his head. "Sorry, Miss. My Momma would snatch me bald for my manners. I'm Bones Jones."

She squinted at him.

"It's not my real name." He settled his hat back on his head. "You may not believe this, but growing up, I was kinda skinny." He puffed out his skeletal chest.

She bit the inside of her lip until she was sure she had control. "Hard to imagine. What's your event?"

"I'm a bull rider, ma'am."

"Cool. I'll see you in the arena, then." The cowboy ahead in line walked away with a cold drink in a bucket-sized cup. She stepped up to the window, scanning the prices. "I'll have a corn dog. With mustard." She pulled her wallet from her back pocket and selected a dollar bill.

A long-fingered hand touched her arm. She jerked back.

"Please, allow me, Ma'am. You'll be saving my bacon later. It's only right that I buy yours now."

"That's sweet, but —"

He looked to the guy in the window who held her corndog. "You put that on my bill."

"I wish you wouldn't do that." She took her corn dog from the man.

"I take my health seriously, Ma'am." He ordered four tacos (no beans) an order of fries, an apple tart and a jumbo coke.

146

"You heard, then." She snatched a few napkins from the dispenser on the ledge.

"Heard what?"

"That I'm the new bullfighter on the circuit."

"No'm." He pulled out his wallet and gave the vendor a five. "I coulda' guessed a safety roper, or a gateman, but you just look like a bullfighter to me." He returned his wallet to his back pocket. "Except for the 'girl thing'."

The compliment was like warm sweet butter, seeping into the cracks in her heart. She tucked it away for some time she really needed it, and beamed at him. "I believe that's the nicest thing anyone ever said to me. Thank you."

He ducked his head and blushed. "Just tellin' the truth, Ma'am."

"Thank you for my dinner. I'll see you in the arena in a couple of hours."

"You sure will. I'll be the one with the winner's check at the end." He took the loaded cardboard tray from the window. "Would you like to have supper with me?"

She took a startled step back, her face flaming like there were jalapenos in her corn dog. "Um. No. Uh, sorry, but I've got to get back —"

"Ma'am, I don't mean anything untoward. I'm a married man." His warm, light brown eyes were soft. "It's just that you'll find that it helps to have friends on the road."

Make that Habaneros. She was embarrassed for assuming he was coming on to her, and even more embarrassed to be caught at it. "I . . . I appreciate it, but I'm going to go get my head right. For tonight."

"Well, we all sure want that. You take care of yourself out there, y'hear?"

"Yeah. You too." She walked away, the cooling corndog clutched in her sweaty fist. If she hadn't been so flustered, she'd have liked to stay and talk to Bones. He probably could have shown her a few ropes.

Damn, was she ever going to stop feeling like a flamingo born into a flock of penguins? She always assumed every friendly overture had an ulterior motive. And, where that kept her safe, it sure kept her lonely.

***

Something about the arena lights, the buzz of the gathering crowd and the smell of popcorn and animals mainlined into her blood. An hour until show time.

Harlie walked between the flat white light and shadows in the chaos behind the chutes, seeking the stock contractor. She dodged contestants toting water buckets, bronc saddles and high hopes; the tension brushed over Harlie in waves, making her heart hammer.

She didn't know a soul, and she still hadn't met the guy she'd be working the arena with.

Maybe she'd run into him back here; best place to look for stock contractors had to be the bull pens, right?

A man with a massive gut and a mouth-obscuring mustache stood alone, leaning against the pipe fence, watching the bulls mill up dust.

"Excuse me, Sir? Are you Cody Miller?"

He turned. "Yeah."

"I'm Harlie Cooper, one of the bullfighters for the weekend." She pasted on a smile and stuck out her hand.

"I heard about you." He looked her up and down.

"Yessir." Making herself hold in front of an oncoming bull wasn't any harder than holding his piercing gaze. She lowered her hand. "I just wanted to introduce myself, and see if you had any instructions for me."

"Before every bull, look for me. I'll give you the lowdown." He looked away, to the bustle of the behind the scenes rodeo prep. Then back at her. "I'll give you a fair shake. Make my bulls look good, I'll broadcast it. You make my bulls look bad —"

"Hearing you, Sir." If he didn't say it, the vibes wouldn't be picked up by the Universe and become reality. "Thank you." She walked away. His heavy gaze on her back was much easier to take than face-on.

"Hey!"

A burly guy strode toward her. "You're the girl bullfighter, right?"

"Yeah." He was one of those middle-aged guys who carried all his weight above the waist. Slim legs, with a stuffed-turkey-chest, sausage-neck and a florid, pancake face.

"Let's go." He veered to the back of the chutes.

She trotted to catch up. "Who're you? Where are we going?"

"I'm Tad Webster, the other bullfighter." He huffed. "They need us to help with the calf tying."

Her brain jammed, trying to process that this guy would be her partner, and make sense of his words. "We're tying calves?"

"Untying 'em."

He clearly didn't have the breath to talk and walk at the same time, so she held her questions; she'd find out soon enough.

He stopped on the opposite side of the arena from the packed stands. She breathed in the smell, the atmosphere, the moment. No matter what happened tonight, she'd always remember this—her first rodeo as a bullfighter.

"They told me this was your first gig. Is that right?"

"Yep."

"Bigger rodeos have more help. County deals like this, part of your job is to help behind the scenes. Just do what I tell you and you'll be okay."

She'd probably end up his go-fer, but that was okay, she wasn't afraid to pay her dues.

"The tie-down ropers will come from there." He pointed to the narrow alley between the bucking chutes. "They'll catch, flank and tie right about where we are, then remount. After six seconds, we run out, pull the rope off the calf's neck, untie his feet, and if he doesn't head for the out-gate, we haze 'em to it. Got that?" The lights highlighted the sheen of sweat on his face.

"I can do that." *But can you?*

The announcer's voice blared. "Ladies and Gents, next up is the calf tying. If you're out getting a beer, you may want to get back here, you're not gonna want to miss this."

She held onto the top rail and bounced on her toes. "By the way, my name is Harlie Cooper."

The next hour she spent freeing calves, setting up knocked down barrels, and chasing down stray goats from the kid's goat-tying event. Lucky thing Banjo wasn't here. It was nice to be the one chasing, instead of the other way around.

"Let's go." Tad took his foot off the bottom rung of the fence. "Bull riding is up next."

She ducked under the fence, her heart rapping a crazed cadence on her breastbone. Showtime.

She veered off. "I've gotta run to my car and get my bag."

"I'll meet you behind the chutes."

Skirting the outside of the arena, she jogged to the shadowed parking lot. She'd been right about Tad. He'd stood guard on the fence the whole time she'd been busting her butt in the arena, saying he had to 'save his energy for bullfighting'.

But she considered it a fair trade. Between trips, he'd regaled her with twenty years of bullfighting stories. This was his last season, and he was only working a third his usual number of rodeos. Forty—years and pounds—were taking their toll. She was looking forward to watching a seasoned fighter at work, and hoped to be able to practice some of the tips he'd given her.

Once she located Yolanda, she was in and out in seconds, running for the back of the chutes, her duffel strap over her shoulder. Trying to get into her gear in the car would take a contortionist, and the line was out the ladies room door. She'd find a dark corner to change.

"Cooper!"

Tad stood waving by a pole fence with contestants' ropes, saddles, halters, gear bags piled along the bottom like tumbleweeds in a windstorm. He wore massive crotchless denim shorts held up with red and white suspenders, multicolored bandanas hanging from every pocket. His t-shirt stretched over his Buddha belly, incongruent with his knobby knees and skinny tube socks.

She jogged up, trying to keep a straight face. "Nice shorts."

150

"Yeah, thanks." He squatted and rooted in a gear bag at his feet and came up with a bath towel. "I'll hold this up so you can change. Hurry. We've got to get to the arena." He shook out the towel, put it behind his back and, holding the ends, turned and faced the chutes.

"Thanks, Tad." Men strode by on their own rushed errands. She ducked behind the towel, opened her bag, toed out of her boots, and stripped off her jeans. Getting into her padded spandex undershorts was like wrestling into a girdle. Thank God no one could see this part —

Tad was a better screen than the towel. His broad torso blocked the light of the sodium lamps. "I'll take the latch side of the arena; you take the gate side. You okay with that?"

She pulled up and tied Hoot's shorts as she stepped into her tennis shoes. "Sounds good." Each fighter was responsible for half the arena, and everything that happened there. She swallowed the memory of her disastrous solo bullfight, focusing instead on the thrill singing through her body. "Done, thanks." She bent to tie her shoes.

"Good." Tad dropped the towel in his bag and without giving her a glance, walked for the back of the chutes. "Let's go save somebody."

Ten minutes later, she stood behind the gate with Tad, stretching her hamstrings and staring into the brightly-lit arena. The weight of responsibility and the loft of adventure entwined, making a brightly colored thread that wove through her and pulled taut. She felt . . . *alive.*

The announcer's voice overrode the crowd. "Folks, you may not have realized it when you bought your ticket, but you've got an extra dose of excitement with your bull riding tonight. Because entering the arena, along with our own Tad Webster is, the PRCA's first female bullfighter!"

Tad flipped the latch, nodded at her, and ran into the spotlight, waving to the crowd. She followed him, skipping all the way. She couldn't help it—her feet wouldn't stay on the ground.

"That little thing with the blond braid is Harlie 'Coop'

151

Cooper, and tonight is her first event. What do you say we welcome her to the Flagstaff Rodeo?"

She waved madly as the crowd cheered.

"Okay people, turn your attention to chute number two, where our first rider, Blake Seaton is gonna do his best to make eight on The Spook."

Harlie took her place near the back side of the gate, making sure to give enough room not to be trapped behind when it swung. She scanned the cowboys on the back of the chute for Cody, the stock contractor.

He made shooing movements with his hands, so she took two steps farther into the arena. The bull must take a long jump out before turning into his spin.

Tad stood across from her, the width of the chute gate between them, crouched a bit, ready to move. He gave her a thumbs-up.

She tried to smile back. *Turn him into the spin, then back off. Watch the rider's feet. Walk to a wreck; don't run.*

Bouncing on her toes and shaking out her hands, waiting for the rider to get set, she heard Hoot's scratchy voice, reciting her priorities. *The rider, the other bullfighter, yourself, the bull.*

The rider crammed his hat down on his head and nodded.

As advertised, the black and white bull took two long jumps into the arena. Harlie waved her hands and his head came around. She took two steps in a circle toward the gate, and the bull turned into a spin. The rider shifted his weight, leaning in to adjust for the centrifugal force, perfectly balanced.

But the bull was an old hand; sensing the cowboy's commitment to the spin, he took a step forward, and swung his head to spin the other way.

The rider couldn't react fast enough. He slid until he hung off the outside of the spinning bull, legs still on the bull, but hanging by his hand, and sliding farther with every step.

Though her hands came up every time the rider whizzed by, Harlie kept her feet planted. If she ran in now, she'd be part of the wreck. Adrenaline hit her system in a rush, even as the scene in front of her shifted to slo-mo.

Wait. Wait. Wait.

The rider's hand popped out of the rope, and he was dumped in the dirt on the outside of the spin, five feet to her left.

Now!

She ran in, but Tad was there first. He put out a hand and slapped the bull's head on the way by. The bull lined out and took off after Tad.

Harlie stayed with the rider until he was up and heading for the fence, then lit out after the pair. She reached them, but forced herself to stop; this was Tad's dance.

The bull closed the distance to the back of Tad's shorts. At the last possible second, he threw a fake and spun, then spun again, kerchiefs flaring. Tad may be a forty-something with a buckle-burying gut, but out here he was Fred Astaire.

The bull turned and came at him again. The ground shook as the two thousand pounds of pissed bore down.

Tad's beatific smile said it all. He crouched, hands on knees, holding, staring down the bull until the head was close enough for Tad to reach out and touch. Then he spun again.

The crowd's *Ahhhhh*, rolled over the arena.

The bull had had enough. He stopped, then tail swishing, trotted to the out-gate.

Laughing, Harlie ran to Tad and gave him a high-five. "You're rockin' the place, partner."

As the crowd cheered, he winked at her. "Home arena advantage. These are my neighbors." The crowd applauded, and Tad took a bow.

Ten riders later, Harlie was catching her stride. Good thing, because Tad's stride had left him, three bulls ago.

Standing in position across from him waiting for the next ride, she could see from the rise and fall of his belly that he was still breathing heavy from the last ride. His sweat-soaked shirt clung. Even his kerchiefs drooped.

Two bulls to go.

When he glanced her way, she mouthed, 'You okay?"

He gave her a thumbs up, but his red, shiny face exposed his lie.

She shot a glance to the back of the chute. Maybe she should tell someone. Cody maybe? But this was Tad's home arena. These were his friends. Wouldn't they know? Maybe he always looked this bad by the end.

And she'd been around enough Alpha males to know he wouldn't welcome her interference.

The latch clicked, and the gate swung.

A small red bull crow hopped out of the chute and, all on his own, turned into a half-hearted spin, kicking at his belly and generally doing little to get the rider off his back. The cowboy started spurring, to show the judges he was in control, and to eke out another half point on what looked to be a dismal score.

When the buzzer sounded, the cowboy loosed his hand and managed to land on his feet, running for the fence. Harlie moved in, but the bull stopped spinning, facing Tad.

Who just stood there, looking confused.

Something's wrong.

"Hey, bull!" She ran in, waving her arms.

Tad's eyes rolled back in his head, and he dropped so hard she heard his knees pop when they hit the dirt.

She pulled abreast of the bull and smacked him on the neck, but he didn't turn; he knew who the vulnerable one was.

He ran over Tad's unconscious body on his way to the out gate.

Harlie stood in a protective stance over Tad until the bull's rump cleared the arena, then dropped down next to him. "Tad! Can you hear me?"

Medic's legs surrounded her, and someone took her shoulder, pulling her back. "Let us get in and work."

She stood and backed up a step. "Check his heart. He didn't look good before that last bull."

They carried Tad out on a stretcher. She stood, hat in hand, as a man walked toward her.

"I'm Bruce, coordinator of the rodeo committee. You okay?"

The red strobes of the ambulance outside the gates reflected off the metal chutes. "Yeah, the bull didn't touch me."

"Good. We've got one more rider. The faster we get to that, the quicker the audience will recover." He patted her shoulder. "Show must go on, right?"

For the first time, she became aware of the crowd's silence. "Sure. You got another bullfighter?"

"No, but there's just one more ride, so . . ."

She opened her mouth as 'Yes', moved down the pathways from her brain.

Hoot's words stabbed her brain. Never go in solo. Loners don't make bullfighters.

Aside from keeping the committee happy, she yearned to do it.

Her head shake matched her hands. And her guts. "No."

"Look, one bull. Cody tells me it's an easy one. You want to make a good impression on the committee, right?"

She glanced to the back of the chute, into the eyes of the cowboy straddling the chute, waiting to see if he'd be getting on the bull. In the bright-white sodium light, she saw the acne on his cheeks.

That made up her mind more than anything. "Look, my first job is to protect that kid." She pointed to the chute. "I learned the hard way, that a solo bullfighter can't do that."

"Really?" The man frowned and dropped his hand from her shoulder. "The committee is not going to be happy. We'll find you a partner for tomorrow night, but I think you can cross this rodeo off your list in the future."

Chapter 14

Stomping out of the arena in a huff probably didn't fall into the 'attitude adjustment' category, but it was better than Harlie's first impulse to sock the committee dude in the eye. Muttering suggestions for the committee involving banned acts with farm animals, she walked to the area behind the gates.

The ambulance was gone. She snagged the shirt of a passing cowgirl leading a saddled palomino. "Hey. Do you know how Tad is? What did the EMTs say?"

The girl slowed, but didn't stop. "Heart attack. They don't know more than that."

Harlie waited for the horse's rump to pass, grabbed her gear bag from the pile, and headed for a women's restroom to change.

Tad had been sweet, holding the towel, telling her stories to calm her down and gently critiquing her technique after each ride. But since this was his home town, he probably had a ton of people at the hospital. She couldn't do anything to help him.

She needed to figure out how to help herself.

Luckily, there wasn't a line for the bathroom. She found an empty stall, balanced her duffel on the toilet seat and began the contortion required to change in the tiny space.

Steve Rawlings would have said she should have stayed and negotiated . . .

There had only been one ride left. Why hadn't she suggested that they start tomorrow night's bucking with that cowboy? He'd get a score, and possibly earn his way into the short-go tomorrow night. They'd probably figured that out by now, but if she'd suggested it, she'd have come across as a level-headed problem solver, instead of a tantrum-throwing little girl.

Why did she never think of stuff like that until later? Probably because she let her temper overrule any sense she did have.

Wriggling out of the padded undershorts, she lost her balance and had to slam her hand against the metal partition for the save. The vibration unbalanced her duffel. It fell in the toilet. "Shit!" She snatched the strap and rescued the bag.

"You okay?" a high-pitched squeak came from the next stall.

"Other than being terminally stupid, I'm fine, thanks." She hung the bag from the hook on the door, giving her even less space to step into her jeans. When would she learn? Getting pissed may make her feel better short term, but it seldom made things better, long term.

Not that she questioned her decision. Harlie Cooper was never again bullfighting without back up. She'd paid the price for stubbornness, back in Chilly. Getting Deuce hurt was more painful than her own injury. She couldn't afford the weight of more guilt. God knows she carried enough already.

Slinging her damp bag over her shoulder, she exited the stall. The parking lot was clearing out, except for the vehicles of the out-of-town contestants. She passed several cowboys with bedrolls, on their way to sleep for free in stalls in the exhibitor barn. The lucky ones had sleepers in their horse trailers. She'd even heard that cowboys would go together, sometimes five to a hotel room, just to have a place to bunk down. None of those options would work for a woman on her own. Much as she dreaded sleeping with the windows rolled up, Yolanda would have to do.

She unlocked the door and tossed her bag into the back, then took a seat on the hood and pulled out her cell phone. She'd make Angel's 'good night' call, and one to give Steve Rawlings a heads-up. Might as well make the tougher one first.

***

It was Friday, so this must be Tonopah. Harlie walked to the rodeo office—a single-wide trailer this time—to check in. Her feet dragged the dust, weighted by a mix of dejected and dog-tired. Cowboys snaked in an unruly line and she fell in at the end, same as she had the past three weekends. But instead of feeling like a comforting routine, it felt like Groundhog Day. Would this ever get easier? Would she ever feel like . . . not like she belonged, she knew better than that, but that she at least had a place here? A tiny corner where she could let down her guard for a few minutes?

Maybe later in the season. Or next year.

After Steve Rawlings had chewed her out for her outburst in Flagstaff that first night, he called the committee and chewed on them, for pushing her to fight solo. He smoothed things over, but warned her that he didn't have time to babysit — aside from nuclear disaster or its equivalent, she was going to have to solve her own problems.

Which really chapped her already abraded ass. Babysit? Really? Harlie Cooper didn't ask for help. Well, almost never. And it *had* been nuclear disaster.

Except that her attitude had a part in moving the situation to defcon one.

The cowboy ahead turned and tipped his hat. "Hey, Darlin'. You must be new. You runnin' barrels?"

Tongue safely between her teeth, Harlie lifted the corners of her mouth and shook her head.

He tipped his head. "You singin' the National Anthem, then?"

That was a new one. She snorted. "That would be a very bad thing for attendance."

"Wait, I know. You're a team roper. Gotta hand it to you gals, competin' with the guys."

She sighed. "I'm a bullfighter."

His mouth opened in an oval of dumfoundness. "Hey, I

158

heard about you." He turned and yelled to the front of the line. "Hey, guys, we got us that lady bullfighter!"

The cowboy hats turned in a wave that could have been choreographed.

"You can save me anytime, Doll."

"Danged bull riders get all the fun."

She let the comments go by, and studied their expressions. Disbelief, curiosity, and, yep, there it was, dismissal. Several turned away. When she realized her chin was jutting, she shifted her gaze to the dirt, using her hat to cut off contact. She *had* to get better at the kinder/gentler thing. Her job depended on it. Keeping her eyes on her feet, she moved up two steps as the line shifted ahead. Angel depended on it. She knew she was going to need new skills with this career. So what if she hadn't anticipated a couple of them? She'd pull up her under-armor and do her best.

She reached up to rub her breastbone, to soothe the ache that had been riding shotgun with her lately. Pressure built behind her ribs. Of course there was the hole where Angel used to be. But the throb of empty had expanded since she'd been on the road: Flagstaff, Winslow and now Tonopah. Cowboys seemed to travel in clumps, rodeo to rodeo. She was starting to recognize some of the faces. They all seemed to know each other.

Friends.

The word echoed through her hollow spaces.

Her personal space had always been more of a bunker than a bubble. Watching other kids hang out on the playground together, make friends, eat lunch side-by-side, Harlie observed, curious as an anthropologist studying a newly discovered tribe.

It wasn't that she didn't like people. She'd just never had the need to form more than surface connections with them. Her family was in her bunker, and that's all she'd ever needed. And since mom died, it was just her and Angel.

But if she faced the brutal truth, until Angel came back, it was just her.

The line moved again, depositing her at the foot of the steps of the trailer. Six hours until the performance tonight. The time stretched ahead, bland and empty.

She hated that ache. It felt like weakness, and she couldn't afford it.

None of the rodeos she'd worked had been large, but this was the smallest so far. The grounds were little more than a roping arena with lights and wooden bleachers. This stock contractor put on several rodeos a summer at his ranch to make money without trailering his stock for a change.

Harlie dressed early, but made herself wait for full dark before she went in search of the head man. The air was cooler, but the ground held the fierce heat of the day, waiting for the dark to release it in a hot sigh.

"Excuse me." She approached cowboys who had to be bronc riders, given the beat-up bare-bones saddles at their feet. "Could you direct me to John Mason?"

They pointed to a clump of men standing around the announcer's table at the side of the arena.

She hiked over. "Mr. Mason?"

A middle-aged man with a big hat and small eyes held up a finger and continued addressing a dusty cowhand. "You tell him I don't give a badger's butt what he wants. If he doesn't get off that computer and get out here in ten minutes, he's grounded. Forever."

"Yessir, I'll try." The hand walked away, shaking his head.

"You manage my bulls. Surely you can corral a high school kid." He tossed at the cowboy's back, then turned to Harlie. "Now what?"

"I'm Harlie Cooper, Sir. One of your bullfighters?"

"Oh, yeah. Good. You'll be working with my son, as soon as that guy tears him away from a video game."

"Hey Merle!" Someone yelled from the chutes.

Mr. Mason's head came up. "What?"

"Where's the flag for the opening ceremony?"

"Shit, I gotta do everything around here?" He walked away.

"Wait, Sir, can you tell me—"

He waved her off and kept walking. "Junior will fill you in when he shows."

Her partner for the weekend was a high school computer nerd. She glanced at the spectators trickling into the stands, then behind, where a line of pickups pulled into the lot, raising dust.

Oh, this should go well.

He wasn't hard to spot. The sullen, downturned mouth, bowed shoulders, and rebellious eyes were a dead giveaway. That, and his high content Rayon blue jeans and untucked plaid shirt. Definitely not cowboy material.

But hey, the kid was a stock contractor's son. He may not have the drive, but surely he had experience. She walked over. "Junior?"

"Yeah." Even his voice slouched.

"I'm Harlie. I'll be fighting with you tonight."

He rolled his eyes. "I can't handle another fight right now. My old man is enough."

She couldn't help it. She laughed. The kid had the downtrodden teen thing *down.*

He crammed his hands in his pockets and glowered, but the corner of his lip quirked.

"You're a funny guy."

"And you're not. A guy I mean. So you and me, we're from the land of misfit toys, huh?"

"Never thought of it that way, but I guess we are." She decided she liked this kid. At least she wouldn't have to play politics with him. "Since you gotta do this, let's figure out how to do it with the least amount of pain. For us, and the bull riders. Okay?"

He gave her a massive teen-angst sigh. "If I gotta."

Turned out the kid was pretty good. Wicked smart and gamer reflexes combined to make up for attitude and lack of enthusiasm. "Fighters ten, bulls zero." She high-fived him on the way out of the arena after the bull riding. "Nice working with you, Dude."

"Yeah, right." Junior put on the mask of disinterest, and slouched as the mantle of teen fell back on his shoulders.

"Whatever."

Mr. Mason stood waiting outside the gate, clipboard in his hands. "You two did good tonight. Just don't make me hunt you down tomorrow night, Junior." He looked up as a truck towing a trailer rolled by. "Hey, you can't bring that in here!" He waved his arms to get the driver's attention. "Go around. Can't you see people walking here?"

Junior frowned, his bushy eyebrows were dark clouds over the storm brewing in his eyes. "I won't be here tomorrow night."

Mr. Mason glanced at his son. "What?"

Junior tisked. "I *told* you. I've got a Dreamhack tournament tomorrow night."

"Oh, you can do it some other time. I need—"

"No. Hello, Dad, this is a competition. Real-time." His volume got louder with every word. "It's scheduled."

"Yeah, well, so is the rodeo. You've known about this."

"And you've known about the tournament." He shrugged, hands out. "You do every time. Only your stuff is important. If I do well tomorrow, I've got a chance to go pro—"

"Pro." Mr. Mason snorted, his face flushed. "You eat. You need clothes. Money for that isn't coming from a *game*. You'll be here tomorrow night."

"Bullshit. This is bullshit."

Several heads turned at the escalating voices.

"Bullshit is what pays for your fancy computer, Junior. You'll be here tomorrow night."

"I won't!" The kid lunged forward, his nose inches from his father's. "You better find somebody else, because I. Won't. Be. Here." He spun, and head down stormed off toward the house.

"Goddamn kid." Mr. Mason swiped his hand over his face to wipe accidental Junior spit.

Her gut tightened in preparation. He was going ask her to fight solo. *Don't forget. Kinder. Gentler.* 'No' and anger didn't have to go together. Other people managed that all the time. Feeling the pressure in her molars, she shifted her jaw from side

162

to side to unlock the muscles. *Going. To. Learn.*

He glanced at her, and whatever he'd been going to say died before it got past his lips. "Give me a minute." He stared at his boots as if they had the answer. "Maybe somebody's got a hand they can spare. I'll make some phone calls."

"I'll be here tomorrow night, Mr. Mason. I trust you'll find someone competent." Watching her feet to be sure they obeyed, she walked away, even though she didn't trust any such thing. And once she got through this weekend, no telling what lie in wait next weekend. She'd been on the road a month, and had worked with exactly one bullfighter who had better skills than her.

And he'd had a heart attack.

The sodium safety lamp in the lot shone off the orange carpet in Yolanda's back window, and she stumped toward it. Tonight, physically and emotionally, she felt like the glass Hoot had said she was made of. No wonder a woman had never done this.

Unlocking the door, she flopped in the back seat, too tired and heartsore to gather her things for a shower. She was tired. Tired of being fragile. Tired of being responsible.

Tired of being alone.

Male voices approached. Her heart stuttered. She popped the lock button with her heel, reaching for her 'plan B'—a steak knife she'd laid under the seat. Two cowboys walked by, bedrolls thrown over their shoulders.

Even before mom died, life had been precarious. Harlie was used to making do. But lately, it seemed she had less and less to make do with. Everything good seemed to be dropping away, until tonight, the last thread ran out. She had nothing left. Physically, mentally or emotionally. It was all gone, leaving yawning chasms in her where her stores used to be.

And that scared her more than getting fired, a charging bull, or even Angel's blank stare.

"I don't know what to do." The whispered admission leaked into the dark. The thought was bigger outside her than in. It filled the car as if it were a living being, exhaling a stench of

163

despair.

"Stop it." She swiped away the tears that tracked to her ears. "Stop it right now." She pulled herself upright. "There's always something you can do."

Wishing, worrying and winging it wasn't going to alter the facts. Anger and a personal pity party wasn't helping, either. There must have been something she overlooked. A choice she tossed aside because she didn't like it. When all other options were gone, you had to consider what was left.

She needed someone she could trust. Someone who'd have her back, in the arena and outside it. But the only bullfighters she knew were the guys from Hoot's school.

And she didn't really like them.

But this isn't about liking.

Which of them could she trust?

"Deuce."

The name was as solid as the seat beneath her. But she remembered what he'd said, in the emergency room.

Besides, after she'd been the one who landed him there, would he trust her?

Probably not. But she had only one ace to play. Maybe.

Hope gave her a surge of energy. She pulled herself up by the headrest and reached for her phone in the console.

Only one way to find out.

"Deuce? This is Harlie . . . Harlie Cooper? From Hoot's—"

When his familiar rolling chuckle hit her ear, the muscles in her shoulders relaxed a bit, making her aware of her watch-spring-wound muscles.

"I don't know too many 'Harlie's'. It's only been a month, Coop. I'm just shocked to hear from you."

Did she really want to ask why? Probably not. "Is this a bad time? Did I wake you?"

"At nine? Hardly. I just came in from the barn. What's up?"

"Are you home? Your dad's ranch, I mean?"

"Yeah, why?"

This wasn't as easy as she'd thought. How did people make small talk look easy? "Are you getting fighting gigs?" She heard a wooden chair creak, and the clunk of boots hitting something wood. She pictured him in a country kitchen, with his boots up on a table, his chair leaned back on two legs. It helped.

"Well, I've been staying sharp, working local bull riding practices. And I'm signed up for the Kinta Rodeo in August."

She remembered his sigh. He always pursed his lips a little when he did that. He wasn't a friend, but she knew this guy. She'd seen him without a shirt, brushing his teeth. This should be easy.

His deep voice rumbled in her ear. "I've got my name in with every rodeo in Oklahoma. But so far, that's it. It's the old Catch-22. You can't get experience without working, and they won't give you work until you've got experience. Hey, how's your shoulder?"

"It's all better. How's your head?"

"No worse than it was before."

"I did tell you how sorry I am about that, right? I didn't mean—"

"Yeah, you told me. And I told you, its fine. Let it go." He waited the span of two breaths. "What's this about, Harlie? I mean, it's good to hear from you, but you're not the call-to-shoot-the-poop kinda girl, you know?"

You think?

She wiped the hand not holding the phone down her T-shirt. "I'm calling with a proposition for you."

Did surprise have a sound? Apparently, because she heard it, before his chuckle.

"You're not the proposition kinda girl, either."

"Don't flatter yourself, McAllister."

"Now there's the Coop I know."

You could hear a smile over the phone too. "So, how'd you like some steady bullfighting work?"

"Oh, heck yeah. You have some?"

On more solid ground, she relaxed enough to lean back against the seat. "I might. I'm booked every weekend this summer . . ." Shit. Her stomach did a back flip. Was he going to think she called to gloat? "I mean, you know, the marketing rep, for the—I mean—"

"I know you're 'in' with the PBR, Coop. We did that, back in Chilly. Just tell me what'cha got."

"I'm working a bunch of small to medium-sized rodeos, all over the Southwest. But the guys I get paired with are . . . sporadic. Their quality, I mean. It can get pretty hairy. So I wondered." She took a breath and pushed the words out with the air. "You want to work with me?"

No smile in this silence. She heard the hollow thump of boots hitting the floor.

"I can't promise. I haven't talked to Steve yet, to see if he could get another guy booked with me. But I thought I'd ask—"

"Oh, hell yes."

Her stomach muscles unclenched. After what happened last time, she half expected him to say no.

"Sorry, I'm a little thrown. I didn't get the impression you really liked any of us, and—"

"This isn't about liking." She took a breath and formed her words softer. "Look, I can't afford to get hurt. It matters more than I can say. I need someone I can trust to have my back in the arena. I thought about who I could call, and . . . can I trust you, Deuce?"

"You can."

There was bedrock in those two small words. Hearing it, she recognized why his name popped into her mind first.

Deuce was solid, down to the ground.

She leaned against the car door and crossed her legs on the seat. Thank God that part was over. "Remember, I don't even know if Steve can get you in, but if he can, how soon could you be available?"

Chapter 15

The weekends on the rodeo circuit were golden. But the days between were quartz—bland, hard and unending. Harlie steered with one hand, as oven-baked wind combed the hair on the arm she draped on the window's ledge. Yolanda was happiest going sixty. Her engine's purring days were in the rearview mirror, but she still managed a throat-clearing rumble as the almost-bald tires ate up the miles. Harlie squinted in the hammered New Mexico sunshine and swiped escapees from her braid out of her mouth.

Glancing in the rearview mirror at the empty road behind, she patted the steering wheel. "Hang in there, Yo-girl. This would not be a good place to break down." She glanced again. She was getting freckles across the bridge of her nose. Great. Like she didn't look like a kid already.

You'll be glad of that when you're old, like me. Her mother's voice and a picture of her cute nose wrinkle floated through Harlie's mind on a wave of sweet nostalgia. Where would she and Angel be right now if Mom was still alive? Would Harlie be in junior college somewhere? Would Angel be a well-adjusted teenager?

She shook her head, dislodging more hair. Not likely. Mack's dairy had just been the end of a slide that started way earlier.

In Harlie's earliest memory, she and mom were living in

a real house. There were flowers out front, and a chain-linked back yard. She remembered riding her Big Wheel in the driveway, and a friendly yellow dog next door. That part was nice.

The skinny guy who owned the house had tattoos, a straggly beard and a scary motorcycle that growled. Angel's dad seemed to like her from the time mom brought her home from the hospital, but he'd never liked Harlie. He wore a mean face whenever he looked at her, and he yelled a lot, when Mom wasn't around. And since he worked days and Mom worked nights at the bar, she wasn't around a lot when he was.

When mom asked about the bruises, Harlie said she fell. And she tried harder to be good. But the time Mom saw a bruise in the shape of a hand on Harlie's face, they moved to a new state, leaving the man, the motorcycle and the house behind. That started the slide—from single bedroom apartments in the projects, to single wide trailers with cracked, newspaper-stuffed-cracked walls. Harlie never saw the scary man again, but she never forgot that it was her fault they no longer lived in a house.

She ripped the rubber band out of her braid and let her hair blow in the hot wind from the car window.

Of course, she understood now that the asshole hadn't liked her because she was another man's leavings. That the slide hadn't been her fault at all.

It only felt that way.

The guilt was cold and slimy, like grease left in a frying pan overnight.

The next day, Harlie stood leaning with one foot propped against the rough boards of the Walker County Fair event barn, hat over her eyes. The sun was warm and the loudspeaker inside announced the FFA Heifer Class winners. It overrode the chug-whine of the midway rides, their engines spitting the smell of diesel, and the sound of kid's screams into the air.

Tonight's Rodeo would be a first on two fronts: her first opportunity to entertain the crowd with her freestyle, and her first night to fight bulls with Deuce. It had taken two weeks, but Steve

Rawlings had come through, getting Deuce paired with her the rest of the summer. Maybe things would get easier now. At least in the arena.

Dr. Nguyen left another voicemail yesterday that Harlie was trying to ignore. She'd told him the last time they'd talked that she had additional evidence that Angel was improving. On their nightly calls, Harlie could hear Angel listening. Harlie couldn't explain it in words he'd accept, but Harlie was certain there was a change in the silence on the line, more so every night. The emptiness was being filled with . . . awareness. Dammit, she *knew* her sister. But the doctor thought it was wishful thinking, or that Harlie was making up reasons to postpone the shock treatments.

Not that she wasn't totally capable of lying to keep Angel from that barbaric treatment, but she *wasn't.*

It was so hard to be here, when much of her attention was there. She could put distraction down in the arena, but this job had so much downtime: traveling during the week, lying in the back seat in rest stops, trying to shut off her mind enough to sleep. Worry was wearing rug burns on her nerves, making her jumpier than a horse at fly time.

"Hey."

At the touch on her elbow, she started, and unbalanced, had to put her foot down not to end up in the dirt.

Deuce's steadying hand came around her arm. "Whoa there. Sorry to wake you."

She tipped her hat back to his familiar grin. "I wasn't asleep." She shrugged out from under his hand.

"Okay." He stood, thumbs in front pockets, looking very pleased with himself.

"What are you grinning at?"

"Just happy to be working." He adjusted his hat. "Did I tell you how grateful I am for calling me? It's really going to be —"

"I owed you, for getting you hurt, in Chilly."

His brows made tildes over troubled eyes. "You didn't owe me. Is that why you called me?"

169

Why was she being such a bitch, when seeing him loosened the muscles at the back of her neck? "I'm sorry. That isn't true." She focused on the red-coated heifer being led out of the barn so she didn't have to look at him. "It's just nice to be working with someone who knows which end of a bull shits."

"I'll try to keep that part straight." His smile was back. "Now what?"

"We get you checked in. Then I'll show you around. I've been here since yesterday, and I know the cheapest place to eat lunch."

She led him to the rodeo office beneath the stands, noting the barrel racer who was giving him the once-over. Twice-over, really, since she turned to check out his butt, too.

"You really haven't worked any rodeos since Chilly? What have you been doing?"

"Just little local stuff. I've mostly been helping my dad on our ranch. And trying to keep my sisters in line." He huffed out a breath. "Going crazy, basically."

"Why do you talk that way about your sisters? Who appointed you Superman?"

"Well, somebody has to."

She squinted at him. "You know you sound like a Cro-Magnon when you say that, right?"

"Okay, this is airing family laundry, but . . ." He reset his hat. "First, there's Pam. She's the oldest. Got pregnant at seventeen, by the county bad boy. Dad woulda' made the guy marry her, but even he thought that punishment was too harsh for her crime. Then there's Patricia. She's still in high school, and trying to sleep with her biology teacher. I had to put the fear of God into him."

He must have noticed her start, because he put out his hands in surrender. "Hey, it was either that, or chain her to the bed. And legally, she still has to attend school, so . . ."

"But isn't that your dad's job?"

He looked off into the distance. "Didn't tell Dad. He'd have killed the guy."

170

"What about the other two? Surely they can't be delinquents in elementary school, right?"

"Oh yeah? Peggy is in fifth grade, and has already beat up every boy in her class. Says she wants to be a lady boxer when she grows up." The side of his mouth quirked. "Either that, or a roller derby queen. She hasn't decided yet."

Harlie had to smile at that. "The youngest. How old is she?"

"Seven."

"How much trouble can a . . ." She watched him shake his head, a full-on smile stretching his lips. "Okay, tell me."

"Penny. She's our dreamer. I had to start taking her to school because she'd wander off, chasing butterflies, and miss the bus."

"Hey, there's worse things than being a dreamer." Angel's smile drifted through her mind. "She sounds sweet."

"You'd think so. But she drives her teachers crazy, drifting off in the middle of a lesson, staring out the window, getting into trouble for scaring the other kids with ghost stories."

"Sounds like she's going to be a writer."

"If she lives long enough. I fully expect her to be wool-gathering and wander out in traffic one of these days."

"Ah, you can't fool me. You love them."

"Of course I love them. But that doesn't mean they don't drive me batshit."

"I can see that. Makes me glad I only have one."

He glanced at her, head cocked. "You have a sister, Coop? How old is she?"

Dammit. That'd teach her to relax. Angel belonged to Harlie. She didn't want to share. There was no way she could explain how special Angel was. Wouldn't explain. It was no one's business anyway. "Hey, look, there's the concession stands. I'm starving. Let's eat." She pointed.

They ate their early dinner while strolling the midway.

Deuce took a bite and rolled his eyes in ecstasy. "The only thing better than bacon is bacon dipped in batter and deep fried."

171

"Someday you're going to be sorry you didn't take better care of your body."

He looked at her, one eyebrow lost in his floppy blonde bangs. "Spoken by a woman who fights two thousand pound bulls for a living." Deuce stepped around a stroller full of screaming toddler, pushed by a frazzled mom.

"But at least I eat right."

He pointed a plastic fork at her little cardboard bucket. "You're eating fried avocado."

She took a bite. "Hey, avocado is a vegetable. Or a fruit. I'm not sure, but either way, it's healthy."

He snorted a laugh. "Here I thought we were in Texas, not the state of delusion."

Harlie stepped sideways to dodge a running kid. "You know they've scheduled time for us between rides to entertain the crowd, right? I'm freestyling. What are you going to do?"

"Like I couldn't have guessed that. Me? I'm telling jokes."

She stopped, and the stream of people flowed around her. "You're what?"

He lifted his chin. "Hey, I'm a funny guy."

"Oh, this is not going to end well." She popped the last bite in her mouth and dropped the tray in an overflowing trash can.

"I've been working on my material. You're going to be rolling."

"Yeah. Rolling my eyes." She didn't remember humor being one of Deuce's strong points.

"Hey, that reminds me. I have to go find the announcer for tonight. He's going to be my straight man." He dropped his container in the trash and wiped his hands on his jeans. "He just doesn't know it yet. Want to come?"

"No. I'd rather be surprised, thanks."

"Okay, I'll see you later."

Harlie'd done enough Friday night rodeos that just the sight of floodlights on dirt shot sparkler flashes of joy zipping down her nerves. Bull riding was next, the last event of the night.

The noisy crowd bulged from the stands, the overflow standing at the perimeter fence.

The chutes were filled with charged-up bull flesh and the air crackled with potential.

Bring on the night.

Hand on the out gate, she waited to make her entrance. Deuce stood at the other side of the gate, his face lit by more than the sodium lamps. He shone from within as he shuffled from foot to foot, grinning like a fool.

And she grinned right back. Damn, it was nice to be able to relax, knowing someone had her back. It felt good to not feel so alone. Not that she'd ever tell anyone that.

"Ladies and gentlemen." The announcer's voice boomed from the loudspeakers. "We have a treat for you tonight, something you've probably never seen before. We got us a lady bullfighter! Meet Harlie 'Coop' Cooper, and her partner, Deuce McAllister!"

Partner. I have a partner! She pushed open the gate and side-by-side, she and Deuce jogged into spotlight that followed them into the center of the arena. When she noticed Deuce waving to the crowd, she did too, and a wave of applause rolled over them. Her heartbeat a drum roll against her ribs; she giggled to herself as she jogged in circles, getting warmed up. When Deuce jogged the other way and their circles met, she noticed a delicate microphone in front of his mouth that had to be part of a headset. He held up a hand and she slapped it. "Glad to have you here, Dude."

"Not as glad at I am to be here. Thanks, Coop."

"De nada. You're doing me the favor." And he was, too. Having him here working the arena with her, felt solid. Like her free-fall slide had ended in a steel platform beneath her feet.

Deuce kept jogging. "Hey, Pete!" His voice was amplified by the sound system.

"Yeah, Deuce." The announcer's voice came from the loudspeakers, but Harlie could see his lips move from where he sat on a raised dais, halfway down the arena fence.

"You know, there's some advantages to having a woman partner."

"There are?"

"Yeah. Coop can give me marital advice."

Harlie stopped jogging. Deuce? Married?

It's possible. You never asked.

"What did you need her advice about?"

"Well see, my wife, Suzie is mad at me."

"Knowing you, I totally get that."

"Yeah, but this time, she's really mad. She claims I don't care about her, because I don't go out and buy her stuff all the time."

"What does she want you to buy her?"

Deuce kept right on jogging. Judging from the quieted crowd, he had their attention. "She told me she wants something that goes from zero to a hundred ninety-five in seconds!"

"Whoa, dude. That is going to take a lot more than a bullfighter makes."

"That's what I thought. But I talked to Coop, and she came up with the perfect gift."

"Yeah? What was it? Maybe I'll get my wife one."

Deuce jogged on, letting the seconds stretch out like ellipses behind him. "Coop told me to stop by Walmart and get her a scale."

The crowd cracked up.

Harlie couldn't help her smile. Deuce was funny. Who knew?

"Okay, people, on to our first rider. Shane Body came here all the way from Colorado, so let's show him some Texas hospitality!" The crowd roared. Harlie took up her position on the latch side of the gate. As the rider scooted up over his rope, she glanced across at Deuce, who bounced on his toes, a look of intrepid expectation on his face. He dropped her a wink, and the gate swung.

A big shouldered black bull lunged out of the chute and headed for her. She ran an imaginary circumference, leading him into a spin. Once he settled in, she backed off and waited.

174

The rider leaned in too far, and began a fall on the inside of the spin.

Though the adrenaline pounding in her veins, yelled *Go-go-go,* she made herself hold.

Hoot's sandpaper voice scratched her brain. *You can't help a wreck you're in the middle of.*

As the bull spun, she caught glimpses of Deuce, crouched and ready.

Dust puffed when the rider fell in a heap into the center of the spin. Harlie took one step, and smacked the bull's head on the way by. He was going so fast; it took a half a spin before the bull recognized the distraction. Which put him right in front of Deuce when he picked his head up.

"Hey!" Deuce darted in, waving. When the bull charged, Deuce ran the opposite direction on the spin, and the bull peeled off, away from the cowboy, who scrambled to his feet and took off for the fence.

Once she was sure the rider was up and running, Harlie took off after the bull, to cover her partner.

Deuce threw a fake and the bull went on by.

By the time he whirled around, he had two humans to choose from, ten feet apart, waving their arms and jumping around. With a confused snort, he gave up and trotted for the out-gate.

Deuce jogged over and high-fived her. "Nice work, Partner."

"Hey. You're not . . . um. Really married, are you?"

"Jeez, it was a *joke*, Harlie." He laughed all the way back to the chutes.

Nine saves and a successful wreck later, Harlie stood in the spot, in center of the arena, facing a black bull with tipped horns.

"This is called freestyle, folks." The announcer's voice blared. "The bullfighter goes one-on-one against a bull for seventy seconds. In competition, the bullfighter is judged on his aggressiveness, and willingness to open himself to risk. His, or in this case, her, objective is to stay as close as she can to the bull, for as long as she can."

You put it that way, I sound like an idiot to be out here. She remembered the explosion of pain in her shoulder, the last time she did this. Her legs weakened with the adrenaline tsunami. The bottom of her stomach fell out.

Hell. I am an idiot.

The announcer started the soundtrack she'd chosen; the swashbuckling theme from Pirates of the Caribbean. The triumphant beat throbbed through her, lifting her onto her toes. She glanced to the fence, where Deuce stood unmoving, so not to attract the bull's attention, but to be close, in case she went down. His hand moved slowly from his side in a thumbs up.

"So whatya say? Let's give this little lady some support!"

The applause was drowned out by the thunder of split hooves, coming at her.

Hold . . . hold . . . haul ass!

She took off running, the bull following two feet behind—one foot behind. She cut right and spun, catching the shimmer flare of the handkerchiefs she'd tied to the elastic belt of Hoot's shorts.

"Ooooooohhhh." From the crowd.

The bull's head was almost in her stomach when she spun again. A horn rubbed the flak jacket over her ribs. She tucked into the bull's shoulder and he pirouetted around her, almost in time with the music. She stood in the eye of the tornado, calm, balanced, transcendent.

This. This was what she loved about her job.

She ducked out of the spin, and ran for the barrel in the center of the arena. She jumped, landing crouched, her feet on the rim, facing the bull. He stopped, lowered his head and pawed the ground, throwing dirt over his back. The crowd fell silent. The music crescendoed.

The animal charged. The instant the barrel shuddered beneath Harlie, she launched. But she hadn't gotten as much forward motion she'd planned.

Short!

She put a foot down on the bull's back as it passed beneath her, and pushed off. Her stomach did a roller coaster drop, but triumph rose, filling her to bursting. It came out in a rebel yell.

She landed, took a few running steps to catch her balance, and spun. A buzzer sounded and the music faded.

"How about *that*, rodeo fans? Someone want to tell that little girl that ladies can't bullfight?"

The crowd stomped the bleachers and cheered.

The bull stood at the other end of the arena watching her.

Giddy with success and the tailing of adrenaline, she turned, bent and dropped her shorts, baring her padded spandex undershorts to the bull.

Laughter from the stands rolled over the arena as she whipped up her shorts and ran, so happy that she practically levitated to the top of the fence. The bull ran beneath her, and out of the gate.

Deuce's exuberant high-five practically knocked her off the fence. But she felt balanced, for the first time on the circuit.

Goddamn, that was fun!

***

The rodeo was over for the night. The next performance would be tomorrow, at noon. Harlie'd just found her duffel in the pileup of gear behind the chutes when a heavy hand landed on her shoulder. She turned.

Deuce stood there, grinning. "Damn, that was a riot, wasn't it?"

"The best." She used the excuse of slinging her duffel to duck out from under his hand. She didn't want to hurt his feelings, but she wasn't comfortable with touching. "I thought you were a goner when that brahma cross caught you on the pass through."

"Yeah, but you picked him up. I didn't get more'n a bruise. Did you see Shane's big move to get back to center on that last ride?"

"Unbelievable. I was ready to step in. Glad I didn't."

He shook his head. "I can't believe he stayed out of the well. Hey, there he is." Deuce slapped the back of a bent over cowboy who was digging through the pile. "When are we heading out, Shane?"

When the compact cowboy straightened, Harlie recognized him from a few rodeos she'd worked.

"Leaving in ten. You riding with me, Deuce?"

"Sure. Saves me gas. Hey, we got room for my partner?"

She backed up a step. "No, I—"

"Sure. And if we don't, I'll make room. She saved my butt tonight." He smiled down at her.

"I can't. I've got a phone call to make." She turned to Deuce. "But thanks for asking me."

"Next time, then." The two guys walked away, chatting companionably.

Harlie watched them go. "Yeah, maybe."

Deuce made buddies on his first night. She knew almost no one after a month on the road. She knew it was more due to her attitude than a guy thing. Deuce and the bull rider met up with several other guys, and they walked away, laughing.

A wave of sorry broke over her as she turned and headed for the parking lot. Not that she'd have wanted to hang out with a bunch of guys in a bar, but . . . It would have been nice to have somewhere to go. Somewhere to be. People to be with.

But she'd have been alone, even if she'd gone.

In school, everyone thought she was an aloof snob when they first met her. She never understood why, since 'snob' and 'trailer park' didn't belong in the same sentence. The aloof part wasn't her, either. She didn't think she was above anyone else.

Just separate.

She dodged a pickup getting in line for the exit. Spotting Yolanda's tattered vinyl roof, she turned down the aisle and pulled out her key. She flung her bag onto the front seat and snatched up her phone, in a hurry to tell Angel about tonight's performance. Leaning against the bumper, she hit speed dial.

"Hey Crystal, its Harlie. Can I talk to Angel?"

"Harlie. I've been waiting for your call." Her excited voice came in little puffs. "Your sister is alert.

Chapter 16

"What?" Her fingers on the phone spasmed, blaring several notes in her ear. She forced her fingers off the keys. "My sister is alert for the first time in six weeks, and you don't call?"

"We have tried. I personally have left three messages."

Harlie glanced at the phone's screen, trying to make sense of the flashing envelope as possibilities zipped through her mind like machine gun fire. Of course, she'd been in the arena. "Oh, right. Sorry." She stuck a finger in her ear to block out the glass-pack muffler of the lifted 4x4 idling by. "What did she say? Is she okay? Did she ask where I am?" The rumble, she realized, came from within. A wad of self-reproach ballooned in her chest, making it hard to breathe. *I should be there. She's going to be disoriented and afraid . . .* "Hello? Are you there? Talk to me."

"Harlie, calm down. I can't tell you when you're firing questions."

She locked her jaw, and waited the longest two seconds of her life.

"I put her to bed tonight. She was the same as always. Two hours later, we heard banging coming from her room." She took a breath. "Now, you know our rooms are designed to be safe for our patients. We go to the utmost efforts to—"

"What? What happened?" A red-splashed, full color snapshot of Angel crumpled and bloody on the floor of the kitchen swept over her. Her muscles went liquid, and her knees gave. *You should have been there.* She clutched Yolanda's exterior mirror to anchor herself.

"When I got to the room, she was attempting to break the bathroom mirror with a chair."

"Is she cut? Bleeding?"

"No, no. We use safety glass. She couldn't break it. We have her sedated."

Like a door opened in a fire, anger roared in. "What the *fuck* am I paying you people for?" She panted. "I leave my sister in your care, and all you want to do is fry her brain with electricity, and now—"

"Harlie." Crystal's voice flowed smooth as warm honey. "Take a breath. Do you need to put your head between your knees?"

Harlie took a deep lungful of Texas night air, wishing she was where the air smelled like smog.

"Angel is safe. She's sleeping. Doctor Nguyen has been informed, and he'll be in at eight a.m. to assess her."

"I'll be there." Harlie did the math. Fifteen hundred miles at seventy . . . over twenty hours. "This time tomorrow."

"The doctor has asked that you wait for his call. We have no way of knowing if she'll fall back into catatonia. Or she may be alert, but non-verbal."

"You don't understand. I've been with her every day of her life, until—lately. If I'm not there, she'll be afraid." She hated the wobble in her voice. But the arrow that pierced her chest was guilt-tipped. It burned.

"Harlie, please. It's late, and I'm assuming you're not in Southern California. Wait for the doctor's call. Then we'll see where we are."

The tide of shock and anger receded, leeching away what remained of her stamina. "I know you're right. I hate that you're right." She slumped over, chest resting against Yolanda's hood. "I'm sorry I yelled at you, Crystal."

"Oh Honey, I've heard lots worse. You're a lightweight." She chuckled. "Now, try to get some rest. If the doctor recommends it, you're going to have a long drive tomorrow."

"I'll have my phone on all night. Call me if there's any change, will you?"

"Of course. But there won't be. Angel will sleep through the night. You see that you do too."

Like that's going to happen.

***

The edge of the world was only a lighter shade of black when Harlie gathered her things the next morning. Luckily, rodeos on county fairgrounds had showers. Free ones.

After staring at the sagging headliner over the back seat last night, the aftershock hit. What about her job? If she left, she'd be leaving Deuce dangling, solo. She knew the nasty feeling of wind on her uncovered butt—and she'd be resigning him to the ineptitude of whoever they could scrounge at the last minute. If they could find even someone.

Working the arena with him felt comfortable. Besides, she was responsible for getting him this job. She owed it to him not to bail.

Besides, what would she tell Steve Rawlings?

She couldn't leave.

But she couldn't stay.

She snatched her phone from the charger, even though she knew there was no way the doctor would call; it was two hours earlier in California. Trudging to the shower, her flashlight spotlighted her way between the horse trailers, RV's and pickups.

Screw it. Her first allegiance was to Angel. She was going, even if she had to quit.

But Angel was going to need a shrink, possibly for a long time. How would Harlie earn enough wearing a paper hat and asking if the customer wanted fries with that?

A cluster of moths beat at the yellow light over the door. Her boot falls echoed in the empty tile-lined restroom. At least getting up early meant she'd have a shower before the tracking of countless boots turned the floor to a decoupage of mud. She walked to the last curtained shower stall, dropped her stuff in a waiting plastic chair, and stripped.

But how could she be on the road when Angel was tackling the demons in her head? Angel would need her sister.

Harlie stepped under the miserly showerhead's spray. The water was hot, but since it was more mist than shower, it took a long time to wet anything.

This was an impossible decision. A puzzle that her mind kept turning over and over, like one of those Rubik Cubes. Only, not exactly—there was a solution to a cube.

And Harlie sucked at puzzles.

Two hours later, the parking lot had gotten busy as the entrants and rodeo people prepared for the noon performance. The cowboy in the next parking slot was grooming his palomino calf-roping horse. Groups of cowboys and girls wandered by, but no Deuce.

She'd already rearranged Yolanda's trunk and cleaned the fast food wrappers and soda cans from under the seats and floorboards. Harlie sprayed borrowed glass cleaner and worked on the road grime on the windshield, her mind still working the puzzle, no closer to a solution.

Her phone rang. Heart slamming, she almost dropped it, trying to pry it from her pocket. "Hello. Hello?"

"Ms. Cooper. This is Doctor Nguyen, from Los—"

"Yes. Doctor. How is my sister?"

"She is cognizant, verbal and calmer, this morning."

"Has she asked where I am?"

"No. She seemed to know . . . told me you were 'on the road'. I didn't know bullfighting was allowed in the states. In Mexico, of course, and—"

"It's not that kind of bullfighting." She leaned a hip on the hood, ignoring the searing heat of the metal through her jeans. "I told you she was listening!"

"It seems you were correct. I need to study this further. There may be a paper there—"

"Doctor!"

"Of course. You want to know about your sister." He cleared his throat. "I conducted an assessment and a preliminary therapy session this morning. Though your sister spoke in short, noncommittal sentences, I believe it is a place to begin."

Harlie put her fingers to the pain points over her eyes and pressed. Hard. "If you think it's okay to wait that long, I can leave here by three this afternoon at the very latest, which would put me in there at. . ." Routes and mileage whipped through her brain like a Dow Jones ticker.

"Ms. Cooper. I know that you want what's best for Angel, and for now, it's best that I work with Angel, one-on-one."

"Okay. I'll just be there to—"

"Your sister won't see you."

Her butt slid off the hood. "What?"

His exhale brushed her ear. "Angel has told me that she doesn't want to see you. Can't see you. Just yet."

A blast of anger shot from her core, pushing out, shimmering off her skin. *She doesn't, does she? I'm out here busting my ass, not sleeping with worry, and the little shit doesn't—* "I'll be there, this time tomorrow." The smoke of anger thinned, but she was the one who was burned. Her only living relative—her reason for going on—had just rejected her. *But why? What have I done?*

"Ms. Cooper, think a moment. Your sister has just come out of catatonia. We have no idea of her mindset, or how she's feeling."

"But this is my *sister*. I raised her . . ." Her voice went loose and wavery at the end, so she made herself stop.

"Ms. Cooper, you shouldn't take this personally."

"Really? Can you tell how to do that? Because I don't think—" She bit her tongue to stop the wail that built at the back of her throat. If it got out, there'd be no stuffing it back. And God knows what lie behind it, but it was big. It bulged in her core, tightening the retaining wall of her skin.

"You entrusted Los Compadres with your sister's care. I'm assuming you researched facilities, and physicians before doing that, yes?"

"I did."

"So please, continue to trust us a while longer. Give me some time to work with your sister. I promise, I'll keep you apprised of the progress here, and will bring you into her therapy as soon as possible."

Thought and emotion tangled in her mind. She didn't know what to do.

"Remember, I trusted you, when you wanted me to delay electro-therapy. Now I'm asking you to trust me."

The blood from her battered heart pooled, congealing into the hurt of a deep, angry bruise. Angel didn't want her. Ultimately, that convinced her. "When will you call me with the next update?"

They agreed on a schedule of twice-weekly calls, and she hung up.

Angel doesn't want you.

She stood, staring at her boots without seeing them, trying to absorb reality. Her only friend. The only person who knew her childhood stories. They shared history. And the past years, they'd shared everything. Her only family didn't want her.

And she'd thought she was an orphan when Mom died. Now, she was truly an orphan.

She took Angel's being there for granted. They'd had to pick up and start over so many times. But now she realized that starting over *with* someone was a whole lot different than starting over alone.

And she'd thought herself a loner, all these years. Her lips twisted in what probably wasn't even close to a smile. She tossed the window cleaner and rag in the back of the car. Pity was a disgusting emotion; self-pity was even uglier.

Pulling her spine straight and her shoulders square, she went to find Deuce.

She found him standing by the roach-coach lunch wagon, drinking coffee. "Where have you been? We've only got an hour before the show starts, and—holy crap."

His skin had a greenish cast, and he squinted through eyes so bloodshot his vision had to be blurry. And if she remembered right, those were the same clothes he wore yesterday. Except for the wrinkles and grease stains. "Are you sick? You look like an extra in a zombie flick."

He put a hand over his eyes, to either block the sun or massage his head. "Kinda. Had a bit too much fun, last night."

His breath washed over her. She took a step back. "Damn, your breath would kill a buffalo. You're hung over." She scanned the menu board. "Wanna split some chili?"

He swallowed. Slowly. "No. I'm good with coffee."

She ordered her lunch. "Man, why would you blow money on something that will make you look that bad?"

"Felt better, going down."

He looked so pathetic she had to smile. "How'd it feel, coming up?"

He belched. "Don't remind me." He closed one eye to block the glare, and squinted at her out of the other. "You don't look so good yourself, Coop. What's up?"

"Didn't sleep real well." She waved him off. "Where's your hat? You're gonna bake out here."

He shook his head. "Damned Ty Baker. He fed it to a bull."

"What do you know? I didn't know they ate straw."

"Well, he didn't swallow, but what was left, you wouldn't want to wear. Trust me on that."

"Come with me." She paid, and took her Styrofoam dish of chili from the vendor. "I'll grab my baseball cap and you can wear my straw hat."

He reared back. "Wear a girl's hat?"

"I'm offering you my hat, not my underwear." He looked so scandalized, she had to smile as she put a hand on his elbow to steer him. "Come on, you big pussy."

Chapter 17

The sun was fast heading for the horizon by the time she and Deuce left the arena.

He held the gate for her as she limped out. "How's that foot?"

"Just a bruise. Luckily that slab-sided SOB didn't land right on it."

"Yeah, and you saved Deke Winter's ass, besides." Deuce tipped his chin to a bronc rider who hailed him. "Oh, and here." He took off her straw hat and held it out. "Thanks for letting me use it."

"Nah, you keep it till you get a new one. It looks good on you, and your brains are overcooked as it is."

"Heeey, Deuce." The cute little cowgirl's two-note love song was as sticky-sweet as the smell of bubblegum lip gloss wafting in her wake. The girl's hips rolled like they were on ball bearings, and she checked over her shoulder to be sure Deuce noticed.

He did. He fingered the brim of his hat. "Hey, Carletta."

Harlie chuffed. "Am I the only one who wasn't at the bar last night?" Her gear bag brushed her leg. Her stomach growled. Maybe she'd have time to eat before getting on the road.

"Well, I couldn't swear to that, but it was pretty packed. You should have come."

"This morning you looked like a poster child for AA. Oh

187

yeah, sign me up."

He chuckled. "You really are a funny lady. That surprises me, after Chilly."

"I wasn't funny at Hoot's?" She spotted Yolanda and headed that way.

He glanced at her. "Really? Intense, yes. Funny? Ummm . . ."

"Yeah, okay, so I admit to a bit of attitude. You would have one too, if you were a woman, trying—"

"*This* is your car?"

She turned to see her car's shabbiness reflected on his face. She hated his judgment. But hated the shame she felt, more. "Yeah. So?"

"It runs?"

She patted the hood. "Don't you diss my Yolanda. This old broad and I have seen lots of miles." She stepped back and swiped paint flakes off her palm.

"Ookay." He eyed the sagging interior and orange shag carpet, one eyebrow raised. "I'll tell you what. Why don't you get ready to roll, and I'll meet you back here at dusk. We'll follow each other to . . ." He reached in his pocket and pulled out a small scrap of paper. "Weatherford, Oklahoma."

"I guess that would be all right." Until now, she hadn't been able to admit to herself how scary her past month had been, all alone on the road. He didn't need to know about the relief that trickled through her worried places.

An hour and a half later, the sun was an aura of gold on the horizon. Harlie sat on Yolanda's hood, waiting for Deuce, going over Dr. Nguyen's phone call in her mind. The memory was already worn smooth from handling, but her mind refused to put it down.

Since she had no idea what Deuce drove, she scrutinized the driver of every vehicle that passed. The lot was clearing fast as cowboys hit the road for the next rodeo.

An older model brown Jeep with a ragged rag top halted in front of her, the plastic passenger window folded down. Deuce leaned over the passenger seat. "I mapped a route. It's only 450 miles. We should be there around two am. You ready?"

"Been waiting on you." She stood, walked to her door, opened it, and slid in. When Deuce pulled ahead, she fired Yolanda up, put her in gear and eased on the gas.

The car rocked a bit, but didn't move. She checked to be sure the red plastic indicator on the dash was on "D". It was.

She hit the gas again. The engine growled, but the tires weren't moving. "What's up, Girlfriend?" Unease rumbling somewhere south of her diaphragm, Harlie shifted the car to park, then back to drive. Gave it gas. Yolanda balked.

"Fucklets." She slapped her palm on the steering wheel. Of the few remaining things in her life that had yet to go wrong, this was the biggest.

The Jeep backed into the now empty space beside Yolanda, and Deuce stepped out. "What's wrong?"

She left the car running and stepped out. "I don't know. I hit the gas, but she doesn't move."

"Did you put it in drive?" His eyes scanned the car.

"Oh, shit." She slapped herself upside the head. "That never occurred to me."

"Okay, okay, no need to get all snarky." He dropped onto his hands and knees and peered under the chassis. "Uh oh."

"Do not say those words. In that tone." Harlie dropped to her knees and leaned over, to see what was uh-oh under there.

Deuce levered to his stomach and wriggled under the car, brushed his hand over the grass, then wriggled back out. He held up his hand for her to see.

"Yolanda's bleeding!"

He wiped his hand on the leg of his jeans, stood and extended a hand to her. "Might as well be blood. That's transmission fluid. Your transmission is gone."

"How bad?" One hand on Yolanda's side, the other on her knee, she pushed to her feet.

"Shot. Kaput. Trashed."

The unease shifted to dread. "How much is a new transmission?"

He stepped to the door, reached in and turned off the

ignition. "I'm not a certified Caddy mechanic, but I'd say at least twenty-eight hundred. Maybe three thousand. And that's not counting the tow."

She didn't even have three hundred, and she needed that to get to Angel, whenever the doctor allowed it. She leaned her hands on the hood. It was warm, like a body that had just exhaled its last breath.

You've been through worse than this.

No she hadn't. Even when Mom died, she'd still had Angel.

And here she thought she'd finally stopped sliding and hit bottom. How much farther down could bottom be? She had nothing left except her job, a few clothes and a tattoo.

She cocked her head back, studying the little broken mirror chips on black velvet. "What else? I mean, really. Whatthefuck else?" It came out matter-of-fact, a tone more curious than mad.

For the first time in her life, she'd run out of anger. That should be a good thing, since it was one thing she wouldn't mind losing. But behind the anger was a bog of soul-dragging defeat. Her neck muscles let go and her hair fell forward. She was too tired to cry. Besides, tears required caring, and she was fresh out of that, too.

"Harlie?"

She felt a light brush on her shoulder, then it was gone. "What."

"This isn't a big deal."

Laughter erupted. Some part of her mind sat back and watched as she collapsed, convulsed with mirth, onto the hood.

This is not good.

But it was better than the alternative. Laughing wasn't showing weakness.

The sodium lamp overhead snapped on. Deuce's worried eyes shone in the flat white light. "No, I'm serious. We're going to the same rodeos. You can ride with me."

She shook her head, tears streaming down her face. She had to get a grip. This was starting to feel like hysteria.

"Yes. Yes, you will." He stepped to Yolanda's back door, opened it, and grabbed her gear bag from the seat. "Cowboys rodeo together all the time. Come on." His hand came under her elbow, and didn't let go when she tried to pull away. "This is better, really. We can split the cost of gas. It will save us both money." He threw the bag over his shoulder and took a step, tugging her by the elbow. "Maybe we could start sharing underwear."

If he hadn't been holding her up, she'd have fallen with a whoop in the dirt. He thought this was about the money. She wished it was about the money.

"I am funny. But not this funny." He handed her up into the passenger seat, and went back to transfer more of her stuff.

She laughed until she was empty inside. Hollow.

Deuce hit the road and just drove.

Harlie watched the pattern of road lights rushing at the windshield in a metronome pattern. Small, bigger, big, gone. She took in the Jeep's perfume of motor oil and sunbaked dust. She listened to the wind rush in the window and the silence echoing from inside herself.

"I can't do this." Her brain hijacked her mouth; she hadn't known she had anything to say.

His face shone pale in the green dash light. "It's not a problem."

"I'm serious."

"Okay then, we can get hold of a mechanic in the morning. Can you call your parents for a loan?"

She would have laughed, but she'd used that all up. "No parents."

"You have a sister. Could she lend you some money?"

She watched the yellow line flash by in the headlights. It made her dizzy, so she went back to the road lights. Small, bigger, big, gone. "I send money to my sister, not the other way around."

"Yeah, but surely in a situation like this—"

"She's fourteen."

"Oh."

Her index finger worried a hangnail on her thumb. "And she won't speak to me." She didn't seem to have any more control of her speech than she had the laughter. "She's why I got this tattoo." Harlie traced the shape she couldn't see in the dark, but knew by heart. "She's why . . . she's why everything."

"What's her name?"

If she didn't stop now, she might spill the whole sordid mess. And above all, she couldn't tell. "You've been nice, Deuce. I appreciate it, really. Can we be quiet now?"

"But—" He shot her a look, and whatever he'd been going to say, died. "No worries."

She considered his tone for reproach, and was relieved not to find any. If not for him, she'd be back in the lot with a dead car.

Ten miles later, the next grenade hit. "Where am I going to sleep?"

Startled from his road Mesmer, Deuce looked over. "Huh?"

The seatbelt morphed to a straitjacket. She leaned forward, pulling it away from her chest, scanning the inside of the suddenly closed-in space. "I don't have a way to get from a hotel to the rodeo grounds. Even if I could afford a hotel, which I can't."

Useless thoughts pinged around the inside of her skull, an endless loop of streaming gibberish. She put her face in her hands. She was done. Physically, emotionally and mentally, toast.

"Hey, it's okay. You can stay in the Jeep."

She stuck her hand out the window and waved it around. "It's not safe here."

"Why not? The doors lock."

"And the windows snap shut. That should thwart those pesky rapists."

"Oh. Guess I never thought of it that way."

"Of course not." She snapped. "You're a guy." She clamped her jaws closed. Much as it would soothe her to vent, she couldn't afford to.

Here was Harlie Cooper, relying on the kindness of strangers. And that felt worse than sliding. It was free-fall.

She lifted her head. "I'm sorry to snap. It's been a long day."

"Have you had problems on the road before?"

She turned her head to the dark beyond the edge of the headlights. "Nothing Yolanda couldn't handle."

"I should have realized. I'm so used to thinking of you like a guy—shit. That didn't come out right. I meant—"

"Thanks. That's the nicest thing you ever said to me." And here she thought she had no smiles in her.

He pushed a hand through his wind-tousled hair. "Ah, Coop, I'm sorry."

"No, I'm serious. I've been trying to prove my sex a non-issue, and you just told me I've succeeded." She took a deep breath of the high desert air and pushed out the words she'd normally keep in. "I didn't think anything could make me feel better. That did. Thank you."

"But there are others who won't think of you that way. I get it." He glanced at the bench seat, then in the rearview mirror. "Simple fix. You sleep in the back seat; I'll sleep in the front. Nobody's gonna mess with you with me here."

This Jeep was smaller than her impermeable bubble of personal space.

"We all slept in the same room at Hoot's."

She opened her mouth. Then closed it. She wanted to tell him she could solve her problems herself. But she had to face the fact that she couldn't. She couldn't fix Angel's problems, now her own. *Oh yeah, this has got to be the bottom.*

Hell, this probably wasn't Deuce's first choice either. But he was willing to see that she stayed safe. He was nicer than she deserved.

"Thank you," she said through gritted teeth. "Again."

***

Deuce snored. Not a hibernating bear snore, more a sporadic rumble, like a big cat's purr that sounded like safety felt. Harlie lay on her back in the pre-dawn, arms behind her head, her

193

knees resting on the support bar for the roof. This wasn't Yolanda's king sized bed, but it would do.

Yesterday's storm had passed. Her mind dawned clear and cloudless. She felt relaxed, and hopeful. One good thing about complete disaster—she'd no longer have the worry of more things going wrong. They already had.

Maybe she should start looking for the positive, instead of focusing on what was bad in her life. Even if it didn't make things better, it was a lot less scary.

Bullfighting fulfilled her in ways she hadn't even understood she needed until she'd set foot in the arena. Deuce was a Godsend. She was doing a job that no other woman had ever done—one of the most dangerous jobs in rodeo, and so far she'd only sustained bruises. If not for Angel's rebuff, life would be good. Great, actually.

Angel.

Her mind went over it once again, touching the ache of the deep bruise like the story of the blind person touching an elephant, trying to make sense of it. She could put it down if only she understood. Angel had no reason to be angry with her.

What if she took the doctor's advice and didn't take it personally?

If it isn't about me, what is it about?

She tried to look around herself, to the darkness beyond it.

The glass. The nurse had said they discovered Angel trying to break the mirror in her room. She'd broken all the glass in their apartment before she cut herself. And . . .

She broke all the glass at the dairy.

Of course she did. Harlie should have seen it way earlier. But she'd been so busy scrambling to patch holes in their dissolving safety net, the pattern was only obvious in hindsight.

So what's with Angel and glass?

Harlie believed the truth in her sister's eyes when she said Mack hadn't messed with her.

If not that, then what? A cold breeze blew through the cracks in her, leaving her shaken. Harlie had been on guard, but

194

what had she missed? Did she really want to know?

Yes. Maybe. No.

None of that mattered though, because she couldn't know more without facts. And Angel wasn't talking. At least, not to Harlie. Was this her punishment for missing something? If so, she was paying. She rubbed the spot over her heart, feeling the bruise. All she could do was trust in the doctors and go on as best she could. Angel had given her no other choice.

All this time, she'd had thought her path precarious. Turns out, the path Angel walked may have been scarier.

Chapter 18

That afternoon the sun seemed brighter, the bulls more nimble, the saves more edge-of-life thrilling. Or maybe it was just her.

This was a college rodeo competition, and it had a different flavor than the Pro rodeos. The cowboys' attitudes were as fresh as their faces. They approached their events with the zeal of wet-from-dunking religious converts. To these kids, rodeo *was* a religion.

Kids. She scanned the knot of cowboys behind the chutes after the last event. Funny how she thought of them that way, though she wasn't any older. Being in charge from a young age added years to her—even if she sucked at it.

"Hey Coop!" Deuce waved to her from a circle of Stetsons.

Damn, that dude bonded faster than superglue. She walked over, tilting her baseball cap to block the late afternoon sun. "Yeah?"

"These guys invited us to dinner. They say they know a great place, and they're buying." He slapped a stocky bulldogger on the shoulder.

"Least we can do. Y'all saved our bull riders' butts and they pulled out the win for us."

"Then, after dinner, they have their annual bonfire, right over there." Deuce pointed to a towering pile of what she'd assumed was junk. Looking closer, she saw it was composed of wood—pallets, old furniture, boards, and heavy logs from God knew where—there weren't a lot of big trees in Southeast Oklahoma.

"Cool, huh?"

She wrapped her arms around her waist. "Way cool. Y'all have a blast."

Deuce frowned, stepped out of the testosterone circle and stopped in front of her. "Come on, Coop, it'll be fun. It'd be rude to say no."

She kicked the dirt, trying to come up with a valid reason not to go.

"Besides, he held out his hands, "What are you gonna do for food? Graze?"

He was right. The catering truck had pulled up stakes right after the calf roping.

"I've got some trail mix—"

"You're not going to sit and mope, mourning that beater of yours, or anything else you got going on that you're not talking about." He leaned in and whispered close to her ear. "This isn't hard if you give it half a chance." He backed up, looking her in the eye. "The Coop I know always takes chances."

She planted a hand on her hip. "Does that toddler psychology thing ever work for you?"

"I don't know. Does it?" He winked.

But it was the busted-little-boy smile that convinced her. "You know what, McAllister? For once, you're right. I'm in." She wouldn't feel so awkward with Deuce there.

It was full dark by the time they pulled back into the rodeo grounds after dinner. The lights of the trucks spotlighted the towering pile of wood, a circle of coeds around its base. As soon as the truck stopped, Harlie stood in the bed where she'd been packed, cheek to jowl with nine other guys, then bailed out over the side.

A little too much togetherness for her taste, but she was thankful for the chicken fried steak dinner that hummed a happy tune below her breastbone. She couldn't remember the last time she'd sat down to a full meal. The chicken dinner with Steve?

197

Yeah, probably.

"Come on, Coop, they're about to light it!" Caleb, a calf roper who'd sat next to her at dinner, grabbed her hand.

She shook loose, then smiled, to show she didn't mean to be mean. "I'm coming."

He led the way to the edge of the crowd. Several cowboys were dousing the lower part of the stack with gasoline.

"See? Told you this would be fun."

Hearing Deuce's voice from behind, the muscles beside her spine relaxed. "So you were right, once." She shot a smile over her shoulder in time to catch his wink. "I'll circle this day on the calendar."

"Okay, everyone, stand back!" She recognized the winner of the bull riding as he waved the crowd away from the pile.

Deuce stood at her shoulder. "That's Brian Custer. Remember the name, 'cuz you're gonna hear it on the PBR when you get there. He's the best in the state."

You could always tell a bull rider. From the angle of his hat to his loose-hipped swagger, his voice commanded respect. Everyone backed up in acknowledgment of his 'top of the food chain' status.

Someone in the crowd handed Brian what looked like a broomstick with a rag tied on the end. He stepped away from the stack, pulled a lighter from his pocket, and lit the rag.

The crowd started chanting, "S. O. S. U." Slowly at first, then speeding up, until the letters ran together. When Brian held up the torch like an avenging sword, they cheered. He tossed the torch on the pile.

Maybe they added a little too much gasoline, because it lit with a *whoomp!* A small fireball rose up the stack, and off the top. Heat rolled forward in a wave, and everyone took a step back.

"Ohhhhhhh . . ." The crowd chorused.

She felt a bump at her elbow and turned.

Deuce held out a sweating bottle of beer. "I grabbed one for you."

198

"I don't drink, but thanks anyway."

He cocked his head and looked at her, too close. "Why not?"

Let her control slip around strangers? She covered her shudder with a shrug. "Not twenty-one."

"Hey, Deuce!" One of the bull riders called from the other side of the stack. "Com'ere and solve this argument, will you?"

"Let's go." He touched her elbow to lead.

She shrugged away. "You go ahead." They hadn't called her. She wouldn't fit in with all those guys anyway.

He gave her an irritated look, then walked away.

Harlie stood mesmerized by the flames, listening to the conversations flowing around her.

"So, I was right, but Professor Engels still wouldn't . . ."

"The coach said that we should end the season seven and six. If we get a good recruiting class . . ."

She wandered the edge of the group, letting conversations drift in and out like late night Spanish stations on Yolanda's radio. Their world was just as foreign to her.

"Okay, its bullshit, but say you're right, and there is no God. What made all this?" A redhead in the group next to Harlie spread her arms, beer bottle pointing overhead.

Harlie stopped. She'd wondered the same thing.

"You've been reading too much Plato, Hon." A lean kid with greasy hair took a swig from a flask. "You first-causers are so last century."

The girl fired back. "I follow the design argument. Everything behaves according to physics—"

"Which is a concept developed by man. You just proved my point."

"The *name* was made up by man. But it was made up to explain something that already existed in nature."

The guy noticed Harlie watching from the edge of his group. "Hey, you, blondie. What do you think?"

Harlie was caught, skewered by the guy's attention. Her face flamed. "I – I'm just listening here. Y'all go on."

The redhead jumped in. "You have to admit, everything we see being correlated to each other suggests a plan."

"I don't have to admit any such thing. You're forgetting randomness. . ."

The second Harlie sensed the two were engrossed in their argument once more, she slunk away to the anonymity of darkness. These kids, with their college education, and daddy's money.

Must be nice.

Hands in her front pockets, she kept walking, head down, tuning out the conversations around her. Besides, who cared about philosophy and how the Universe got here? It was here. And it was hard enough dealing with that reality, without getting into dumb discussions that no one could win anyway. These kids had the luxury of 'is there a God' philosophical discussions. Hers was more the school of, 'is there a next meal?'

"Hey, Coop." Deuce waved to her from a clump of cowboys. "Come on over here. We need your opinion."

Her stomach clenched, but she forced her feet that way. Deuce wouldn't put her in a tight spot.

"We're talking about the PBR rule about riders being 'put on the clock', for taking too long in the chute."

Brian, the bonfire conductor, leaned in. "Everybody knows they just did that because of the Brazilians. It's not fair."

"How can it not be fair, when it applies to everyone?" Deuce said.

"I know, but it never even occurred to them to do it, until the Brazilians were so methodical—"

"Methodical?" A short rider with a big hat and a florid face asked. "Holy shit, they got a TV schedule. Those guys were taking *minutes* in the chute, messing with the tail of their ropes, and their chaps. If I was a stock contractor, I'da been pissed."

"Shut up you guys. I want to hear what Coop thinks." Deuce raised his beer, as if to hand off the conversation baton to her.

Time stretched out. "I . . ." her throat worked, but instead of words, saliva filled her mouth. She had an opinion. Of course she did. Why couldn't she spit it out?

Glancing around the circle of fire-lighted faces looking back at her, she shook her head and backed away. There was no way she could just slide into this group like Deuce did.

She was halfway to Deuce's Jeep by the time her heart stopped trying to beat its way through her ribs. *It doesn't matter. Just a bunch of blowhard kids, spouting opinions like they actually know somethi*— a hand came down on her shoulder and she whirled, fists up.

Deuce stopped and held up his hands in surprise. Or maybe it was surrender. "What is it, Harlie?"

She lowered her hands, but not her guard. "What? Because I don't see the point in jawing with a bunch of cowboys?"

He waved a hand at the group behind them. "They're nice guys, and they were just talking. Would it hurt you to try to fit in a little?"

She put a hand on her hip and rolled her eyes, acting, to cover the hurt. "What difference does it make what I think. Or what they think?" She threw her hands up. "The rule was put in place by the PBR. Why do y'all waste time flapping lips about it?" She turned and took a step.

"Why are you afraid?" His voice was soft. Knowing.

Shame rushed to her face. She whirled on him. "I'm not afraid. Don't you say that!" She squared her shoulders and tried to look down her nose at him. She had to tip her head back to do it. "You don't know me. You don't know anything about me."

"How would I, when you won't talk to me?" he spoke quiet and slow. "We're partners. We're supposed share stuff. And I'm not talking underwear." His face held hurt, not humor. "I don't even know your sister's name." He stood, waiting for her to say something.

This was Deuce. He was worthy of her trust. He'd proved that, as recently as last night. She *wanted* to tell him—to see what the words would be like, outside. But they just built, in her mind, in her throat. 'Don't tell' was so ingrained, she couldn't, even though she wanted to. Tried to.

How do you let loose of what you've worked for years to keep in?

His expression stiffened to his tough bullfighter face. A stranger's face. He turned and, hands in pockets, walked back to the bonfire.

She watched his back until it disappeared in the crowd. She whispered, "her name is Angel."

It was quiet in the Jeep the next morning on the way to Albuquerque.

When Harlie couldn't stand her conscience nagging any longer, she tucked her hands under her thighs and spoke to the windshield. "About last night."

Deuce held up a hand. "You don't owe me an explanation."

"But I—"

"Look, Harlie. You and me are going to be in close quarters for the rest of the summer. If we start trying to be all polite and do what we think the other person wants, it won't be real, and we'll probably end up killing each other, right?" He glanced over at her. "We are who we are. Let's just work stuff out as we go, okay?"

Seeing softness around his eyes, the muscles in her shoulders released. She knew she owed an apology, but politeness rules always tied her up in knots. Even if the feeling was sincere, under pressure, it always came out fake. And he deserved better. "How did you get to be such a nice guy, McAllister?"

He draped his wrist over the steering wheel and chuckled. "You forget; I have four sisters. If I weren't mellow, I wouldn't have survived."

She leaned back, resting her stocking feet on the dash. "Tell me some sister stories."

"Well, let's see. There was the time that Peggy, she's our ten-year-old tomboy remember, beat up the fifth grade class President because he was trying to buy votes with chocolate bars. The principal was going to expel her for lying, until she set up a sting, and got the kid busted."

Harlie pulled windblown hair out of her eyes. "I think I'd like Peggy."

"Oh, you two will never meet. Are you kidding? You'd become her biggest hero and she'd give up wanting to be a roller derby queen to become a bullfighter. I'd never sleep again." He mock-shuddered.

"You can't fool me. You're not the caveman you make yourself out to be."

"Hey, there's worse things than cavemen."

Harlie scanned the brushy landscape rushing by the open window. "Angel got ejected from the science fair one year."

"Your sister?"

"Yeah." She watched the clumps of mesquite pass by. "She made this board, showing how everything in nature is linked. You know, a cow eats grass, and its waste is used by the plants. When it dies, its body becomes fertilizer."

"I think I know where this is going."

"She used real dog poop, and a pancaked squirrel she found on the side of the road." Harlie smiled, remembering. "They had to air out the gymnasium afterward."

Deuce chuckled and flipped on the turn signal to pass a beat up farm truck. "I think I'd like your sister, too."

Harlie picked at the ragged cuticle of her thumb. "She's in a mental facility."

The surprise in Deuce's look slid over her.

"It was kind of a breakdown; I guess you'd call it. She's been . . . away, in her head for a time." Harlie couldn't make herself say the medical name. It was too cold, too removed. Too un-Angel.

"Jesus, Harlie. What do the doctors say?"

"She's awake now, but . . ." She tore off a strip of skin and blood welled up. She put her finger over it, both to stop the bleeding and hide the cut. "They're working through it."

"Well, you have to trust that they know what they're doing, right?"

She coughed a chuckle. "This is me you're talking to."

The corner of his mouth lifted. "Yeah, trust isn't really your thing."

She put her thumb to her mouth to suck off the blood.

They drove a time, silence swirling in the Jeep's interior. Silence felt different with Deuce. It wasn't the usual prickly-oh-shit-what-next not-talking she felt around most people. It was as clean as the breeze that tugged wisps of hair out of her braid.

But silence changed, and like a storm front, words gathered. She didn't want to say them. No one wanted to hear them. She was so not 'poor little me.' She checked her thumb. The bleeding had stopped. "My mom had this loser-radar. She was so pretty she could have had so much better, but she always picked the hopeless ones: the good 'ol boys without jobs, with drinking problems . . ." She tried to shut up, but the storm had broken and the words poured down. "With anger issues." She inspected her fingers. "I was twelve, and Angel was six. We were living in Ohio when Mom's radar messed up. Howey was a good guy in a loser costume.

"He was laid off, but he didn't hang out in bars. He only stopped in the bar where Mom worked because his car died, and he came in to wait for a tow truck." She found a callous on the pad of her finger, and worried at it. "He was so nice. And not just to my mom. He liked us, too. Since he wasn't working and mom worked nights, he'd pick us up and take us on 'adventures': a picnic in the park, a scavenger hunt, or he'd chase us, playing kick-the-can." The memories lifted the corners of her lips. "You can't fool a kid—he really *did* like us. He had big plans. He was going to get a job—a good job, and we were going to get a house. He was going to marry mom, and adopt us. None of the losers ever said that. They didn't need to—they could have mom without all those pretty lies.

"Turns out, he must've been a decent salesman, because he got that good job. Before you know it, we moved into a house. It was small, and not on the cushy side of town, but it had a yard. He talked about getting Angel a little dog. Mom was so happy. It was just like we were a normal family." She ran a finger over a grease stain on the leg of her jeans. "He said he'd put me through

204

college. Wherever I wanted, he said." The downpour of words slowed. She could stop them, but found she didn't want to. They felt better, outside.

"Did they break up?" Deuce's gaze stayed focused on the road. She was grateful for that.

"I guess you could say that. He came home one day around ten months later, all sad. Only I could tell he wasn't, really. I mean he looked sad, but under that was all this excitement, wanting to burst out, you know? He told us he'd gotten this promotion. He was going to be a sales manager in the home office, in Chicago."

"Angel got all excited. We were going to move and then she'd get her puppy." Harlie snorted. "He looked at mom, all teary-eyed, and I knew. *We* weren't going anywhere."

"What?"

"Yeah, see, he was on his way up. On his way to being a big shot. Mom worked in a bar, and Angel and me, we didn't even have the same father. We wouldn't fit in, in Bigshitdom."

Deuce's neck was red, his eyes murderous. "He *said* that?"

"Of course not. He was a nice guy. He gave mom some bullshit excuse, and we were hustled out of that house in a week. He was really sorry, but had to be in Chicago see, and the lease was in his name."

Deuce muttered what had to be a filthy word under his breath.

"Maybe I never went to college, but I learn fast. I couldn't save mom from losers, but I could keep me and Angel safe. We never believed again. I taught her. See, the ones who are bad on the outside are easy. You see them coming. It's the ones who act all good who can hurt you the most." She looked out the window, wishing she could leave it at that.

But even if she looked like a 'poor me' loser, she had to say it. "You asked me last night what I was afraid of. That's it. You trust someone else with your dreams, you're handing them the knife to stab you with."

"Yeah, but Harlie, you gonna condemn the whole human

205

race because of a few assholes?"

"It's worked so far." She stared out the window, knowing she'd said too much.

Chapter 19

Four hours down the road, suburbs replaced mesquite and road signs replaced the oaks passing the Jeep's window.

Deuce pointed to the tall buildings in the distance. "Amarillo's coming up. I need to make a stop. Do you mind?"

Harlie raised her arms and stretched, feeling the vertebrae pop in her neck. "Are you kidding? I think the stitching on my pockets have tattooed my ass."

The word-storm, miles ago, had loosened her, as if the telling unwound something deep inside. Funny that, but even stranger, it seemed to have loosened Deuce as well. The careful tightness around his eyes relaxed, and his lips lost their taut line. She hadn't realized until now that he'd only looked like that around her.

She'd never considered how her 'rough edges' could rub other people. Never cared.

The Jeep slowed as Deuce took the exit.

"Where are we going?" She took her feet off the dash and stuffed them into her boots. "Do you think they'll have a bathroom?"

"There was a sign back there for . . . there it is." He turned right. "And I'm sure they'll have a bathroom." About a block down, he turned left into the parking lot of 'BootNation'. "I've got to get a bull-proof hat."

"What's wrong with using mine?"

He braked in a parking slot and rolled his eyes until they rested on her. "Because it's yours?"

"There's nothing wrong—"

"God, woman, will you stop?" He unbuckled his seat belt. "Your hat is great. I appreciate you letting me borrow it. But it's your only straw hat, and I'm going to return it. Okay?"

In his droll stare, she saw more rub marks her edges made. "Oh, yeah. Sure." She unsnapped her seatbelt, and felt between her feet for her phone and her wallet.

Not that she was going to buy anything.

When Deuce held the glass door, she stepped into cool air heady with the scent of new leather. "God, I love that smell, don't you?"

"It's right up there on my list. Only problem is, it makes me want to pull out my wallet."

"Has the same effect on me." She glanced around, and headed for the metal door marked 'Cowgirls'.

Deuce kept walking to where hats covered the back wall.

Once the most pressing matter was handled, she strolled, hands in pockets, ignoring price tags and dreaming.

Her phone rang. *Compadres Mental Health Center.*

Her pulse rate zipped up. "H-hello?"

"Ms. Cooper, please hold for Dr. Nguyen."

She put a finger in her other ear and paced the empty aisle. Waiting had never been easy for her, but lately, it was excruciating.

"Ms. Cooper? Dr. Nguyen here."

"Yes, doctor. Is Angel all right?"

"We are making progress. Your sister is beginning to participate in our one-on-one therapy sessions. This is encouraging."

"Can I come, now?"

"I'm afraid not."

"Why?" When a shopper on the next aisle's head snapped up, she lowered her voice.

"I am not at liberty to discuss details, Ms. Cooper. But I

can tell you that Angel's problem is not with you. You are tangentially involved, of course, because you are her guardian, but—"

"Tangentially? What does that even mean? Will you stop spouting doctor shit and *tell* me something?"

His heavy sigh did not sound patient. It reminded her that her Angel was in his hands. She made herself wait. And breathe. And wait.

"You are not your sister's problem. She loves you, and misses you. But she is consumed with trying to come to grips with her situation. Facing this is difficult for her. She's not able to deal with more than that right now."

"It was Mack, wasn't it?" God, if that bastard wasn't dead, she'd kill him. She hoped he suffered in that fire.

"That is all I can say. I'll talk to you again on . . ." She heard pages turning. Wednesday, around this time. Please, try not to worry. Your sister *is* making progress."

Muttering a not-altogether sincere apology for snapping at him, she hung up.

And paced the aisles, walking off some pissed. It wasn't his fault that Angel needed him, not her. But helplessness was her mother's thing—not her daughter's.

When her focus turned outward again, she found herself standing in front of a pair of boots. Not just any boots. *The* boots. Brick red, low heeled working boots with the traditional simple loop overstitching on the toe. But above the ankle, the stitching got intricate, swirling and branching to a flying bird pattern on the shin. They were perfect; all business below, pretty, above.

And they were *red.*

You can't afford them.

The yellow markdown sticker drew her eye. Sixty-nine dollars! She sucked in a breath. The price was better that she had any right to expect, and way more than she could afford.

But you have the money you saved for a Yolanda breakdown that you won't need any longer. And you're only paying half the cost of Deuce's gas.

But soon, she'd have the cost of a trip to California.

Hopefully soon.

I could eat less.

She stroked the toe with her finger.

I'll just try them on. They might not even fit.

Pulling a size six, she stepped to a bench and sat. Opening the box, the new boot smell wafted up and she stopped long enough to pull in the rarified perfume of New.

She pulled her old boots off. They were scuffed, creased, dusty and needed reheeling. Turning one upside down, she noted the almost hole where the ball of her foot rested. She dropped it, tucked her big toe back through the hole in her sock and pulled on the red boot. Her heel settled in a perfect-fit-sigh. So did the second. She stood, and walked to the end of the aisle, where a floor length mirror stood.

They looked good. Traditional, but the color was just the other side of normal.

Maybe there was something to this 'retail therapy' thing because she was happy, just looking at them. Jazzed wrestled with practical as she walked back to the bench. She'd been working since she was fifteen, and the few extravagances she'd bought had been for Angel. Not that she begrudged one bit of that.

But dammit, she deserved *something* for herself. Something that made her happy. Practical was on the mat, down for the count. Smiling, she dropped her old boots in the box, and sashayed to the checkout register.

She met Deuce on the way.

He let out a long whistle. "Pretty snazzy zapatos, Miss."

Grinning, Harlie mock-curtsied. "Why, thank you. You're looking pretty dapper yourself."

He tipped his new straw hat and when he held out a forearm to escort her, she took it.

***

The rodeo in Albuquerque was part of the New Mexico State Fair, the largest venue Harlie'd worked so far. A cush job too, since she and Deuce didn't need to help with the other events in the big, indoor arena.

210

The bulls were better too. Gear bag in one hand, she limped to the exit after the rodeo, her other hand supporting her bruised kidney.

Deuce trotted up. "Are you okay?"

"Nothing that aspirin and a hot shower won't help." She hoped, anyway. She'd probably be peeing blood for a couple of days, but saving the rider had made it worth a hooking.

"Damn, that was a great save. Shane was half out. He'd've been stomped for sure, if you hadn't shot the gap—even though there wasn't a gap." He slowed his steps to match hers. "We're lucky it happened on the last ride. No way you could've kept fighting."

"Oh, I could have. It'd just have hurt a lot." She lifted a corner of her mouth in what she hoped didn't look like a grimace.

Deuce held the door for her, and she stepped into the cool, high-desert night air.

"Give me that." Deuce grabbed the handle of her gear bag.

The pull jerked her back. She sucked air through her teeth and let go.

Shit, that hurt.

The Jeep was in the first row behind the barn, thank God. They'd gotten there early enough to cop a coveted spot under a safety light, so they wouldn't be groping in the dark for their stuff.

Deuce opened the back and tossed in their bags. "The guys want to buy us drinks over at the band stage later." He closed and locked the window, then walked to her, hand held up. "I know, you don't drink beer, but I'm sure they have soda."

"How do you do that?" She opened the back door and reached slowly for her towel and shower kit.

"Do what?" He stepped past her, opened the front door and rooted around, looking for his towel.

"We've been here less than eight hours, and you're fast friends with every cowboy in the damned rodeo." She tried not to groan when she straightened. "The only one I know is Bones Jones, and only because he bought me a hot dog, once."

211

He slammed the front door. "And you let him?" Shaking his head, he inserted the key and locked the door. "I'm shocked."

"Very funny." She closed the flimsy door gently, to not jostle her screaming back. "He wouldn't take no for an answer."

"Harlie." Deuce's stare was no less probing for its softness.

She sighed. "I feel a lecture coming on. Can you make it a short one? I really need that hot shower."

"I get why you feel the way you do. But it doesn't have to be that way." He locked her door. "Not everyone will let you down. And besides, you don't have to let everyone in all the way." He swept a hand, ushering her in the direction of the showers. "There's more than black and white in the world, you know."

"Not in the world I live in, there isn't."

"You just don't choose to see the gray. But it's there if you look, I promise you. Come tonight. I'll prove it to you." She felt his look slide over the side that faced him.

She raised her hand, a stop sign. "Don't start with the, 'The Coop I know always takes chances'. That only works once."

His teeth flashed in the security light. "You'll come?"

Lately, her old solitary ways seemed more lonesome than loner. And from the feel, her back wasn't going to be happy about lying down. "If it'll make you shut up, I guess I'll go. You nag worse'n an old woman."

His smile proved he saw through her grumpiness. "Cool. You'll have a good time."

A half hour later, feeling half human and half presentable, she walked out of the shower room to find Deuce waiting, towel over his shoulder. "Did you think I'd try to run off?"

"Nah. My partner is brave—faces down pissed off bulls."

She snorted. The aspirin were kicking in, holding the jackhammer in her kidney to a dull throb.

He walked beside her, head up. "Love the boots."

The corner of her mouth lifted. "Oh shutthehellup."

After dumping their shower stuff, they headed for the midway, which was rocking, from the sound. The crowd was

212

older after dark. Boots and Wranglers ruled; for the cowboys and their dates. The rides and the food booths all sported lines that snaked into the Midway traffic.

"God, what a zoo." Harlie let Deuce break trail, keeping one eye on his plaid shirt, and the other on anyone who would jostle her back.

"Hey, lighten up. This is what is commonly referred to as 'fun'."

"Where I come from, this is a mob."

The bass thump of an amplified drumbeat began as they neared the lights of the covered stage, increasing until she could feel the reverberations in her chest. The band swung into a Rockabilly song.

Deuce scanned the huge pod of picnic tables inside a fenced off area labeled, 'No Alcohol Past Here'. "I think I see them. Come on."

A beefy bouncer in a black cowboy hat blocked the entrance. "Hold up there. Need to see your I.D."

Deuce pulled his wallet, and flashed his license. The guy scanned it with his penlight, then nodded him in.

Harlie knew how a calf felt, cut off from the herd. "I'm not twenty-one, but I'm not drinking."

He pulled a hot pink plastic bracelet from his pocket. "Hold out your wrist."

She complied and he fastened it on, then waved her in.

Feeling sorted and branded, she followed Deuce through the crowd of couples and groups of buddies. The bracelet wasn't the only thing setting her apart. She felt as out of place as . . . a wallflower at a party. Why had she come? What did she think she'd find here?

The Kiwanis Club beer trailer was doing a bang-up business, its ropy line meandering along the fence. The yeasty smell of beer hung in the cool air, and the noise of dozens of conversations competed with the band.

"Deuce, Coop, over here." Bones Jones waved from a table near the fence, as far from the band as possible. "I saved you seats."

"You sit; I'll get us drinks. You want a diet, right?"

"Yeah." She reached for her wallet.

"I think I can handle the cost of a soda, Coop."

"Okay, but I'm paying you back."

He rolled his eyes, then set off.

Harlie recognized most of the bull riders who had commandeered one table for themselves. She lowered herself gingerly to the seat. "Nice ride today, Bones."

"I'm on a roll with the good draws. Tomorrow, I've got Deacon Blues."

"If you can make his first corner on him, you can be a ton of points." Cody Lindsay said from across the table. "I drew Zippity, and that's most likely gonna be my score."

"That SOB danced on me in Tucson last year." Rod LeBlanc said. "Trust me, you don't want to hang up on that one."

"You're hurtin' aren't you?" Bones said under his breath.

"Nah, I'm fine." She raised her voice. "Anyone hear how Shane is doing?"

"Sheeit. He's up there dancing with a local bunny. He's fine."

She rubbed her sore side. The aspirin were wearing off already. *Hoot was right. These guys bounce. I shatter.*

"Hey Cody, remember that trip to Eulah, Oklahoma?" Rod asked.

"I'm breathing, ain't I?"

"What happened?" Harlie shifted to her other hip.

Rod chuckled. "We left the Tucson rodeo as soon as we bucked off, and drove straight through to make it in time. My bull was in the alley when we pulled up, and I threw my rope to an old boy to put on 'im while I got in my spurs and chaps."

"And I'm up right after him." Cody said. "On the way to the chute, somebody tells me I drew Sid Vicious."

Harlie smiled. "Is that as bad as it sounds?"

Bones jumped in. "That sombitch would try and hook you even before you were in the chute. I knew a cowboy who got bit on the leg. Never knew a bull to do that before."

Cody scooted up on his seat, arm in the air to

214

demonstrate. "So I lower myself on that bull real gentle, snuck up on my rope and nod my head 'fore he can get pissed." Cody shook his head. "He blew out hard and took a turn into my hand. I let loose and spurred 'im with my right foot and I'm seein' dollar signs whiz by. But about five seconds in, he pulls a gear I didn't know he had, I blew out my left spur and 'afore I know it, I'm in the dirt, paddlin' like a turtle on my back, and that mother is bearing down on me like the 8:15 freight outta hell."

Rod said, "The bullfighters ran in, but 'ol Sid, he knew which one had been on his back. The second time that bull runs him over, Cody decides it might be a good idea for make for the fence, so he gets up about the time Sid comes back for another pass."

"Damned bull hooked me in the behind and threw me onto the fence, but not before ripping me outta my Wranglers."

"Might nota' been so bad, 'cept Cody here, he weren't wearin' no underwear."

Harlie put her hand over her mouth to cover her laugh.

Cody ducked his head. "I was so embarrassed it took me ten minutes to realize I broke my collarbone and two fingers, hitting the fence."

"How about that time in Casper, when . . ."

"Here you go." Deuce sat beside her and slid over her diet drink.

"Thanks." She put a knuckle to the small of her back, to ease the ache.

"You got pain pills?" Bones asked.

"Nah. I'm okay."

Bones shot a glance around, then pulled a metal flask from his pocket. "Here." He unscrewed the cap.

She shook her head.

"A swig'll just dull the pain."

This ache in her kidney was getting old. It wasn't enough to take her down, but too much to concentrate. Killing some pain sounded pretty good. She grabbed the flask and took a tentative swallow. Her eyes teared up and it burned on the way down, but she managed not to choke. When she could breathe again, she wheezed, "What *is* that?"

"Everclear 190." Bones took a pull. "Damn, that'll fix what ails 'ya."

Bob Farris yelled from down the table. "Hey, Bones, tell them about the time you lost your rope in Denver."

An hour later, Harlie stepped around crowded, shadowy tables, walking against the flow of traffic on the way to the bathroom. The Rockabilly band had been replaced by a tribute band, thumping out oldies and trying to imitate legends.

She hummed along with the singer's dismal attempt at Johnny Cash.

Deuce was right. This is kinda fun.

She didn't know if it was the company, or if the stars were in a once-in-a-century alignment, but tonight she'd slipped into the social waters with barely a ripple. Okay, so she just sat listening to the bull rider's stories, but for the first time in her memory, she actually felt a part of a group.

And it felt good.

A burly guy squeezed through the narrow aisle ahead, a tray of drinks in one hand, a tray of chips and queso in the other.

She turned sideways and pressed as close as she could to the crowded picnic table, smiling as the guy passed, repeating, 'Sorry, excuse me', every two steps.

Large hands bracketed her waist from behind, and pulled. She tumbled into a lap.

Her kidney bellowed. "Ouch. Goddamn it!"

Arms snaked around her and she turned to see and smell that she was nose to nose with a slack-jawed drunk.

"Weeell boys, lookie here what I got. Caught me a pretty cowgirl."

"You gonna share, Steve?" The equally bleary drunk across the picnic table eyed her like she was a steak dinner.

Beery halitosis washed over her, and she recoiled, pushing her hands against his chest. "Let go, asshole."

His arms tightened. "Aw, tha's no way to talk." He tried to pull her close enough to snuggle her neck. "I jess want a kiss."

Sitting crossways on his lap, she had no way to knee his

groin. His friends were obviously not going to help her. Options ricocheted through her brain. For the surprise factor, she chose the most dramatic. Taking one hand from his chest, she used it to rabbit punch him in the face.

It couldn't have hurt much—she couldn't get a wind-up. But his surprise, coupled with drunken reflexes, drove him back, and they fell backwards off the bench.

"Let me go, you sonofa*bitch*!" She thrashed, trying to get free.

Arms came around her and lifted. She fought them too, until she got a glimpse of Deuce's square jaw in the lights from the stage. Behind him, she saw Bones, and the other stony-faced bull riders, filling the aisle between tables.

Deuce set her on her feet. "What did he do?" A muscle jumped in his jaw.

"It's over. Let it go." Now that the danger had passed, she became aware of her kidney, singing high contralto, thrumming through her body. She bent, put a hand to her side and moaned.

"He was jest bein' friendly." His buddy stepped over the bench. "She punched him. That's just not ri—"

Deuce's fist stopped him, mid-word.

The table emptied, the bull riders waded in, and it was game on.

Chapter 20

Harlie woke to a sky of gray felt. From her prone position in the back seat, it looked as if someone had thrown a blanket over the mountains. She shifted her hips, testing her injury. A twinge, but nowhere near as bad as she'd expected.

Rustling from the front, then Deuce's face appeared over the seat. "How do you feel?" His left eye was a painful eggplant lump, swollen shut.

"Better than you look." Groaning, she struggled to a sitting position. "I cannot believe you guys got in a brawl last night."

"It was fun." His smile was incongruent with his split lip.

"And unnecessary."

A crease appeared between his brows. "You don't get it."

"I get that y'all went all caveman." She whisked her hair behind her ears, then reached back to pull out the scrunchie. "Any chance to save a damsel in distress, huh?" She raised a finger. "Which I do not cop to, I might add. Any day I can't take out a drunken—"

"It wasn't because you're a woman." The parts of his face that weren't purple, tinted red. "I mean, only partially. Mostly, it was because someone messed with one of us. And if you mess with one of us, you get us all."

Me? One of them? A warm spot opened in her chest.

218

Since when did people liking her, matter? She flashed him a gang sign she learned from her days in Santa Clarita. "Do we have a special handshake?"

He slapped on his new hat. "Cowboys on the rodeo road are more a family than a gang." He leaned over, unlocked the door, and slid out. "Gotta pee. Be right back."

She watched him walk the deserted space between the parking lot and the arena, comfort and confusion warring in her chest. Fitting in couldn't be as simple as the fight last night. No, thinking back, it had started earlier—the moment she'd slid onto the picnic bench.

And yet, nothing had been different last night than the zillions of other times she sat in a group, alone.

Except maybe her.

That bore thinking about. In the shower. She unzipped and dug through her duffel at her feet for a fresh change of clothes. They were going to have to hit a laundromat on the way to Wyoming. She was down to one pair of clean underwear. Pulling her thin towel from the roof brace where she'd hung it to dry, she eased out of the Jeep.

Her phone rang. She snatched it up from the seat. *Steve Rawlings.*

She clicked send. "Hey, Steve, what's up?"

"You are, Coop. I've been hearing good things from the rodeo committees."

"You have?" Already smiling, she trilled up in a 'tell me more' ending.

The door to the men's bathroom banged and Deuce walked toward her, one eyebrow raised in question. She gave him a thumbs up.

"They say y'all are on time, you work hard and put on a hell of a show. Having a woman bullfighter is putting butts in seats, and they couldn't be happier. Two of them called me special, just to tell me."

Joy rocketed up her core, firing a burst of pride in her chest and pulling her lips into a grin. "We're trying hard."

"You keep this up for another month, and we'll see what

219

the PBR thinks about a bullfighter team that includes a woman in the Touring Pro Division."

If she weren't worried about waking her kidney, she'd be bouncing around the parking lot like Tigger on crack.

All those days of worry on the road, feeling as if she hung on a cliff's edge, the weight of responsibility and her own fragility prying at her finger-hold, the cold breeze of failure on her bare butt cheeks. Sure, a bull could take her out in the arena today. But it wouldn't take away this. She'd done what she hadn't known she could do.

What no one thought a woman could do.

"You were right about McAllister. He was just the partner you needed."

Grinning, she glanced at Deuce. "Yeah, I guess he'll do."

Deuce stood, hands spread in the physical version of 'what?'

"He's right here, Steve. You tell him." She handed over the phone.

"Hello?" His face lit up as he listened. But then he frowned, shot a glance at her and walked away. Far enough away that she could hear the rumble of his voice, but not the words.

After a few minutes he hit a button, and with a lower wattage smile, walked back to hand her the phone.

"What was that about?"

"He just . . . uh, thanked me."

She slipped her phone into the pocket of her t-shirt, and threw her towel over her shoulder. "For what?"

He ducked into the Jeep and rummaged in his duffel for clean clothes. He mumbled something.

"What? I didn't hear you." Knowing Steve, she had an idea of what he'd said, but she wanted verification.

Deuce backed out, but his focus was on his duffel. "For keeping you . . . from using your spurs on people."

He was so painfully uncomfortable, she had to laugh.

His head jerked up.

"He's right. You are a good influence. And a good partner. I appreciate you, every day."

His brows came down as he considered, looking for a trap.

"Now get your stuff together. Because, trust me, Dude, you need a shower."

His mouth opened, then closed, as he were if chewing the words to help him understand them.

She picked up her shower stuff and walked away, her step light, attempting to whistle through a smile. She took a breath of the rarified air of accomplishment. It was like opening a window closed all winter, letting out the tired, stale air and taking in a fresh spring breeze.

Hanging with Deuce had given her a different perspective to consider. She liked the world she saw through his eyes. It was simpler, cleaner . . . lighter. Not that she was ready to abandon her view of the world. But it hadn't hurt her yet to consider his, had it?

The last performance was at noon. Harlie stood behind the chutes, stretching, and watching the towering flat-bottomed purple clouds scud overhead. The color guard galloped into the arena to cheers and fat raindrops. The audience was sheltered by the roof overhang, but not so the competitors. The rodeo queen's western satin shirt was stained with dark stripes by the time she galloped out and handed the stars and stripes to a waiting hand.

Distant thunder rumbled in the hills. The bulls milled in the pens, uneasy.

Bareback riding was first, which was a good thing. Horses spooked easier than bulls, so it was best to get their events over first. Because, from the looks, the weather wasn't due to improve.

Cody Lindsay leaned with one foot on the fence, a bruise from last night darkening his jaw. "Hope you like mud, Coop, because by the time bull riding comes around you're sure gonna be in it."

Fat drops pattered on her straw hat. "If this gets bad, they'll have to cancel."

"It'd have to come a real toad-strangler." Cody scanned the clouds. "They won't call it unless we're in the middle of a lightning storm." He pushed his hat down on his head. "Cowboyin' happens in every weather."

Maybe, but she didn't like the looks of that sky.

Deuce jogged by. "Come on, Coop. They need help setting up the team roping."

An hour later, Harlie swiped water out of her face and ran into the arena, waving to the crowd. The footing was loose as gooseshit. It'd be a soft landing for cowboys, but mud wouldn't be a good footing for the bulls, or the bullfighters.

Thunder boomed and a blast of wind hit, plastering Harlie's shorts to her legs. She slapped a hand to her hat as the rain let loose, increasing from a shower to a drumming downpour.

"Ladies and gentlemen, those funny looking people are your bullfighters. Harlie 'Coop' Cooper, and—Holy cripes, is that you, Deuce McAllister?"

Deuce swept off his hat and bowed, clicking on his mic on at the same time.

"You look like the hind legs of destruction, boy. Where'd you get that shiner?"

"Well, see, that's kind of a strange story. Maybe you can help me understand it."

"What happened?"

"After dinner last night, I was just sitting on the couch, watching a program, minding my own business, when my wife came in and asked me what was on the TV."

"Well, what'd you tell her?"

"Dust."

"Oh, man, Deuce, you never learn." The straight-man announcer chuckled. "Now, let's get on to the bull riding, before the bulls end up dogpaddlin'. In chute number one, we have our local cowboy, Cody Lindsay, up on Zippity."

They moved into position, Deuce on the latch side of the gate, her on the hinge side. She tipped her chin at the stock contractor, who smacked his fist to his palm, the sign that this was a mean bull.

Hoot's voice rang in her mind. *The mean ones are the*

*best. They're lookin' for a target, so it's easy to get their heads
up. It's the smart ones you have to watch for.*

She sent up a quick prayer for a pen full of dumb bulls.

Suddenly there was a lull in the storm. The air went still,
and the rain slacked off. Goosebumps raised on Harlie's arms
and she shivered, her body humming with energy that seemed to
come from the air itself.

She shifted her feet, feeling a slight sucking as her heels
came out of the mud. "Mean 'un, Partner. Watch him."

Deuce nodded, eyes on the gate man.

A hiss split the air, followed by a concussing crack. The
world lit in an unholy blue-white light, and a transformer in the
parking lot exploded in a shower of sparks.

Shit! Lightning!

The bull lost it. It reared in the chute, trying to climb out.
It looked like he was going to make it, too. The cowboys
scattered.

Hand tied to the bull, Cody dug his spurs in and hung on.

It happened in slow motion. The bull fell back into the
chute, slipped in the mud and went over backward.

The gateman ripped the gate open, but it was too late. The
bull landed with a squelching thud, on top of Cody.

The bull struggled to his feet. Deuce was right there,
smacking him on the nose, luring him out. The second the bull
cleared the chute, the gate man swung the gate closed.

Cody was safe. Harlie took off after the bull, who was
chasing down Deuce.

Deuce threw a fake, but the Zippity wasn't buying it. His
horn barely missed her partner's ribs.

Fucking bull wasn't just mean, he was smart, too.

There was a roar in her ears but whether from the crowd,
the wind, or thunder, she didn't know. The next time Deuce
turned back, she was there. Deuce spun one way, she turned the
other.

The bull chose her.

This was no time to be playing. She threw one fake and
ran for the fence. The mud shook under her feet. She didn't dare

223

look behind her, but she didn't need to; the bull was closing.

Deuce was atop the fence, his mouth open in a yell she couldn't hear. One step from the fence, her foot slipped. She reached and caught the top board as her feet went from under her. Biceps and stomach muscles straining, she pulled her knees up. Deuce grabbed her under the arms and lifted.

The bull veered off, but not before his horn grooved the boards where her legs had been a nanosecond before. Heart redlining, she struggled for a toe hold as Deuce hauled her up.

His job done, the bull ran through the out gate.

"Ladies and gentlemen," the announcer's voice boomed over the loudspeaker. "The remainder of the event has been cancelled due to the storm. Please proceed carefully to the exits, and y'all drive home safe now, y'hear?"

Deuce held her, patting her back until she got her breath and her heartbeat quieted to where she could hear the rain pounding the cemented area in front of the stands.

He backed up enough to look down into her face. "You okay?"

"Yeah, thanks to you." she panted. "You?"

"I'm fine. Let's go check on Cody."

They jumped from the fence onto the cement and headed for the chutes.

The ambulance was loading when they got there. Rain pounded on the cowboys who stood, hats in hands. A few knelt, one knee in the mud, praying.

Her stomach took a nosedive. *Oh, shit. It must be as bad as it looked.*

She snatched at the back of Rob's shirt. "How is he?"

He turned away and put his hat back on. "He was alert, but couldn't feel anything from the waist down. It doesn't look good."

The ambulance slid in the mud, but when the rear wheels caught, it slid to the exit,
hit the lights and the siren and pulled onto the highway.

"He's got a wife and a new baby at home," one of the cowboys said.

224

Bones reached in his pocket, pulled out bills, and dropped them into his hat. He handed it to the guy next to him, who pulled out his wallet, and added more bills.

You do not have the money for this.

More money fell into the hat.

Your first priority has to be Angel. What the hell had she been thinking, buying herself new boots?

When the hat came their way, Deuce dropped in two twenties. "This is from both of us."

She reached into the interior pocket of her shorts. "I've got it."

"No. You need your money for—"

She remembered Cody laughing, telling stories last night. Young, full of life. Now he may not walk again. "I said, I've got it, dammit." She growled and dropped in a twenty.

Dejected, dispirited and dirty, they trudged through the rain to the Jeep. When Deuce unlocked the doors, she reached for her things for a shower. God, it would feel good to get the mud off, and get dry. "I have to stop at a laundromat tomorrow. I am officially down to no clean underwear."

"TMI, Partner." Deuce snatched his rain jacket from the front seat and shrugged it on. "But so am I. What's the next stop? I can't keep them all straight."

"Gunnison, Colorado. One heck of a hike." Remembering her phone, she retrieved it from the seat. She'd plug it in to charge while she was in the shower. "Steve would have scheduled the rodeos closer, but he couldn't book them until he was sure I got my PRCA card, and by then, he had to take what was available."

Deuce wadded his towel, tucked it under his rain slicker, and closed the door. "That's okay. I like road trips." Water dripped from his straw hat.

"Speaking of that, you've got to let me drive on the way to—" Her phone rang in her hand, making her jump. *Angel!*

It was an 800 number she didn't recognize. "You go ahead. I'll take this and be right behind you."

Deuce jogged through the puddles to the bathroom.

She sat in the Jeep to get out of the rain. "Hello?"

A deep male voice asked, "Is this Harlie Cooper?"

"Who is this?" No way she was verifying her name to an unknown caller.

"This is Floyd. Of Floyd's Wreck and Tow? I got a '93 Caddy in the yard, plates registered to a . . .Harlequin Cooper. That you?"

Shit. In all the drama, she hadn't thought about Yolanda since she abandoned her in the Albuquerque parking lot. If he'd towed her, there was going to be a bill.

Her thumb was moving to 'end' when she thought better of it. If he tracked her through the plates, dodging this call wasn't going to make him go away.

"Hello? You there?"

"Yes," she sighed. *And the hits keep coming.*

"What you want me to do with this beater? Tow it to a mechanic?"

Yolanda was family. She, Angel and Yolanda had history. "Can you keep her for me?"

"Sure. That's ten bucks a day."

Screw sentimentality. She didn't have the funds for it. "Junk it."

"That's a disposal fee of two fifty."

"Two hundred fifty *dollars*?"

He chuckled. "Well, it ain't two bucks fifty."

A panicked hamster scrabbled around her guts, doing laps. She didn't want to know . . . "How much do I owe you, so far?"

"Well, let's see . . ."

She heard the rattle of an old-fashioned mechanical calculator.

"There's a hundred for the tow, and storage till today. That'll be," The calculator whirred. "Two hundred ten bucks."

She sucked in a breath as the hamster clawed, trying to get out. That left her fifty bucks to her name. And she'd owe Deuce for half the gas all the way to Wyoming. That didn't count little things like eating and washing clothes. Her salary would direct deposit next week, but the Compadres bill for Angel's care would take most of that. "I'm screwed."

She wished she had the money back she'd spent on those damned boots. Not to mention the twenty a too-soft emotion had made her drop into the hat.

No, not the twenty. Cody needs the money more than I do.

"I'll tell you what." Floyd said. "Cuz you're in a bind, I'll scrap the Caddy, and split the metal recycling fee with you. That'll bring the bill down to . . . let's say a hundred."

That still sucked, but at least she could breathe. "Oh, thank you." She got his information, promised to transfer the funds when the bank opened in the morning and hung up.

She'd just remembered the danger to seeing the world through Deuce's eyes.

He could fall back on the support of a loving family.

And she was still glass.

Chapter 21

Three weeks later:

Deuce checked both ways then pulled out of the Wyoming rodeo grounds. "You know, when you first called me to come on the road, I was happy to get out of Oklahoma. But I have to admit, that rodeo made me miss home."

Harlie laid her straw hat in the back seat and pulled on her baseball cap. "Ten Sleep is a pretty cool town. That rodeo was more like a big reunion, with the pickups backed up to the arena and everyone tailgating."

"And the parade through downtown? I think more citizens were in it than were watching."

"I liked the wild horse race best. Most of the teams were related." She shook her head. "That was a hell of a way to spend the Fourth."

"Sure was. Enough to make you homesick." He sighed. "Hey, Coop, we're only booked through Labor Day. *If* we get to go to the Challenger PBR division, they don't start up until the end of September. Wanna come home with me? I could to introduce you to the fam, and show you around Kinta."

"I appreciate that, but I'm hoping I'll be back in L.A. by then." She turned away from him, and the endless, useless loop of questions that ran through her mind. Dr. Nguyen was still cryptic when she called, saying they were making progress, and no, she couldn't visit.

"I hope you are too. But think about it, just in case . . ."

"Yeah. Thanks." She toed off her boots and rested her feet on the dash. She'd shared a broad-stroke picture of Angel's situation with Deuce. Only seemed fair, since he shared so much with her. Besides, they were partners. She'd trusted him not to pry for more details, and so far, he hadn't. "How far is it to Idaho?"

"About six hundred fifty miles. Why don't you get some sleep, and I'll wake you when it's your turn to drive?"

"Sounds like a plan." She pulled the brim of her hat down to block the sun's glare. "If y'all wouldn't have kept me up so late, drinking coffee and jawing around that campfire—"

"If I remember right, I was the one who reminded you it was getting late."

"Yeah, but you're the one who brought up the PBR scoring changes. Damn, I thought Brody would never shut up."

"You shut up. Go to sleep."

"Yessir." She crossed her arms over her chest and relaxed. The warm air swirling in the windows ruffled the pages of the rodeo magazine on the floorboard. She let the rush of the engine and the whine of the tires empty her mind. Within a few minutes, it all blended to a long hum.

She wasn't aware it was her phone's ring that woke her until she already held it to her ear. "Hello?"

"Harlie?"

Harlie thought she knew how much she missed her sister. She thought she knew how to go on without her. She thought she knew how lost felt.

But she didn't. She didn't realize it until she heard that voice, saying her name.

It slammed into her. All she hadn't let herself feel— couldn't afford to let herself feel—all this time. She heard a hitch in her own breath. She felt almost afraid, as if there was a ghost on the line.

That's when she knew, deep in her darkest places, that

she'd never really expected to hear that voice again. *"Angel."*

The world narrowed to a tunnel. An electronic corridor that suddenly seemed so fragile, so tenuous, that she cradled the phone gently in the cup of her hand, careful not to touch any buttons that could shatter the connection.

"Harlie." The sweet sound of her sister's sob sounded in her ear. "Can you c-come? Now?"

"Angel, are you all right? Angel? Angel!"

"Yes. No. I have to talk to you. Will you come?"

"I'm on my way. Do you hear me? I'm on my way, Littlest." When her muscles let go, she leaned over, chest on knees and whispered, "Just don't go away again. Don't leave before I get there. Promise me, Angel. I can't take it if you do. Please? Promise?"

"I don't know how to promise, Harlie." She sniffed. "What if I can't help it?"

"Just hold on. I'm coming. I *love* you Angel. You know that. Right?"

Another sob. "I love you too, Harlie."

Click.

She hugged her knees and rocked. Rocked on the outside, to calm the rocking inside as she soaked in the few words Angel had spoken. Not their meaning, but the timbre, the cadence, the essence of her sister that had come through the phone. They seeped down to the parched soil of her soul.

Angel was back. And she wanted her sister there. Nothing was going to keep Harlie away.

You have to get to Los Angeles. Now!

She jerked upright, her shoulder blades slamming the seat back. The Jeep was pulled to the side of the road, the engine off.

Deuce sat looking at her with a worried expression. "Your sister?"

"My sister." Numbers and logistics ticked through her brain. "I have to go. I have to get to an airport. I have to—"

"Here." He leaned over, pulled a white handkerchief from his back pocket, and handed it to her.

That's when she realized tears were dripping off her chin.

230

He cleared his throat. "Now, let's think a second. Have you got enough for airfare?"

Money. She mopped her face as the bottom of her stomach dropped away. No. Not near enough.

He must have seen her answer, because his chin went hard. "Okay then, we'll drive there."

"No way." Deuce was her partner, and the closest person to her outside of Angel, but this was family. *Besides . . .* "You have to be in Pocatello in two days. No way in hell you could get to L.A., then make the rodeo on time." An oily sheen of guilt leaked into the ocean of need to get to Angel. "Oh hell. What are you going to do without a partner in the arena?"

He reached across her, rummaged under her seat and pulled out a compact road atlas. "I'll look up the closest airport."

"Deuce, wait." She put a hand on his arm. "You won't go in the arena alone, will you? Promise me?"

"I only know one person dumb enough to do that." He looked up, one side of his lip curled. "This is a small rodeo. If they can't find anyone, the bull riders will step in. They take turns fighting in practice pens at home. They'll help me out." He looked back at the atlas, turning pages. "I can lend you money, but I don't have much. And the full cost of gas to get to Idaho will be on me—"

"Thanks, Partner, but I'm not taking your money." Her brain sorted and discarded solutions at supercomputer speed. "I'll call Steve. Get an advance."

He riffed to the back of the atlas. "Oh, good thinking."

She felt like she could run all the way to L.A. *I'm going to see Angel!* Her knees rebounded with the beat of her toes bouncing on the floorboards. Her body hummed with adrenaline. She opened the door and stepped out, thumbing up Steve's number. She started walking and hit 'send'.

I'll need enough for the plane fare, and a taxi. Hopefully they'll let me stay with Angel, because I can't afford a room, and I'll still need—

"Harlie. What's up?" He sounded stressed. And in a hurry.

"Hey, um, hi Steve. Can you float me an advance?"

"Harlie, this is the third time—"

"And I have to take some time off. I have some personal business that won't wait." She said it fast, hoping if she got it out fast, it wouldn't sound like a big deal.

"What? Wait. You'll have time off at the end of the season. You can't take time off now."

"You don't understand—"

"You're right I don't. A rustling, and she heard him speak away from the mouthpiece. "You go in; I have to take this." Then he was back. "Are you out of your mind?" Those rodeos are counting on a lady bullfighter. What could be more important than the career you swore to me you wanted?"

"I . . ." She tried to string words together to explain, but they weren't there. Because it would be telling. And nothing good ever came from telling. Harlie took care of things, not looked outside for help.

He'd judge. The social worker's pinched face appeared in her mind, mouthing, *mentally unfit.* The taunting kid, calling Angel crazy. And that would hurt worse than whatever was going to happen next. "I have something I've got to do." Even those vague words had to escape from between her clenched teeth.

"Jesus, I'm under the gun here. I've got bosses who've put out a bunch of money on my say so. You can't walk out now. Don't you want a shot at the PBR?"

Anger heated her body, burning from the inside out, like at shot of Bones' Everclear. "Of course I do. It's me out there risking my life every day, remember? But I've got something I *have* to take care of."

"Yeah, I know. Something you can't tell me about." His sigh was loud in her ear. "No, you know what? Don't tell me. It doesn't matter. It's always something with you."

"Hey, you said yourself that things were going well, and the contractors are happy—"

"Yeah, that was when you showed up and did your job. You get to that rodeo in Idaho, or you're out."

She pulled the phone from her ear and just stared at it. Out? As in *fired?* Well, she should have expected this. It was the way the world worked. But that didn't make it hurt less. Losing bullfighting would be like turning her back on the one shining thing in her life.

No, the second shining thing. First was Angel. Her shoulders dropped. "I *can't.*"

"Fine. I'll deposit your final pay now. Then we're done."

"Steve—"

But he'd already hung up.

A wind slap of panic hit. What the hell was she going to do now? The money from this job kept Angel safe.

And you love it.

She'd lose the health insurance that was helping to pay Angel's doctor bills.

And you'll go back to being a nobody. A powerless, faceless nobody.

The best job she could expect to get next came with part-time wages and a paper hat.

You'll never get to feel the thrill in the arena again.

The loss of her dream was a great open space inside her, a cold, empty cavern. She clamped down the muscles of her core, compressing the space to contain it, then turned and began the hike back. She'd let it matter later. Right now, Angel was counting on her.

The Jeep sat, sparkling in the sun, the circle of Deuce's yellow hair catching the light as he looked down, probably finding the directions to an airport.

What the hell was wrong with her? While she was having fun, living this dream world, her protective bubble had popped. She, of all people, knew better. You let people in, they let you down. The fact that Deuce was a nice guy only made him more dangerous. Because it would hurt a lot to lose him.

The world she saw through his eyes was friendly and amiable. And that wasn't reality—not for a hardscrabble mutt like Harlie Cooper, anyway.

If she told Deuce she was fired, he'd go all save-the-day

on her. He might even quit himself, to try to save her job. And she couldn't let her dream dying kill his, too.

So, lie. Hell, she'd stolen money, a car, and run from the law to keep her and Angel together. What's a little lie to keep Deuce safe?

It sounded simple, but it wouldn't be easy. In the weeks they'd travelled and fought bulls together, Deuce knew her moves as much as she knew his. He heard what she didn't say as well as what she did – and knew that they were sometimes opposites.

She hadn't known that would happen.

She'd have to dance at the edge of the truth. It would take a much better actress than Patrice to pull it off. But hell, she saved cowboys from two thousand pound bulls. She could do this.

Deuce was measuring distances with his finger on a map of Wyoming when she slipped into the passenger seat. "Did you get an advance?"

"Yeah."

"We're in luck. The Jackson Hole airport is only two hundred miles away."

"Two hundred miles? That's lucky?" She tried to relax her jaw, though he'd probably write off her tension to wanting to get to Angel. And God knows, that was part of it.

"Have you seen how huge and unpopulated this state is? As it is, Jackson Hole is probably a local airport for skiers. You'll have to take a puddle-jumper to a hub, most likely, Denver." Without looking up, he handed her his phone. "Here. I know you don't have data on yours. Look up what a ticket will cost, then call and book a seat. I've got to start putting on miles."

God, she was going to miss him. Next to bullfighting, having someone to share it all with was the best. Someone to argue with, joke with, share collective memories with. But that was the dream, not reality.

When she didn't move, he looked up. "What?"

It wouldn't hurt to tell him. To act for these last few hours, like the world was as he saw it. She'd be gone soon enough. "Have I told you how much it means to have you as a friend, Deuce McAllister?"

His smile was warm. "Ditto, Coop. Ditto." He turned the key in the ignition. "Now, don't distract me. I have a damsel in distress to save."

Damn, she was going to miss him.

***

The lights of L.A. spread like a bright blanket of stars beneath the plane, as if the world had flipped upside down.

It was hard to believe how much had happened since her first plane ride. Buckling into the vinyl seat brought the emotions back, full force. Her heart's wrench of loss at leaving Angel. The fear of what she'd find at her destination, and not measuring up. The weight of being alone, and solely responsible for whatever happened next. But still and always, the pull of the thrill – the prospect of facing danger, head on, and triumphing over it.

That had only been two months ago. Now she was feeling the mirror image of the emotions. Fear of what she'd find at her destination, and what Angel had to tell her. The wrench to her heart, leaving the rodeo, and her partner.

The danger this time was to her heart. And it wasn't thrilling.

It'll be okay. Angel is better. She'll keep improving, and won't need therapy. Money will go farther. I'll work my way up some job, and we'll get a place to live.

She wished Deuce was beside her, instead of the businessman with buffed nails and the perfect power tie. But this was hers alone to do.

Her metro-sexual seatmate pulled out a laptop and started typing. He had a job.

She felt the edges of the ragged hole in her life, where bullfighting used to be. In retrospect, she could see that it meant a lot more than money and thrills to her. The rodeo was the first place she'd ever really fit. The people accepted her for what and who she was.

Of course she'd be there for Angel. She'd always be there for Angel. But still, walking onto the plane was one of the hardest things she'd ever done. Her mind screamed, *No! Don't do it!*

She was afraid. More afraid than she'd ever been in the arena—hand shaking, gut churning, weak-kneed fear. Because she knew that whatever happened in L.A., it would change her life. And she was just starting to love her life.

Days Made of Glass

"Where there is ruin, there is hope for a treasure."

"Why do you stay in prison when the door is so wide open?"

Rumi

Chapter 22

Harlie paid the driver and stepped out of the airport shuttle. The tired façade of Compadres looked the same. The warm light spilling onto the sidewalk even looked welcoming. But her feet still didn't want to take the steps to the door.

Crystal, the nursing supervisor, was behind the desk. "Welcome back, Harlie. It's good to see you."

"Thanks." Was she being paranoid, or did Crystal's eyes flick away a moment too soon?

"Angel's been waiting up for you. Would you like me to unlock an office, so you two can be comfortable while you talk?" She looked kind. And concerned. "Bring you coffee, maybe?"

Formal politeness from Crystal, who'd always been friendly and jovial, convinced Harlie she wasn't paranoid in the least. "Thanks, Crystal, but we'll be fine." She gathered what courage she had and strode for the hall that would lead her, at last, to her sister.

The door was open. Harlie halted at the edge of the light, watching. She was so used to her on-the-road-memories of Angel as a little girl that her mind bumped against the sheet of glass reality; Angel was now a teenager. A young woman. Her rounded cheeks were gone, melted to longer planes and smooth skin. Though her mouth had lengthened, her lips retained their fullness. It was her eyes that changed the most. Rather than a little girl's awe, or a teen's anticipation, they held a woman's awareness. A woman much older than her sister's years.

Angel stepped around the room, straightening a pillow, smoothing the bedspread, sliding a paperback on the nightstand a few millimeters to the left. When there was no longer anything left to do, she clasped her hands in that familiar wringing motion Harlie remembered from the last time. Angel must have realized what she was doing, because she curled them into white-fingered fists, before relaxing and shaking out her hands.

Heart beating a timpani in her chest, Harlie stepped into the doorway. "Angel."

Angel turned, and her face lit up, then darkened. She ran the four steps, and her hug almost knocked Harlie off her feet. Angel leaned down, but Harlie still had to lift her chin to tuck her sister's head under it. She fit different, but even blind, Harlie would have recognized Angel's shape, her smell, her . . . spirit. The piece of Harlie that had been missing, clicked back into place.

They held on, shaking and silent, sheltered in the tiny space between the past and the future.

Before Harlie would have, Angel let go and stepped aside.

The book on the nightstand looked familiar. The bent, ragtag cover showed a young woman in a disheveled ruby velvet gown, reclining on ivory satin sheets. "You're reading Mom's romances?" She hadn't meant it to sound like a slam, but it came out that way.

Angel ran a finger over the cover. "Books are safer than real people."

Hard to argue with that.

"I know they're pretend, but while I'm reading, I can pretend too—that things do work out, sometimes."

"Things do work out, Angel." Harlie took her sister's chin, lifting it, so she could see her eyes. "Don't you remember? We're going to live in a big old country house, with animals, and laundry on the line, and we'll never eat mac 'n cheese from a box, ever again."

Angel twisted away, eyes on the floor, her hands twisting together in their obsessive dance. "Oh Harlie, how is that story any different than the ones in Mom's books?"

The words hit with a slap. *She doesn't know what she's saying.*

Harlie took her sister's hands. "Let's sit." She led the way to the window, where two cheap plastic chairs sat separated by a floor lamp. She lowered Angel in one, then pulled the other alongside, and sat. "I can't tell you . . ." When her voice wobbled, she paused until the clot of emotion passed. "God, I missed you, Littlest." Her hand bridged the gap to touch Angel's thigh. That helped. "Why did you have to go away in your head? Do you know?"

Angel sat quiet for a while. "When I was little, I knew that things didn't come just because you wanted them. You had only what you got. Not things. I don't mean things. I mean . . . joy, I guess." So I learned to be happy with what I had. And that worked, for a while."

She looked to the wall across the room, as if the words were printed there. "But then I went to school, and I realized it wasn't like that for everyone; having to wait to be happy. I was different."

"No you were not." Her voice slammed out of her, hard and brittle.

"Yes. I was. The kids knew it too. It's like I existed out of the corner of their eyes—like if they looked at me straight on, I'd infect them, and they'd be crazy too."

"Stop it. That's not true."

Angel shrugged. "You asked."

She had. If she was going to help, Harlie was going to have to bear listening. "I'm sorry. Go on."

"I kept trying with what I had left, and sometimes it worked. But then Mom died, and it was you and me. But the more time went on, the world felt more and more like a painting, flat and not real at all.

"Then the colors started to fade. It scared me. I tried to get the color back Harlie, but I got so tired. That day . . . in the

241

kitchen." She hitched a breath. "I thought that if I could bleed the color back into the world, maybe things would be okay again."

"God, Angel, why didn't you tell me? All that time . . . I could have done something. We could have—"

"If I'd have told, it would've proved I was crazy." The words were whispered, and her eyes darted away. "And I tried so hard not to be crazy."

"Angel, it was just—"

"And I was afraid. Nothing was ever real until I told you. What if, when I told you about the colors bleeding away, you saw it too?" She looked up, and the depth of lostness in Angel's eyes tore holes in Harlie. "I was afraid I'd take you down with me."

"Aw, Angel . . ." Nothing else would squeeze through the bottleneck in her throat, but that didn't matter. Words hadn't been invented for a situation like this, anyway. Reaching over, she pulled her sister into her lap. She came willingly, curling like an ungainly baby around Harlie's body.

She wrapped her up, and lips to her temple, rocked her as heartbreak fell out of Angel to wet Harlie's shirt.

Later, in bed, the sightless dark made words easier. They lay under the covers, connected by their entwined fingers.

"I've been talking to Doctor Nguyen, but it's hard." Angel's words faded to a whisper. "It feels like *telling*."

Another hole opened in Harlie. In trying to keep them safe, had she encouraged Angel to bottle up her fears? Her fingers tingled. There was something in there. Something she needed to consider. Later. "You don't have to worry about that any more, Angel. You tell." She squeezed her sister's hand. "You hear me? You tell him everything. From now on, you tell."

"I don't know if I can, Harlie. I'm scared, and my teller is rusty."

She put an arm over Angel's chest. "You don't have to be afraid, Angel. I'm here, and I won't let anything bad happen to you."

"I know I hurt you when I said for you not to come. I'm sorry. I just—"

"We'll talk later. You rest now." Angel rolled onto her side, and Harlie did too. She stroked her sister's hair, like she always did, to relax Angel to sleep. "I'm here."

But Harlie lay awake a long time, sorting through the broken glass of the past.

Chapter 23

Coming awake to a ceiling rather than the Jeep's canvas top, Harlie was jolted to a present that felt a lot like her past. How could her life have changed so much in less than twenty-four hours? Yesterday, crazed to get to Angel, she hadn't had much time to consider what she was leaving. She pressed a hand to her chest, trying to compress the hollow place where the rodeo used to be. Pieces of what she'd lost were like bits of space junk in there, careening into the walls, leaving dents, making more holes.

Watching that world recede, she could see more clearly what it meant to her. And it turned out to be about a lot more than the money.

Bullfighting had changed her. In all that hard work, she'd proved something to herself. She may not have a degree, but she was smart. She didn't have the strength of a man, but she could do a man's job. She was a loner, but . . .

God, she missed Deuce. And the people she'd met on the road. She hadn't understood how having friends could lighten your burden, even if you didn't lean on them. Just knowing someone was there who cared, and would step in if you called— that was enough.

Not that she'd let herself call.

But it was even more than that. With distance, she could see how the connections between cowboys were like woven threads, creating a community unto itself. Cowboys helped their own. In little ways, like lending gear, or giving a ride to a stranger, or wading into a fight. In big ways, like chipping in to help the family of an injured rider buy groceries.

In spite of herself, and mostly thanks to Deuce, she'd been a thread in that community. And though it felt strange to admit, she was proud of her place.

What used to be her place.

Well, deal. L.A. is your place now.

For the first time in her life, she'd had something that had been hers, alone.

Was that what she'd felt the night of the bonfire? Jealousy for kids who were free to have their own lives? Smaller responsibilities? Was she that small a person? Maybe she was, because right now, she'd give anything to be staring up at the inside of that ratty Jeep's roof.

Angel's face looked younger in sleep, innocent, as if ugly reality couldn't penetrate her dream world.

A poignant tenderness filled Harlie, so pure and deep that it ached. She blinked back the emotion. Angel needed her now more than ever.

How could she love her sister so much, yet still mourn not having her own life?

Angel's wasn't the only shattered life. Harlie's had broken in two, and now the pieces could never fit back together. She was going to have to pick up this piece, and learn to go on without the other.

Highlights of her rodeo memories ran through her mind as she lay, tracing the design on the inside of her forearm.

"You got a tattoo!" Angel's sleepy eyes were open, watching her.

"Yeah." She stared at the ceiling, not wanting to tell, but knowing she had to. "Angel, I'm so sorry. Your glass box got broken."

"Oh." She made the two letters sound sad. "I thought they kept it from me, because it's glass."

"I shouldn't have taken it." She rushed on, to get it out. "But I saw it right before I left, and grabbed it, thinking it would be something of you to have with me. I took it, and now it's gone. I'm so sorry."

"That's okay, Harlie. I'm glad you had it, if it made you feel better." She reached out to trace the yin-yang. "This looks like my scar."

"I got it in the same place on purpose."

Angel withdrew her hand. "I don't know if that's a good thing, Harlie."

"I was at bullfighting school, and missing you, and the box had just gotten broken . . ." There was no way to explain the jumbled emotions she'd felt that day. But this was Angel, so she probably didn't have to. "All the guys got tats."

"You were the only girl there?"

"Yep."

"I missed a bunch." Angel pulled the covers up and snuggled in, hand under her cheek. "Tell me a Harlie story."

This was so the old Angel that Harlie had to chuckle. They used to do this all the time as kids. She snuggled in too. "The school was in Chilly, Texas, on the ranch of a legendary bullfighter, Hoot Leonard."

"Oh you're making that name up."

She mock-glared at her giggling sister. "Hey, do you want to hear the story, or not?"

"Okay, okay." She squirmed under the sheets, settling in. "This is going to be a good one. Tell me."

***

When Harlie first heard Angel's voice on the phone, she'd assumed that Angel was, if not cured, at least well on the road to it. They could start planning their future.

Proving once more, that Harlie Cooper was an Olympic reality-dodger.

She stood outside Doctor Nguyen's door, trying to make herself knock. She raised her hand, then hesitated, wanting to remain ignorant a while longer.

If they wanted to keep Angel much longer, Harlie had big problems. No job meant no money. And no medical insurance. But she sure wasn't telling anyone that. She rolled her shoulders. Not until she had to.

If Littlest is brave enough to face this, you've got to be.

She let her knuckles fall.

"Come in."

Nothing good ever came out of this room. She forced her courage forward with her feet, and sat on the sunny slice of the couch. The doctor sat in the high-backed chair, like a king on his throne. Or maybe that was just her attitude.

"Ms. Cooper. It's good to see you once again."

After the crap she'd given him when he forbade her to come, she doubted that. The diplomas on the wall opposite looked down their glossy noses at her, judging. Realizing the staccato sound she heard was her boot tapping on the polished wood floor, she made it stop. She didn't bother telling him it was good seeing him—he'd told her last time she was a bad liar. "When do you think Angel can be released?"

He looked down. "I think you should be prepared to temper your expectations." Opening the much-bigger-than-last-time file in his lap, he adjusted his reading glasses. "The definition of dysthymia is chronic depression. By chronic, I mean—"

"I know what chronic means, Doctor."

He looked over his glasses. "You are your sister's guardian. It is important that you understand her long-term treatment plan. I'm not judging your knowledge, or lack thereof. I'm not going to make any assumptions." His gaze pierced her skin, probing beneath. "This is too important."

She held her squirm inside. "Okay. I'm listening."

He put on his glasses and referred back to the bible in his lap. "As I told you on the phone, due to your sister's earlier than early-onset, her long-term prognosis is difficult to assess. Especially since we are only in the—"

"Just tell me." God, didn't he know this was torture?

247

"Your sister will need institutional support for the long-term, possibly for the rest of her life."

"For the rest . . ." There was no air for more words. It had whooshed out with the gut punch.

"That's not as bad as it sounds. I do believe that, given time, she may advance to a
Community living facility. A halfway house, so to speak."

Harlie's balloon of hope lay wrinkled on the floor. She focused on breathing.

"Communal living environments are very supportive. Patients do very well there."

Turning her sister over to someone else's care was the hardest thing Harlie had ever done. Now he was saying they weren't giving her back? Ever? That was unacceptable. "Whose fault is this . . . dysthymia? What the hell caused it?"

"It's impossible to say, but there are risk factors." He crossed his legs and sat back. "First is having a close relative with dysthymia, or major depression."

"Mom wasn't like that."

His eyebrow raised. "Her father, then?"

Shit, who knew? All Harlie remembered of Angel's father was his tats, and his angry hands.

"The second is stressors, such as loss of a loved one, or financial problems."

"I believe we've got those covered." She looked away. Little did he know.

"Last is low self-esteem, coupled with an interpersonal dependency, where the person relies excessively on approval and reassurance from others."

"But Doctor, you said yourself that you couldn't predict what would happen. Angel could improve. This has just been a really bad patch for her, but she's going to work really hard. She told me. She . . ."

A head cock told her he was seeing behind her words. Seeing too much.

Goddamn it, they weren't just two more bugs to put under his microscope. "You don't understand. We have a life. We have *plans*."

"Ms. Cooper, I know this is hard for you to accept, but those plans are *your* reality. They're not Angel's." He took off his glasses and rubbed the bridge of his nose. His eyes looked kinder without them. More human. "She has been trying for years to keep her mental problems from you. Trying to live up to your expectations." He put his hands out, palms up. "That's what led to her suicide attempt."

Harlie snapped straight so fast her spine popped. Hearing him say that ugly word out loud was a firecracker compared to his hand grenade implication. "Are you saying this is *my* fault?"

"No, of course not. I'm trying to get you to understand. Angel's trying to be who you want her to be. But she can only be who she is. The only way you can help her is to accept her for who she is. *Whatever* that is."

In spite of her taut muscles, the truth hit its target. She flinched as the grenade's shrapnel ripped through her guts. "You're giving up on Angel, aren't you? Maybe I need to take her somewhere else for treatment." It was a hollow threat, since she had no money for this care, much less somewhere better.

"You're welcome to do so, of course." He put his glasses back on. "But I suggest that first, you talk to your sister. Let her tell you what she's feeling. Open yourself to her point of view."

The shrapnel hit the ammo bunker of her temper. "I don't listen to my sister, is that what you're trying to say? What do you think, that I drag her the way *I* want to go, kicking and screaming?" She was on her feet, all her blood pounding into her head. "I've only wanted what was best for Angel. Always and first. That you'd insinuate—"

"Ms. Cooper. Harlie. You need to calm down." He pushed himself out of his cushy chair. "Angel will see your distress as her fault."

"Oh, I can't do this anymore." Her voice cracked like a calving iceberg. "No more. I can't take one. More. Thing." She strode for the door, ripped it open and fled, before he saw that weakness filled her eyes.

Thoughts whirring, she hustled down the hallway, and pushed out the front doors. Sultry sunshine, L.A. smog and a whiff of garbage dumpster greeted her. The sun was warm on her thighs below the hem of her shorts. She squinted, wanting her ball cap, but that was in Angel's room.

You have to talk to Angel.

That doctor may not know Freud from Foxworthy, but he was right about one thing; she had to calm down first. She palmed her eyes, and started walking.

Dammit, she may only have a GED, but she knew her sister better than anyone.

But do you?

Had she put more pressure on Angel than she could handle? As much as she wanted to shy away from that blind dark alley, she knew she had to at least look down it.

Their bedroom at the dairy had been on the sunny side of the house. When Harlie got done milking in the morning, she'd wake Angel up for school. Angel had never been a happy-waker. Harlie would tickle, coax and jolly Angel out of bed. Sometimes it even worked. But more often, it hadn't. Was that only the earliest symptom of this . . . thing that had taken her sister?

She stepped around an exploded fast food bag of trash.

What was she supposed to do, let Angel lie in bed all day, feeling sorry for herself? Yeah, she pushed, but Angel had to work too, if they were going to get out of that damned place and on their own, where they'd be safe.

Yeah, right.

In light of what happened, she'd hardly kept Angel safe. Acid sloshed in her empty stomach. Guilt was a poor breakfast.

Give it up. You can't change the past anyway.

She took a hopping step, then, balancing on one foot, pulled off her boot and dumped out what felt like a piece of glass, but turned out to be a chunk of quartz. A car honked, and kids yelled out the window something about her ass, then sped off.

"Little assholes," she grumbled, and stepping into her boot, trudged on.

She watched as cars whizzed by, tires humming, going somewhere. A battered Jeep chugged after them. Green, not brown.

Wonder what Deuce is doing right now?

Wednesday. He was probably on the road to . . . Phoenix. Homesickness for the road washed over her. That life was over. She had a much more pressing issue than the past to think about. Money.

Doesn't help wanting.

The smell of fresh donuts wafted over her, waking her stomach with a snarl. She was passing a dingy strip mall with a ten-foot donut with stucco sprinkles perched on the roof. Her hunger guided her feet to the door. She stepped in to the chill of air conditioning and the smell of spent grease. The morning rush had taken its toll—the floor was dingy, the tables didn't look clean, but the glass case displayed colorful fat pills, so it was good as far as Harlie was concerned. Checking out prices, she stepped up. She wanted a bear claw. But if she got a plain donut, she could get a small coffee too. Her caffeine-jones won out. She counted change into the cashier's hand, then took her little paper bag and cup to a table overlooking the parking lot.

The last diner had left the morning paper. She found the want ads and spread the pages on the table to read while she ate. Her phone buzzed in her back pocket. She pulled it out. It was Deuce. Again. She let it go to voice mail. Again.

I'll call him when I figure all this out, and have something to tell. And when she could listen to his adventures without it hurting quite so much.

Earn thousands working from home on your computer!

Yeah, probably. Even if she wanted to be a spammer, the job would require a computer. And a home.

She scanned through the columns. Retail clerks, fast food, grocery checkers and baggers. Even the ones that were full time didn't have medical benefits. Or wages that would pay enough for an apartment in this neighborhood, much less food.

There were better jobs. Just not ones she had the skills for.

But she had yet one more problem. No transportation. Even if she found a good job, unless it was close to Compadres, she had no way of commuting.

She abandoned the paper to stare out the window.

She was a problem-solver, and a hard worker. With time, she could surmount one or two of these barriers. But all of them, all at once?

This is impossible.

She couldn't go back. She didn't see a way forward. And the ground between the two was crumbling beneath her feet.

Chapter 24

When there's only one thing left that you can do, you have to do that thing.

Given her truckload of troubles, calm was beyond Harlie, but she was at least composed when she walked into Angel's room. Pulling the stopper from the bottom of the door, she let it fall closed.

Angel sat in the plastic chair by the window, reading.

"Dr. Nguyen thinks we need to talk." Harlie managed to say it without sarcasm. Well, almost.

Angel put down her book, but didn't look up. "Yeah?"

They talked about this. Harlie's heart fell and she let her body follow, dropping into the other chair. She wanted to rip into his words—to argue them into so many pieces they'd be carried away on the breeze from the open window. But she couldn't. Because that would make him right.

And from Angel's hunched shoulders and troubled frown, she had something to say. Something she didn't think Harlie would like. She sat like a guilty puppy, waiting for the rolled newspaper to descend. Harlie recognized the familiarity in that posture.

A tender ache bloomed in Harlie's chest, melting her hard attitude. How could she want to be right, when Littlest was hurting? She reached over and took her sister's hand. "The doctor says that I need to listen. And you need practice in telling. So practice on me. Tell me Angel. Tell me everything."

253

Angel sat silent for a space of time. Her sigh deflated her further, bowing her shoulders. "It's my fault."

"What's your fault? Nothing's your fault, Angel. You just . . ."

"Can you just listen?" Angel didn't look up, but took her hand back. "I don't think I can say this if you talk."

She's right. You're doing what you always do. "Sorry. Go on."

"You always wanted to know whose fault it is that I'm the way I am. Mom, Mack, whatever. I never was brave enough to say it before. But there's no one to blame but me."

"Oh now, that's just bullshit." The words escaped from behind her lip-bitten barrier.

"It's not. And you know it." Angel looked up, eyes wild. "I'm crazy, Harlie!" It was a wail, a haunted echo down an insane asylum's hall.

As she did in the arena when a bull charged, Harlie made herself hold. But she couldn't hold back the negation in her shaking head.

"You knew it. Back in third grade. When you beat that kid up. You did it to keep him from telling. From telling the truth."

Harlie put her fingers to her mouth. "Oh, Angel." How had her little pixie been able to hold this in, all these years? "Baby, I beat him up for hurting you, and spreading lies."

For the first time, Angel looked into her sister's eyes. "But he wasn't lying, was he, Harlie?" She spread her hands. "I know you don't want to admit it, but look around. Is this where normal people live?"

Harlie couldn't spin away fast enough—awareness hit like a horn to the gut. Angel had taken Harlie's protectiveness, not as love, but as proof of madness.

She claimed that she and Angel were two parts of a whole. How could she not have known something this . . . huge? The answer popped, as if her brain had been waiting for her to ask the question.

Because that's what you do.

Harlie Cooper decided the way the world worked, then marched off to fight the world and right wrongs. Instead, she should have been listening—really noticing how *Angel* saw the world. Looking back now, she saw the signs. Angel's low self-esteem. Her black, silent moods. Her words, that day in the kitchen, when she almost died.

I had to let it out.

Harlie closed her eyes, to try once more to not see, but found the truth blazed in neon on the backs of her eyelids. Angel had been asking for help. It was there, if only her sister had the courage to see.

The stuff everyone else thought hard and scary, those were easy for her. The squishy emotional stuff? She ran from that, every time.

Everyone thought she was so brave. Truth was, deep down, Harlie Cooper was a coward.

Shame burned worse than guilt. "Angel, the glass . . ."

"I tried so hard to be brave, Harlie. To be the Angel you saw in your head, because I knew that was the Angel you loved. So I tried." The words came out wobbly with pain. "I tried so hard. Then I'd look in the mirror, and see that I was only pretending. I couldn't stand it, seeing that crazy girl."

Harlie sat stunned. "Angel, I never wanted you to be anyone but who you are."

Her head was shaking, even before Harlie finished. "No, you loved that other Angel. You wanted so bad for me to be like everybody else. Remember my science project? When I stunk up the gym? I saw how you whispered to the principal, and my teacher." She tucked her chin. "I saw how you looked at me out of the corner of your eye. Like everybody else did."

I couldn't have. I didn't. She thought back to that night. The principal had wanted to take Angel out of class. They'd suggested a special school . . . God, had she? What if she'd have accepted help back then? Would Angel have been spared all the agony?

But no, Harlie had decided; they didn't need help.

Regret squirmed in her chest, squeezing her heart. But that wasn't the worst part. The worst part was that Angel believed her sister's love was conditional.

And it wasn't. It never had been.

How could she have been so sure, and so blind at the same time? She felt around inside, but everything she knew was in ruins, as if destroyed by a massive earthquake. All the landmarks were gone.

If you can't trust your own view of the world, what can you trust?

"What're you thinking, Harlie?" Angel's voice was a timid mouse in the dark.

She swiped at her eyes. "I think that we're both broken, Littlest."

"Not you, Harlie. I always wanted to be like you."

The surprise came out in a snort. "Oh, Angel, you do not want to be like me."

"You don't see yourself clear, Harlie. You always know what's next to do."

"But I don't!" Angel's hand-squeeze stopped her from going on.

"I didn't say you always know the answer, or that you're always right. But you're not afraid to take the next step. Even if it means you're going the wrong way, and you'll have to back up later. You're still brave enough to move."

"I'm just starting to see that I don't know anything, Angel." Her energy had leaked out with the guilt. She was utterly, bone-deep tired. "I'm sorry, so sorry for it all, Angel. But there's one thing you need to know. And it's the most important thing. Are you listening?" She lifted her sister's chin to catch her eye. "There is nothing you could do that would make me stop loving you. You could murder people. You could steal. You could run naked down the street."

The last brought a small smile. "I'm crazy, Harlie, but not that crazy. Mom would come up from her grave and kill me."

"You don't have to be anything but Angel for me to love you. Okay?"

"Okay." Angel's face relaxed into another look Harlie recognized. Her big-sister-hero-worship look. Angel would follow her sister anywhere—for as long as she was able. She'd already proved that. But for the first time, Harlie saw through the look, to where it led, for both of them.

She never realized that she depended on Angel's following. That she leaned on that trust, and belief to shore herself up when she was afraid, or lost faith in herself. Insight broke over her, clear as the view through a magnifying glass.

A weak leader needs the follower at least as much as the follower needs a leader.

They'd been running this treadmill forever. Angel had gotten so tired, she fell off. And still, Harlie kept running, faster and faster, never realizing she had a choice. But a treadmill didn't actually take you anywhere, did it?

Fuck it. Today, I'm stepping off.

It was okay if she didn't have all the answers.

She didn't know what would happen now. But it didn't matter, because she'd used up all the answers she had inside herself. Maybe if she listened, she'd hear the answer from somewhere outside herself.

She saw the love in her sister's face. She still loved and trusted Harlie, even after all this. Angel didn't belong to Harlie. She belonged to herself.

"How about if we make a deal, Angel? From now on, if we want to, we're going to tell. We're going to be brave enough to ask for help, when we can't do it alone. Okay?"

"You're already brave, Harlie. You would never have done what I did."

"I made my own mistakes, Angel. I should have asked for help. I should have told, way earlier. I was dumb, and I'm so sorry for that." She put on a hopeful face. For both their benefits. "Besides, Angel, you are brave. You came back from that place you went to hide. And now you're going to deal with this. That takes more courage than anything I've done."

Angel tipped her head, and the pixie was back in her small smile. "I'm not brave, Harlie. I had to come back. I heard you calling me."

***

Harlie and Angel sat in the cafeteria the next day, drinking coffee.

Smiling, Harlie shook her head. "So I'm on the ground, and all the bull riders wade in, fists flying. You should have seen Deuce's shiner."

Angel leaned in, like she used to, hearing stories about movie stars. "So, are you sweet on Deuce?"

"What? No. He's a friend." The word may sound funny, but it felt good on her lips. "A good friend." She glanced to the clock on the wall. He'd be in Phoenix now, probably hanging with the bull riders, telling lies, waiting for the performance tonight.

"Why do you like the danger, Harlie?"

"With this hard head? There's not much danger." For the first time, that didn't feel right. She owed her sister more than the usual flippant answer. Squinching up her eyes, she thought about what it felt like; that thrill. "It's kinda like standing at the top of a really high place. Most people are afraid they'll fall. I'm afraid I'll throw myself off." She shook her head. "Man, that sounds stupid, but it's something like that."

Angel swept a few crumbs off the table. "When are you going back to the rodeo?"

"I'm not." Inside, she cringed, remembering the ignored voice mails from Deuce on her phone.

Angel's head whipped up. "What? Why not?"

She couldn't tell Angel about getting fired. She'd think it was one more thing that was her fault. "I'm getting a job close by, so I can be near you."

"Oh no, Harlie, you can't." Angel's eyes were huge.

"Why the heck not?"

"Because you love the rodeo. You don't see what you look like when you talk about it. It's like there's a light behind

258

the skin of your face, and it shines through your eyes. I want you to have that, Harlie."

"We'll see what comes down the road, Angel. But for now, you've got a session." She pushed herself to her feet. "I'll see you later, punk." She walked out and headed down the hall for the front door, her flip flops slapping the tile.

Today she felt different—as if the vows she made yesterday had firmed like cement in the sun. She was done pushing, trying to figure out the answers to everything. For a change, she was going to keep her eyes and ears open, and let the answers to come to her.

She'd snag a paper to see what the want ads had to say today. She rounded the corner to the lobby.

A filthy brown Jeep sat parked at the front doors.

Her heart banged, once, twice, on her ribs as a thrill shot through her.

Nah. There's tons of old Jeeps on the road.

But at the reception desk, a familiar set of broad shoulders. Deuce stood, back to her, talking to Crystal.

New cowboy hat in hand, he wore a plaid shirt, his good pair of Wranglers and his dusty cowboy boots. Seeing his cowboy uniform made her realize how much she missed hers. It was like that kid had said – she was from the land of misfit toys; and *that* was where she fit.

But it was more than the clothes that loosened her guard - it was the guy inside them. Her friend. Happiness rose in her like a dancing Las Vegas fountain and broke over her in a huge smile.

She took two steps before the fountain shut down, mid-spray.

Why is he here? How did he know where I am?

She had part of the answer when he turned.

His light brows gathered over the clouds in his eyes. His jaw was so tight she could see a muscle tic close to his ear, and the cords stood out on his reddening neck.

He was pissed.

He strode over, grabbed her upper arm, and kept walking, half dragging her to the door.

"Deuce, what the—"

"Come with me."

Crystal picked up the phone. "Harlie, do you need me to call security?"

"It's all good." She hoped it was, anyway. She waved Crystal off with her free arm as Deuce hit the metal bar on the glass door and flung it open.

She twisted her arm out of his grip and walked into the slanting sunshine. Guilt squirm or no, he wasn't going to intimidate *her*. Stopping at the Jeep's grill, she turned and dropped her butt against it. "What is your problem, McAllister?"

"*My* problem?" The red spread to his face and pooled, getting darker. "You can't answer one freakin' phone call?" He paced, taking a few laps back and forth in front of the Jeep, his jaw working. "A week and five voice mails, and I still hadn't heard from you. So I call Rawlings to see if he knows anything." He stopped in front of her. "Imagine my surprise when he told me that you quit!" His head-cocked squint said he thought she should be a patient here. "*You* quit bullfighting?"

"Depends on how you look at it. How did you find me?"

"Really? That's what you want to know?" He shook his head. "I was there when you gave the shuttle service the address, remember?"

"Oh. Yeah." His steady glare was starting to burn through her. "Aren't you supposed to be on your way to Arizona?"

"Quit trying to change the goddamn subject. Why didn't you call me?" He stuffed his fists in his back pockets and looked to the smoggy sky, as if praying for the patience not to strangle her.

Guilt spread like a grease stain on a white wall. She slapped a trowel of indignation over it. The best part of her defense had always been her offense. "I didn't have a choice. You know I had to get back here, and Rawlings told me that if I didn't make Idaho, I was done."

"Oh, that's bullshit. If you don't want to be a bullfighter, fine. If you don't want to be friends, fine." He poked an accusing finger that stopped just short of her face. "But don't you lie to me, Cooper."

She'd never seen him mad before. Even wading into the brawl at the rodeo, he'd been smiling.

She met his eyes and made herself hold. "I didn't know how to tell you."

"I knew you needed time with your sister. I didn't want to make you feel bad about leaving me alone on the road. I even felt bad about calling, knowing it'd remind you of all the bullfighting you were missing." He tipped his hat back and the look he gave her pierced her. Then tugged. "Rawlings asked me what your 'personal business' was."

She felt caught, like a fish on a hook. "Did you tell him?"

"Of course not. If you didn't see fit to, he sure wasn't hearing it from me."

Proof that he still had her back made the hook dig deeper. "I had to get back to Angel. He gave me an ultimatum. What was I supposed to do?"

He didn't move. Didn't blink.

The fuse on her temper sparked. Anger felt better than guilt. It wasn't like manning a french fry basket or cleaning toilets were her first career choice. "Where the hell do you get off, McAllister?" She crossed her arms over her chest and fought the hook. "If one of your sisters needed you at home, are you telling me you wouldn't have done the same?"

"Of course I would. But I'd have taken care of business first. I'd have told Rawlings what was going on. If you'd explained, he would have understood. Even I know that, and I've talked to the dude exactly twice." He looked down on her like she was a bull patty pile he'd stepped in. "I never knew you to be a coward, Coop."

Little does he know. So much easier to just bite the line in two, and swim away. The hook would fall out eventually, and she'd be left with just a scar. And what the hell was one more?

"Let it go, McAllister. It's none of your business."

261

"None of my business?" Even his squint looked disbelieving. "Goddamn it, all I've ever tried to do is be a friend."

"I never asked you to!" She threw up her hands, suddenly furious. He wasn't the only one having to live with disappointment. Blood hammering, she leaned in. "Do you think I'm partying over here?"

He leaned in too, until his was face inches from hers. "Harlie Cooper, you are the stubbornest, independent little shit I ever met. I tried to be patient. To give you space. *Four* times I called. I knew you'd be dealing with heavy stuff, and thought you might need to talk. That you might need a friend." His upper lip peeled back from his teeth. "But not Harlie Cooper. She doesn't need *anybody*. You treat friendship like a bank balance, and you can't accept anything you don't have the funds to cover."

She winced when that dart hit home. "No shit. Where I come from, that's the way things work."

He threw his hands up. "How the fuck would you know? How many friendships have you had in that closed-off little life of yours?"

She tried to think of a comeback. Nothing came.

"Not everyone is out to stomp you down, you idiot. Some people even might like you, if you only showed them you're human. At Hoot's you were like a mean little dog, snipping at everyone who tried to get close."

"Get close? Are you kidding? I didn't have the balls required for membership into y'all's little boy's club."

"The Coop I know had more than enough balls. You were just afraid to take a chance—to put yourself out there."

"Those guys didn't give a shit about me." Seeing dots of her spit on his cheek, she backed up an inch or two.

He pointed to her forearm. "Did you know that 'those guys who didn't give a shit' all kicked in to pay for that tattoo?" He nodded. "It was Cash's idea. We said the guy threw it in free because we knew you wouldn't accept it otherwise."

She stood, shocked wordless.

"You can douse me in a bucket of shut-up. But that doesn't make you right." He shrugged, hands out. "So what now?

Are you going to stay here busting your ass for minimum wage the rest of your life?"

Was that pity in his eyes? "What's it to you if I do?"

He huffed out an exasperated sigh. "Why do you think I scooted out of Kinta as soon as I had the chance? I saw that same life, sitting waiting for me."

"Why are you doing this?" Damn him, now she sounded like a victim.

"Because you're making a mistake. Because you're a gifted bullfighter. Watching you in the arena—"

"Quit!" Didn't he know that she'd love to grab her gear bag, hop in the Jeep, and make that rodeo in Arizona? That she wanted that life so bad that her guts shook with the wanting? But it was too late.

He still waited, his eyes boring through her. "Is minimum wage going to get you the money you need to get Angel the help she needs?"

Her chin dropped. She couldn't even argue that point. "No."

"Then what is the problem? This isn't like you. Talk to me, Coop."

"I'm afraid. Okay?" Noticing her fingers shook, she hid them behind her butt once more.

"Afraid of what?"

She bit the inside of her lip, trying to dredge up words that would explain . . . what she didn't understand herself. "All I know is that leaving feels like the easy way out."

"Do you think that by punishing yourself, it'll make Angel's suffering less?"

"No." But she realized even as the small word slipped out, that's exactly what she'd thought.

"You're allowed to be happy, Harlie. If you're not, how can you be strong enough to help your sister?"

"It's easy for you to say. You have the support of a big family . . ." She stopped. The weakness made the words sound whiny. And damp. She bit the inside of her cheek. The pain helped.

He cocked his head. "So do you, dummy."

She bit her lips to stem the words, afraid if she tried to ask, it would spill out.

"The rodeo. You've seen how cowboys hang together. You've even helped them that needed it. They'll be there for you, too, if you let them." He touched her shoulder and smiled a smile as soft as his eyes. "A family can be more than the one you were born into, Harlie. Shared blood may define a family, but spilled blood can too."

The desperation and hopelessness of the past weeks rose in a liquid rush to her head. The pull of longing she'd been fighting amped to a power-line hum, running under her skin. She wanted to go back, where she fit. If only she could put down her burden for a few hours and rest, maybe she could see what was right.

To her horror, the wanting broke from her in a sob she tried to smother with her hands. Her partner took a step, wrapping her into a sheltering hug that made it okay to let go. Like in the arena, he stood over her, protecting her until she could stand again on her own. It seemed like a long time later when she did.

How odd life was. She'd tried to save her sister, and failed. She tried to save a bunch of cowboys, and succeeded.

Maybe it was time for her to save herself.

She sniffled, palmed tears off her cheeks and asked, "You have your phone on you?" If Angel was brave enough to face her demons, her older sister had damned well better be willing to step up.

Deuce pulled out his phone, handed it over and turned to walk away, to give her space.

Reaching out, she touched his forearm. "Would you stay?"

His smile warmed her. "I'd be proud to."

She dialed the number she knew by heart. When Steve answered, she kept her promise; she told.

Ten minutes later, in spite of being on probation, she had her job back. She had a partner.

264

She had a future.

Just yesterday, she'd decided to keep her eyes open and look for answers outside herself. Today, the answer showed up, in faded, creased jeans and a new cowboy hat. Coincidence?

Sure didn't feel like it.

She looked inside, to see how she felt about all this. There was joy, gratitude, comfort, fear, guilt and regret. The only new emotion was the comfort. Maybe the percentages had skewed a bit, more to the positive. She grinned.

Deuce stepped beside her, leaned his butt against the Jeep, arms crossed, his smile saying 'I told you so'.

She looked up at her too smug, too smart partner, took a breath and a chance. "Do you want to meet my sister?"

Better Days

Optimism is the foundation of courage.

Nicolas M. Butler

Epilogue

Three months later:

An old trail drive song played on the radio, as an autumn-tinted breeze blew into the window of the Jeep. Harlie swiped dancing wisps of hair behind her ear and glanced in the rearview mirror while her toes sought her boots on the floorboards. "We're almost there. Are you ready for your first rodeo?"

Her sister's worried eyes met hers in the mirror. "Now I'm not so sure."

Deuce eased off the 101 at the exit that would take them to the Santa Maria Rodeo grounds. "Nothing to worry about, Sugar. These guys are big 'ol teddy bears."

When Harlie had asked Angel what she wanted for her fourteenth birthday, she said she wanted to go to a rodeo. Deuce was all in, so she'd worked out a pass from Angel's halfway house to take her on a road trip. Stopping to pick her up had made them late, but it was worth it.

Doctor Nguyen said Angel was progressing, but she still had her dark days. Probably always would. She wasn't shy, exactly. More watchful. Wary.

It made Harlie's chest ache to feel that hesitancy. She mourned the lost innocence.

But today would be a happy one. Harlie would see to that.

She glanced at her partner as she pulled on her boots. "You ready for your last rodeo of the year?"

267

"Oh, hell yeah." He shot a look in the mirror. "Heck yeah. Especially since the PBR Challenger Tour starts in two weeks. You ready for the big time?"

"Well, the Challenger Tour is more the medium time. But Steve thinks if we excel this season," she looked from under her brows at her partner "which we will, it could mean we're full-on PBR come next season."

The cheap seat section perked up. "You'll be on TV?" Angel asked.

"You always did love your celebrities." Harlie shook her head

Angel's head popped between the two seats. "And now I'll be related to one."

"Hey, I have a movie credit. Even if it was only a shot of the back of my head on a horse galloping into the sunset."

Deuce turned in at the entrance to the packed rodeo grounds. "You were in a movie? You never told me that."

"You don't know everything, McAllister." She winked at her sister. Her rare giggle hit Harlie like the first warm day after a long, gray winter.

Deuce pulled the Jeep to the stables, and trolled the aisle of pickups, looking for a parking place.

"Hurry." Harlie released her seat belt and donned her straw cowboy hat. "Mutton-busting is first, and Angel can't miss that."

He pulled the Jeep into a spot against the back fence that surely hadn't been made for parking. He shut down the engine and pulled the keys. "Then we are going to have to hustle. Let's hit it."

They piled out, scrambled for their gear bags and jogged for the area behind the chutes. When Harlie realized Angel wasn't on her heels, she stopped. "You go ahead, Deuce. I'll be right there."

She walked back to where Angel dragged her toes in the dust. Maybe she was wrong. Maybe this was throwing too much at Angel too soon. "Are you okay?"

"These are your people, Harlie. I'll just go sit in the stands."

She took her sister's hand and tugged her forward. "They're my family, Littlest. That makes them yours, too. Come on. They're just ol' country boys." She leaned over and whispered, "Some don't even have all their teeth."

Harlie's hope rose with the corners of her sister's mouth. It was a small smile, but Harlie would take it.

When they got to the staging area behind the chutes, cowboys lounged, stretching and prepping gear while they told each other lies.

"Hey, it's Coop." Rod LeBlanc called. "Thought we were gonna have to hold the rodeo."

"Had to be there to save your slow butt, LeBlanc."

"Yeah, but you're leaving us, so next week our butts will be bare, hanging out there for any brahma that comes along." Shane wrung his hands in mock worry.

Bones walked up, rope in hand. "Watch your mouth, cowboy. There's a little lady present." He doffed his hat and bowed. "Howdy, miss."

Seeing his gap-toothed grin, Angel shot a look at Harlie, then gave him a shy smile.

"Angel, this is my friend, Bones Jones." She raised her voice. "Everyone, this is my sister, Angel."

The cowboys tipped their hats.

"Hey, looka' that - a mini-Cooper!"

"You gonna be a big bad bullfighter like your sister?"

Angel ducked her head. "Harlie's the brave one."

Deuce stopped pulling gear from his bag and walked over. "The Duke said that courage is being scared to death, and saddling up anyway. I'd say all the Coopers are pretty darned courageous." He held out his arm to Angel. "May I escort you to the mutton-busting Littlest?"

Angel looked up at him. "So is this what it's like to have a brother, too?"

Harlie watched them walk away, her new family and her old, wondering when the two had merged.

Angel had a long way to go, still, and they both had to accept that she may not improve much beyond where she was right now.

Harlie had come to accept that the dreams they'd held were children's dreams. Her dreams now were smaller, and farther out.

But they were no less sweet for that.

Dear Reader:

Thank you for reading *Days Made of Glass*. If you have a moment, I would love an Amazon or <u>Goodreads</u> review from you. It doesn't have to be long, just your honest opinion of the book. Reviews help authors more than you know!

Most of my books split the line between Women's Fiction and Romance. If you liked *Days Made of Glass*, I think you'll love my RITA winner, <u>*The Sweet Spot*</u>. Here's a snippet of the beginning:

> *The grief counselor told the group to be grateful for what they had left. After lots of considering, Charla Rae decided she was grateful for the bull semen.*

Charla Rae Denny wiped her hands with her apron and stepped back, surveying the shelves of her pantry. This month's *Good Housekeeping* suggested using scraps of linoleum as shelf paper. It had been a bitch-kitty to cut, but cost nothing, would be easy to clean, and continued the white-pebbled theme of her kitchen floor. And for a few hours, the project had rescued her weary mind from a hamster-wheel of regret.

The homing beacon in the Valium bottle next to the sink tugged at her insides.

She sipped a glass of water to avoid reaching for it and glanced out the window to the spring-skeletal trees of the back yard.

Her gaze returned to the two-foot wide stump the way a tongue wanders to a missing tooth. Tentative grass shoots had sprung up to obscure the obscene scar in the soil.

She hadn't thought that an innocent tree could kill a child.

She hadn't thought that an innocent coed could kill a marriage.

And if those pills could kill the thinking, she'd take ten.

At the familiar throaty growl of a Peterbilt turning off the road out front, Char jerked, realizing minutes had passed. She'd been listening for that deep throb for hours. She always did. As the cab and empty cattle hauler swept by the window, she wound her shaking hands in her apron, as if the sturdy cotton would hold her together.

A ranch wife could stretch a pound of hamburger farther than anyone, but Daddy's new medication cost the moon, and the bills in the basket beside the computer were piling up like snow drifts in a blizzard. Hands still shaking, she untied the bibbed apron and pulled it over her head. She'd rather clean bathrooms at the airport than ask her ex for money, but then, most of her choices these days were like that. Sighing, she walked to the mud-room, shrugged into her spring jacket, yanked open the back door, and stepped into the nippy air.

For more about me and my books, visit:
http://LauraDrakeBooks.com

Want to hear about future releases? You can sign up for my quarterly newsletter:
http://lauradrakebooks.com/contact-laura/

I love hearing from readers!
Email me at: LauraDrake@LauraDrakeBooks.com

Made in the USA
San Bernardino, CA
12 August 2016